The Larger Conversation

The University of Alberta Press

The Larger Conversation

Contemplation and Place

TIM LILBURN

Published by

The University of Alberta Press
Ring House 2
Edmonton, Alberta, Canada   T6G 2E1
www.uap.ualberta.ca

Copyright © 2017 Tim Lilburn

LIBRARY AND ARCHIVES CANADA
CATALOGUING IN PUBLICATION

Lilburn, Tim, 1950–, author
     The larger conversation : contemplation and
place / Tim Lilburn.

Includes bibliographical references and index.
Issued in print and electronic formats.
ISBN 978–1–77212–299–2 (softcover).—
ISBN 978–1–77212–360–9 (PDF). —
ISBN 978–1–77212–358–6 (EPUB).—
ISBN 978–1–77212–359–3 (Kindle)

     1. Human ecology—Philosophy. I. Title.

GF21.L53 2017   179'.1   C2017–904967–4
                             C2017–904968–2

First edition, first printing, 2017.
First printed and bound in Canada by Houghton
Boston Printers, Saskatoon, Saskatchewan.
Copyediting by Michael Lahey.
Proofreading by Joanne Muzak.
Indexing by Mary Newberry.

The University of Alberta Press is committed to
protecting our natural environment. As part of our
efforts, this book is printed on Enviro Paper: it
contains 100% post-consumer recycled fibres and
is acid- and chlorine-free.

The University of Alberta Press gratefully
acknowledges the support received for its publishing
program from the Government of Canada, the
Canada Council for the Arts, and the Government
of Alberta through the Alberta Media Fund.

Contemplata aliis tradere

—ST. THOMAS AQUINAS, *Summa Theologica*, Part 2-2, question 188, article 6

Contents

Introduction

I TEACH A CLASS every few years called "Settling the Mind in Wilderness: Nature Writing in Ancient Asia and Contemporary North America." Since the course focuses on writing about place, I sometimes will start the first session by asking students where we are. This question provokes some nervous stares, some eye-rolling, but then a few attempts at an answer, "Victoria," "Saanich," local political names. The university, in fact, lies in a Garry oak meadow, from which most of the oaks, camas lilies and native grasses have been removed, on the north slope of what municipal maps call Mt. Tolmie, the name borrowed from a nineteenth-century Hudson's Bay Company employee. The mountain's name in SENĆOȾEN, the Indigenous language in much of the Saanich Peninsula, is W̱MIEȾEN (place of the deer); at its foot, in large pipes sunk under asphalt is Bowker Creek, a former salmon stream. The slope and all of the area around it are unceded territory. There are more geographically and historically close descriptions possible, I have no doubt, but I don't know them, or know them yet. A student once remarked that though she'd lived in the city for many years and had driven past the mountain countless times, she'd never really *noticed* it. She was stunned, in the weeks after the first class, to truly see it. This is what it is to be a colonial subject—you move in a sort of daze in the place you call home.

This book represents a ragged beginning at a personal attempt at decolonization. This venture will strike some as peculiar, idiosyncratically marginal, though I see it as necessary work. I have no confidence the book's ambition will be met, but hold a conviction that the effort it pursues must be taken up as a way of life. With this sort of undertaking, the notion of completion is foreign, but this inconclusivity is not cause to step aside from its challenge. The difficulty, if not futility, of this project, as I see it, is part of its charm and its durability.

In the work of Taiaiake Alfred, Glen Coulthard and others collected in Leanne Simpson's *Lighting the Eighth Fire: The Liberation, Resurgence, and Protection of Indigenous Nations,* and in the thought of Neal McLeod and his collaborators in *Indigenous Poetics in Canada,* I read an account of a parallel, yet far more advanced, work taken up from a quite different point of view. Indeed, I received the notion of decolonization as an individual renovation, in the light of horrendous political pressures and amnesias, from the writings of Taiaiake Alfred, in particular his *Wasáse: Indigenous Pathways of Action and Freedom* and his introduction to *Lighting the Eighth Fire,* and from others joining him at the University of Victoria and elsewhere in thinking about how to undo forms of thought and behaviour implanted by colonialism in First Nations communities. Alfred identifies this task as the work to undermine "our disconnection from what it is to be Indigenous. This problem has been framed in many complicated ways, but really, what is colonization if not separation of our people from the land, the severance of the bonds of trust and love that held our people together so tightly in the not-so-distant past and the abandonment of our spiritual connection to the natural world?" ("Opening Words" 9–10).

How to approach the work of autochthonicity from the side of settlers and their descendants, the supposed imperial victors? A certain form of rule, as Socrates makes clear in his exchanges with the disquietingly audacious Glaucon in the *Republic,* is itself a psychic illness, from which a score of additional maladies rapidly develop. The "feverish city" that arises in the dialogue as an expression of Glaucon's unexamined desires is aggressively expansionist, violent within and without, just as it is luxurious and pleonexic. The presenting symptoms of the disease this sort of rule provokes are a breathtaking presumption and the appearance of behaviours that are more or less untouched by moral consideration. But there are deeper problems. I have long sensed, and recorded in previous books like *Moosewood Sandhills* and *Living in the World As If It Were Home,* that I was stuck in a deep cultural malaise marked by a sense of alienation from where I stood and a feeling of pronounced existential floating. This rootlessness is the capitalist psychic predicament, pointed out for me by George Grant in his prescient essay "In Defence of North America" in his book *Technology and Empire.* I float over the land, but also float in an intellectual tradition that offers no chthonic or sapiential mooring. The insight that my condition is, in significant part, the result of my occupying and deriving benefit from a colonial situation is, I am abashed to say, a relatively recent one. This account of my difficulties is deeper and more extensive than the epistemological connundra I have explored in earlier books, though I remain convinced these epistemological matters and their connections to politics remain central. Their remediation is crucial in undoing the imperial knot, in both its existential and political forms. For this reason, the decolonization project on the settler side, I believe, is foundationally contemplative and involves a psychic archeology and apokatastasis that are both philosophical and mystical theological, at least insofar as that latter pursuit is ascetical, because it is within these strata that the problems, the misalignments, that fashion the colonial appropriation of the world reside.

This sought contemplative proximity to the world should not preclude a pursuit of justice, nor should it make justice wait, but chthonic activism in support of First Nations may grow from this quest. A recent example of such supportive, cooperative activism was the trek to the top of the peak in Mt. Douglas Park in Victoria, on May 22, 2013, by W̱SÁNEĆ people and newcomers. There, as hundreds looked on, elders and leaders set aside the old colonial name of Mt. Douglas and ceremonially restored the ancient name of the mountain, P,KOLS. Non-Indigenous witnesses were in attendance because they saw the justice in the W̱SÁNEĆ reclamation of the name *and* because they loved the mountain. And they loved it because they had interiorly tasted it.

The essay and the lyric poem are perfect instruments in this psycho-political undertaking of a contemplative return to being in the form of one's place because both essentially refuse as bogus the confidence that underlies a complete account. Each rests on the sense of the fragment as sufficient—at the heart of one is the non-comprehensive confession, a shard; the epiphanic apostrophe lies at the center of the other. Neither literary form conceives a band of veracity beyond these two inconclusive interior experiences. Both, therefore, are toppling forms, inducing tentativeness and humility and, inevitably, permeability. They, in their incompleteness, promote conviviality and conversation—you need to talk to fill in the greater picture—thus both are heuristics and goads for a larger, a pandemic, conversation.

A book of essays can jump around as much as a collection of poems often does. Its strength is not expressed in the reach to a complete argument, but in repeated awkward plunges of orphic exploration. A collection of such interrupted, partial attempts can be unsurprisingly heterogeneous. Essays on Chinese poets, contemporary and ancient, rub shoulders in this book with observations on paleo-neurology and Christian monastic theology from late antiquity. The presence of much that may seem arcane—Sufi angelology from the twelfth century, for instance—is not as peculiar or anomalous as it may first appear. This impression merely indicates the extensive philosophic poverty of the West. The book's heterogeneity, however, is not diffusion: the entire work has a single focus that possesses both a psychic and political arm. There's much in our intellectual tradition that's been jettisoned or misplaced that needs to be retrieved. This operation often cannot be a matter of mere addition since the categories that would receive the recalled understandings and practices have been lost themselves and must be resuscitated or rebuilt (how to accommodate those Ibn 'Arabian presences?). So there is a roughness and wildness in what follows for which I apologize, but I see no way around this situation. To try to domesticate these necessary understandings would produce not exegesis but reduction: the returning insights must be allowed to keep as much of their autonomy as possible and, with this, their capacity to surprise. So they retain their full power to teach and form; they keep their political daemonism.

The book builds on two previous essay collections, *Living in the World As If It Were Home* (1999, 2015) and *Going Home* (2008), as well as conversations I have been having over the last thirty years with a range of poets, thinkers, liturgists and ceremonialists. I offer a partial list of these essential sharers of talk—Jan Zwicky, Fr. James Gray OSB, Joseph P. Cardinal, Louise Halfe, Don McKay, Dennis Lee, Warren Heiti, Peter Butt, Francis Whiskeyjack, Xi Chuan, Sheri Benning, Helen Marzolf and Kevin Paul—and thank them for their intellectual hospitality and nourishing friendship.

The essays do not adequately address directly the issue of compunction for colonial theft and violence. The guilt is deep. I would like to say this goes without saying, but it does not. The guilt is too deep to adequately address and I do not know the whole of it even now; possibly no one does. Anyone who attended recent Truth and Reconciliation proceedings or read reports in the summer of 2013 of medical experiments conducted on First Nations children and adults in the 1950s will have felt this remorse. Meanwhile, the extended and present imperial act goes on, producing its own annihilations, a form of revenge that worldview wreaks upon the very culture and world from which it grows, and upon which it relies for nourishment—climate change, pollutions of all sorts, a gnawing sense of the absence of meaning, emptying churches or filled churches increasingly fundamentalist, an endemic and starving lightness in behaviour. Certain dispositions are giving birth to their own furies. As I've said before, I believe the atomic source of these conditions is epistemological. Guilt without an attempt at renovation in this area, an alteration of cognitive disposition, is enervating, indeed is itself an imperial result.

|| Louis Riel, the founder of a polyglot, somewhat mystical polis in Western Canada called Assiniboia, in an unpublished memorandum on the Hudson's Bay Company's sale of Rupert's Land to Canada, expressed incredulity at the audacity of the two participants in the agreement. The exchange had obliterated the visionary political condition he had conceived. Yet in Riel's view, no actual sale had taken place, because what was offered to Canada was unsaleable. "[T]he Company does all in its power to deliver us," Riel observed on the events of 1869–70, "and Canada threatens that if we do not yield gladly their army will come; beyond the fact that the merchandise is not saleable, the Company sold an object that does not belong to it; the rights it sold never belonged to it" ("Memorandum"). The moral nullity of the agreement means that even now this space is still available for imaginative re-occupation. This book wishes to re-enter that space, Riel's Assiniboia, "a spiritual if not territorial community" (*Czesław Miłosz* 130), as Irena Grudzinska Gross describes Milan Kundera's and Czesław Miłosz's depictions in the 1990s of the new "Mittel Europe." This imaginal re-entry, like Kundera's and Miłosz's writings on Central Europe, is an attempt to shape a new embodiment in one's place.

I draw the notion of "the larger conversation" from Robert Duncan's symposium of the whole, but the exchange I wish to take up is broader than Duncan's, which was chiefly sociological and revolutionary, drawing the most marginal persons, "all that has been outcast and vagabond" (Rothenberg 20), to the center of the cultural discussion. The symposium I have in mind is even more spreadingly convivial, is indeed pan-ontological and multi-temporal, including the non-human and, of course, the dead, who, like Carl Jung's god, called or uncalled, come. The talk has no terminus, no center, no telos and sets in place no unamendable understanding, but efficiently builds a courtesy, a gratitude and an absorption in what lies beyond the self.

The pieces that follow are formally varied—confessions, exegetical treatments, a review, an interview and various lectures. The conversation now required, because of its urgency, inevitably assumes a range of shapes. Talk is all: yet in this, meaning is not primarily uttered but heard. Though I say much here, much of this was incited or molded by interlocutors speaking to me over kitchen tables, in poplar forests, around fires, in seminar rooms, in sweat lodges. The insight building in conversation often seems to have its own genius; its meaning is not mine, not my interlocutor's, not even a precise and exhaustive synthesis of both our views. I also owe a more general debt to the monks of St. Peter's Abbey and their hospitality during the fourteen years I taught philosophy and writing at St. Peter's College in Muenster, Saskatchewan. From them, I learned the Benedictine spirit of welcoming amity and physical work, as well as a broader version of quotidian interior practice than I could claim before.

I

1

The Ethical Significance of
the Human Relationship to Place

Michael Keenan Memorial Lecture, St. Thomas More College
University of Saskatchewan, 2010

THE MOST ANCIENT VISUAL ART is 32,000 years old.
It appears on walls over scatters of cave bear bones in Chauvet cave in the
south of France, charcoal and ochre figures drawn beautifully on calcite
walls. The oldest musical instrument, a flute made from the wingbone
of a vulture, is slightly older, around 36,000 years old, and was discovered recently in a cave in southern Germany. Language, likely the place of
the first human art-making—seasonal and love songs, ceremonial instructions, invocations, tales of heroes, accounts of creation—is very much older,
though the date of its actual emergence is hard to pin down, of course, since,
before writing, there are no linguistic artifacts. We do know, though, that
the appearance of language depends on the advent of bipedalism, which
occurred around 1.6 million years ago, during which time the spine underwent a realignment so that it entered the skull at its bottom rather than at
its back, which caused the larynx to drop. This change, over time, permitted
hominids to emit a greater range of sounds. Once these anatomical

alterations were in place, complex language use was possible. One theory for the origin of linguistic communication, proposed in the early 1990s by the paleo-anthropologist Leslie Aiello and the evolutionary psychologist Robin Dunbar, is that oral communication emerged to extend mutual physical grooming in the building of social cohesion once hominid hunting and breeding groups became too large for grooming alone to be an effective political tool. These larger groups appeared around a million years ago, during the time of *homo habilis*. Community building is a function that language retains to this day.

Our forms of art-making have remained roughly unchanged over the millennia: we still use paint and brush, still sculpt, still dance, sing songs, fashion metaphors and compose narratives, though we have acquired a few newer technologies in which to express these formal skills. The content of contemporary art, however, is much different from that found in the Upper Paleolithic. The walls and ceilings of Chauvet and Lascaux caves are filled with animals; our galleries, screens, novels and poems are equally crammed with the human self.

This shift in dominant theme need not be read as solipsism, an artistic folding into a numbing self-absorption. Rather it may mark a serious inquiry, stretching from late antiquity to the present day, into the roots and complexities of human interiority. How to come to one's most developed self, to the fully individuated self? This is a question that has preoccupied philosophers from Plato to Descartes to John Stuart Mill to Charles Taylor and absorbed writers as diverse as Hildegarde of Bingen, Herman Melville, George Eliot, Simone Weil and Anne Michaels. It is also a central concern in all twentieth-century psychologies. It can be understood as a religious question too, touching on salvation, since the self that is maximally real is likely to be the nearest approximation to the individual in the divine mind. Mill saw the nurturing of the genuine self, particular, spontaneous, vital, courageous, as our pre-eminent political responsibility. A society resting on such selves, he argued, would be the freest, most tolerant, most creative and most lasting.

I'd like to make a rather broad claim about the conditions under which such a self, what we may call the well-formed self, appears. This claim is unprovable, but, I believe, easily confirmable by most people through self-reflection. The claim is that the more fully realized self is not invented or even made in an extended act of bricolage; it has little to do with innovation and will—but instead is given. It is given, that is, through recognition by others, a gift from another's imagination. This experience of receiving one's self from another's generous, sympathetic construal is extraordinary. It constitutes knowledge that is exigent, seemingly irrational; it provokes startled, though eventually grateful, conviction. We are heard or seen into a larger presence. Often this recognition comes in conversation; in the space between ourselves and our interlocutors, a new apparitional figure appears, a fresh version of what we might be, and we walk toward it, realizing it as we go. Here is the essence of good teaching, good spiritual direction, nourishing talk among deep friends, inspired psychoanalysis. This means that individuality is not a solitary or selfish achievement, but the artifact of some sort of convivial community. As art is. I realize in making this last point that I speak against Kant's depiction of the artistic genius in his *Critique of Judgment*, where the supreme art maker is presented as autonomous, singular, one of nature's elect. The paintings in Chauvet and Lascaux caves involved the efforts of large numbers of people, some, it is true, astonishingly talented. But the building of scaffolds, the maintaining of juniper wicked lamps, the mixing of pigments, the grinding of ochre, the holding of a belief in the import of certain images all needed a group's persistent, muscular commitment. Even the provision of plain company in the dark and dangerous caves contributed to the art.

The community that is the school of the truly formed self, in my view, the self that may be an exposition of divinity, is very large, the "symposium of the whole" (Rothenberg 20), to use the phrase of the American poet Robert Duncan. This is a gathering that includes everyone, especially "all the excluded orders," which Duncan, writing in the 1950s, lists as "the female, the proletariat, the foreign, the animal and vegetative, the unconscious and the unknown, the criminal and failure." This larger conversation, says Duncan, following Plato's conviction in the moral efficacy of dialectic, of exchange, is the shaper of elemental desire and the foundation of virtue. A crucial participant in this larger conversation—and here I would like to make an addition to Robert Duncan's list—is locale.

Each of us, I believe, has a particular place to which she or he is pleased to return; some are lucky enough to have a small range of these. We may "have" these places without knowing in detail we do. Still, even outside acute self-awareness of embeddedness and indebtedness, we may instinctively view these locations, these situations, as curing and cheering, close to us, dear. I invite each of you to take a minute or two now to picture one of these, a location deep in your affections, the South Saskatchewan River, perhaps, admired from the railway bridge to the west of the university in late July; the Moosewood Sandhills, to the southwest of Saskatoon; land near Pike Lake, in winter; a grove of aspen poplar; some long grass behind a house and out-buildings where you liked to lie and hide as a child and that you still may visit; a corner you prefer to sit in because of the way light falls across your chair in the early morning; the room containing most of your books. Hold this scene in your mind a moment, letting your eye pass slowly over it.

Standing, sitting, lying in or walking through locations like these, either actually or imaginatively, can be as reviving as taking a long drink of water. The experience of dwelling in these places is restful, vitalizing; they can make us feel lodged in ourselves. They calm us, inform us concerning essence, allow us to feel undispersed, gathered. It can seem that we belong to them, as Coast Salish peoples say of certain salmon rivers and certain families, not the other way around. There is a particular be-friending or fostering going on with these places: here we are taken in, at home, and, oddly, this at-homeness feels like being *seen*. Seen with truth but with a degree of graceful inflation: home, we are more than the atomic self by the measure of the place and its range of connections. We are the self in chthonic and local relationship, the self as an ampler ecology.

Almost every day when I am not teaching, I take a walk up a small mountain in Victoria, toward the south end of the Saanich Peninsula, near where I live. I have numerous routes to the area of rock above the trees, a south route through salal and Douglas fir, a dry west route through oak, wild grass and flowers. In the course of nearly every walk, it is as if the mountain presents a new version of my self; I go there to find what I really think. I am eventually the tone that comes from seeing these trees in this light, from this smell of ground. From the generosity of place to us comes identity, as I have said, but also ethics or at least its dispositional rudiments, gravitas, decorum, a grateful humility, that will build into a complete ethics, for we cannot harm something or someone whose idiosyncratic beauty has become our domicile; and if we cannot harm this, we may begin a habit, or discipline, of not harming in general. Such places quiet us, place in us the rhythms of courtesy, and prepare us for an elemental conviviality.

If these benefits, arising from an experience of place, foundational in an interior sense, sound like the effects of prayer, it is because they, in fact, are—the existential residue of the practice that the Egyptian monk Evagrius Ponticus, and other early contemplative authors, called *theoria physike*, contemplation of nature or prayer as a "participation" in physical things. This prayer, said Evagrius, is the Christian polis, the Kingdom of Heaven. "The Kingdom of Heaven is *apatheia* [the freedom from personal, acquisitive desire] of the soul along with true knowledge of existing things" (par. 2). By knowledge, Evagrius means theoria or contemplation, interior absorption, the full fructifying gaze at stones, rivers, trees. The Kingdom of Heaven, he seems to say, is precisely such looking.

But there is another account explaining our strange intimacy with prairie coulees, river systems, light-filled chairs and granite erratics that comes from Plato's great cosmological dialogue, the *Timaeus*. Here the human soul is described as being formed in the same receptacle in which the Soul of the World had been formed earlier. Plato's maker of things mixed in this bowl what was left over from the previous creation—bits of stones, leaves, bark, wave crest—so that human innerness, the soul, is in fact composed of scraps of everything in the universe (*Timaeus* 42). Plato, of course, is not so much doing ontology here, as he is attempting to construct an account of a deeper layer of human emotion. This sameness, a felt homology, or at least a family resemblance, between nature and humans and within nature, between our deepest capacity for savouring and all physical things, is what drives praise in lyric poems, the linguistic eruption arising from insight into rough, startling familiarity, shared shape. This felt homology also drives the delight of playful anthropomorphisms and is the basis of all Pythagorean hunches, perhaps the source of the confidence of science itself. It is what makes theurgical practice in ceremony, the ritual use of objects made of stone, wood and cereals, deeply transformative and divinizing. Everything seems amicable, truly connectable with everything else. A tree rises in the ear, as Rilke says in his *Sonnets to Orpheus*; bees strip the udders of the meadow. The world is built for metaphor. And metaphor, we discover when we think carefully of Plato's account of the source of things, is not mere aesthetic embellishment, but probing, true description, a sagacious form of realism.

Since places that are personally remarkable to us seem to take us in, filling us out, giving us our higher minds, our deeper selves, our richest identities, shaping our language and our bodies, the loss of such a place through relocation, bankruptcy or theft is truly disabling, like losing a friend, a loved one, or part of oneself. We have no name for this particular interior wreckage around lost land, and the general culture overlooks it. Permit me a small example. When I moved to British Columbia from Saskatchewan over six years ago, something essential left me, and I became quite ill as a result. This illness lasted four years and involved multiple surgeries. My story is perhaps a trivial example, but it says in miniature what land loss does. I missed the prairies I knew—the South Saskatchewan River between Saskatoon and Batoche, the aspen stands of the Moosewood Sandhills, the coulees of the Palliser Triangle, the Cypress Hills, Grasslands National Park. I thought perhaps I would not write again; I didn't know how to breathe or act or name things outside of the old place. But in this leveling I was privileged with good luck, and met the low mountain I mentioned just now or, rather, it presented itself to me after I hung around it abjectly for a time. Such a place is integral for me to the "larger conversation," a force congruent, it seems, with inspiration, Ibn 'Arabi's agent intellect (more on this particular function later), the will prior to my will, in its formational, defining power.

Certain qualities are helpful in order to be seen in this way, seen home into an ampler self, to engage in the more reaching conversation with land, which has, I believe, an immense personal and political significance. Two of these qualities needed to engage in this conversation are permeability and the activation of one's interior senses, so that a contemplative savouring of things, a feasting attention, is possible. Where can these qualities, or training to acquire these qualities, be found? No place in our current culture has them, but, among other occult, recessed locations, they can be excavated in the Platonic contemplative tradition in its Christian, Islamic and Judaic manifestations, a tradition marginalized if not almost completely forgotten in our day. Permeability, we learn in this tradition, may come from a jolting shrinking of the self, from kenosis, that is, or what the fouteenth-century beguine Marguerite Porete called "annihilation" (Porete 135), or Simone Weil, the twentieth-century philosopher, named "decreation" (Weil 28). A description of the interior senses, their operation, can be found in the writings of both Origen and Evagrius, third- and fourth-century contemplatives and philosophers, and in Benedict of Nursia, who all speak of the interior sensorium, a complete person within, an inner sense of smell, taste, sight, hearing, touch: exercising these senses, Origien and Evagrius tell us, is the sensuous life of prayer, the delight of contemplative focus. We need to read the works of these authors and re-enact their phenomenologies. This is a political or communitarian need, as well as a need of the soul. We must work to resuscitate the treasure of this contemplative lore through scholarship and through the practice of ascetical and mystical theology, which is the true knowing of contemplative prayer. Perhaps our building desperation around the state of the natural world will quicken the impulse to attempt these retrievals and re-enactments.

Conviviality is another of the virtues deepened interiority brings, and it is a third quality necessary for participating in the larger conversation involving all things we have been examining. It is important since it breeds openness and calmness around exchange: *convivium*—relating to feasts and guests; sociability: conviviality—given to hospitable, pleasing concourse among equals; the quality of being keenly conversational, avid to eat the bread of conversation. Christianity is essentially a religious practice marked by conviviality, marked, that is, by a spirit of conversation and reciprocity. The exchanges in the Gospels illustrate this quality; the conception of the Trinity as a sort of community or family does as well. St. Augustine's notion of the mind or self in *De Trinitate* as a colloquium of memory, understanding and will, along with Marguerite Porete's version of the self in her book *The Mirror of Simple Souls* as a collection of impulses and allegiances in conversation both reveal this deep dialogical, Christian trait. *The Divine Comedy* is a continuous series of colloquies, while the form of Aquinas' argument shows a history of exchanges with mentors and critics. The various collections of apothegmata, the sayings of the desert fathers and mothers, show that teaching in early monasticism was as much conversational as it was exegetical. In all of these instances, knowledge and identity are mediated, extended and routed by conversation. It is as if thought and feeling are helplessly unprotean, non-motile, unless shared. Again we find ourselves coming up against the Kantian notion of genius. But not all forms of Christian practice can be characterized this way. Two exceptions to the rule of conviviality are dogmatic theology, following the great Christological debates culminating in the Councils of Nicea and Chalcedon, and Christian missiology over the last four hundred years.

It should be clear to all of us that there has been a virtual absence of yielding, attentive talk at the orphic band of experience between Christian churches in North America and First Nations communities, from the days of earliest contact, described by Jesuit missionaries in the *Jesuit Relations* of the 1630s, to the present. What has been lacking on the European side has been a discipline of a plunging kenotic alertness, a permeability to the view of the possible interlocutor, a savouring alacrity for discovery, an ecumenical and syncretistic spirit, a spirit of hunger, humility, poverty that carries the hunch or hope that one's completion or necessary augmentation may arise in speech with another, an interest in, an availability to, surprising, vivifying, novel explanatory shapes.

The great French phenomenologist Emmanuel Levinas writes of two behaviourial styles, which he calls "totality" and "infinity" (48). With totality, exercised between lovers, within a family, a state, among peoples, between humans and the environment, the impulse is to "make the other the same," to homogenize all difference under a single paradigm, to colonize, in other words. So is removed the strangeness on the other side that makes for a bracing partner in exchange. The behaviour he calls "infinity" is quite different, the roots, he argues, of ethics itself, in fact. This behaviour, disarmed, tentative, occasionally toppling, keen, grows from what he describes as an experience of the "Face," the deep recognition of the indissoluble individuality of another and a subsequent decorum and attentiveness toward the other growing out of this arresting experience. Christian missiological behaviour in North America and elsewhere has been almost entirely totalizing.

I hope a true exchange between feral European mystical thought and Indigenous communities in North America at some point may occur. It seems to me crucial to hope for this exchange. But I believe we are far from it happening. The best we can wish for now is that we enter a state of pre-conversation, a preparation for talk. A necessary conversational precondition will be genuine compunction on the settler side for residential schools, which were, we see clearly now, a form of cultural colonial war.

It is likely the exchange I hope for, in fact, will not come about; perhaps there is too much unresolved hurt for forgiveness to be offered, for people to feel safe enough to be open and speak. Nevertheless, the responsibility to prepare for it remains. An apt book considering the dynamism of remorse that dares not hope for resolution, but that is nevertheless required, is *Guilt about the Past*, a collection of lectures on German Holocaust guilt, by the novelist and jurist Bernhard Schlink. I suspect that if the conversation

between the two cultures does take place, it could be part of a new politics in this country, one that attempts a decolonization of settler relations
with First Nations and a new relationship with the land. I further suspect or
hope that at some point people in the European diaspora will recover and
speak from within the sociability, the keenness for conversation, of our own
wisdom tradition. A new imaginal world could come about, a new way of
thinking, of being revived. Call to mind the rich exchange between Taoism
and Buddhism in medieval China and the novel form of comprehension that
emerged, or the marriage of Greek and Christian insight in the early Church,
which gave the West one of its greatest treasures: Christian contemplative
thought. Something of this order could happen here, without the fundamental autonomy of either conversant tradition being marred; a new politics,
a new ecology could be the result. Let me emphasize, however, again,
that this must be an exchange, a growing through the spiritual exercise of
conversation, not a homogenization or a blending that extirpates either
mythopoeic side. Its chief labour would be the practice of attentiveness. Its
eventual outcome would be impossible to predict in detail.

But, as I say, we are at best in a state of pre-conversation now, a long way
from actual talk, a talk that, of course, may never occur. The resurgence of
ancient ceremonies in First Nation communities, over the last few decades,
and the appearance of incisive critical thought around decolonization
among Indigenous scholars connected with such schools as the Indigenous
Governance Program at the University of Victoria and the Indigenous
Studies Program at Trent University are forming a compelling side of a
possible future exchange, but there has been scant comparable formation
on the European side. I'd like to propose four activities, lifelong, life-shaping
practices or vocations, each of which amounts to a participation in this new
politics and a shaping toward its full expression. Each of these activities is
personally and eventually politically transformational. I should state explic-
itly, before I describe these four exercises, what may already be clear to many
of you—that I regard this new politics as an orphic politics, a politics, that is,
of descent (into the past, into the self), retrieval and return.

The first of these transformational activities is scholarship or a particular type of exegesis or reading or retrieval of what is culturally lost from the deposit of Western wisdom literature in the form of its various mystical and ascetical theologies. Here is where the most acute thought on desire in the West has occurred. The sort of work I have in mind is modeled by, among others, Thomas Merton, Jean Leclerq and the scholars whose work appears in *Cistercian Studies*, both the magazine and the book publishing series. I'd add Kevin Corrigan, former dean of St. Thomas More College, to this list of crucial exegetes and philosophers, both for his translation of Gregory of Nyssa's *Life of Macrina* and his more recent work on the anthropologies of Evagrius and Gregory (*Evagrius and Gregory: Mind, Body and Soul in the Fourth Century*). Other writers could be included here as well—Pierre Hadot, Benedicta Ward, Henry Corbin and Caroline Bynum come to mind. From this scholarship or retrieving reading, the wealth of the Western contemplative tradition is resurfaced, said again in and for the life of the present. From this revivified tradition may come exercises building to dispositions within which we experience a keen sensitivity to the land and a delectating receptivity to other lineages of thought and feeling. These exercises or disciplines, however, do not inevitably arise from such reading. A shallow scholarship, touristic, careerist, is always possible.

The second activity that prepares for and enacts this new way of being is ritual, Christian liturgy or the ceremony of the sweat lodge. Both ritual practices teach decorum and yearning, both bring gravitas, especially toward things and gestures, rooting us in materiality, its concord with us. I want also to mention poetry here as one of the engines of this new politics, poetry that chants us into generosity, into our nature via the ampleness of metaphor and spreading cosmic and chthonic lists. All books, fiction, drama, non-fiction, "written on the back and on the front," as it says in Ezekial (2.10), but perhaps pre-eminently poetry, theurgical writing, have this power, and are thus a form of ecological activism. Lastly, I would recommend a savouring and a valuing of our individual, special places; in this practice, the self and much of its perduring, defining desire is formed.

At nearly every point in the history of the Church, when thinkers have pursued a renewal of contemplative prayer, a freshening of interior focus in a contemporary context, they have turned to the initial Christian experience with monasticism in the Egyptian desert of the fourth century. Benedict, Bernard of Clairvaux, and Thomas Merton all illustrate this impulse. This gesture of return is caught equally in the documents of the Second Vatican Council, in the *Decree on the Adaptation and Renewal of Religious Life* in particular, where the argument is made that growth depends oddly enough on travelling backward "to the original inspiration behind a given community" (par. 2). This action is a conservatism that propels one into fresh, more inclusive terrain, clarifying and deepening one's dispositions in the present. It is not a romantic or nostalgic conservatism that wishes to resuscitate an idealized era and impose it by force of will. We in Canada recognize the former spirit of conserving as Red Toryism, the view that one attends to the past to comprehend the genius of dwelling well now. Many of us mourn the eclipse of this particular political possibility in the present. This spirit of moving forward by remembering and reviving is found also in modern political philosophers like George Grant and Gillian Rose, he attempting a retrieval of Plato to learn the appropriate gracefulness of the state and she returning to Hegel to discover the true conversational, synthesizing ethos of genuine politics. We find the same impulse of retrieval in the work of the novelist and ethicist Marilynne Robinson. It is close, I would argue, to what Origen and others in antiquity meant by apokatastasis, a recovery of essence, our state of nature.

I believe a similar return to the roots of the West's wisdom tradition is appropriate now as we seek a new relationship with the land. By reading authors like Evagrius and John Cassian, Ibn 'Arabi, and aphorists like the monk Poemen, or lives like Macrina's or Teresa of Avila's, staging their words and acts in the theatre of our imaginations, we will have the practice of kenotic attention, daemonic conversation, hospitality to all persons and animals, and profound affective and intellectual humility performed before us, performed within us, and the beauty of these acts might insinuate their rhythms into us. Such reading, then, is theurgical.

Let me say a brief word about theurgy and its operation, especially in ceremony and poetry. The word first appears in the Neoplatonism of the second century, yet it describes an activity probably as ancient as human symbolization itself. The word means "god work," or spiritual exercises by which human beings are lifted and altered, made, that is, more richly human. In Iamblichus' work *On the Mysteries (De mysteriis)*, we hear of the ritual use of various objects, grains, stones and so forth, to remind participants in ceremony of divine presence and the common origin of all things, to bring us home to the community of all things, the kinship of everything. In Proclus, theurgical transformation is largely linguistic: the sacred statues of words and the beauty and delirium of their arrangement work anagogically on readers and auditors. These linguistic acts have transformative force. Poetry retains this power; its repetitions, musics, metaphors and speeds are a boat that may carry us into a new politics.

What we manage to retrieve of our now subterranean sapiential tradition and convert into act may be the substance of the settler portion of a possible future conversation between those who draw on the spirit of contemplative Platonism within and without European Christianity and those who are members of First Nations. There is little else that would be appropriate to bring to the psychagogic, dialectical exchanges for which I dare to hope. An evolutionary philosophy of history and the fineness of Eurocentric religious culture are two topics that settler society has tried and that have failed, and now have been unmasked as imperial ploys. And, of course, we can't be said to actually possess this singular conversational substance, what our wisdom tradition gives us to say, since the contemplative idleness, for example, non-eristic, objectless exchange, full absorbing attentiveness to things, unappeasable eros, among other states of heart, have little place in modernity. We are therefore in a state that precedes conversation, as I've said, precedes even perhaps the state of pre-conversation; we may be left, at best, simply desiring to desire these states.

Yet still I hope, as others do, for a quickening of appetite and affection for place in descendants of European settlers, a yearning for the ground where one stands, a life based on a valuing and treasuring of the places that appear to recognize one, places with which the heart exchanges glances. This could be an important beginning for us. Such locales seem to choose and form us, as I have said; if we do not take in the genius of these places— that is, open ourselves to the transformations they can work, as some of the old Egyptian apothegmata assert—these places will throw us out or set us aside. This is a serious matter: placeless, our identity is never fully developed and our anger, thus unnamed, is rampant, diffused. Without a relationship to land and the respect and ethical regard that come from relationship, we are dangerous and savage to land, as well as bereft within, nameless, unhoused. Our incompleteness makes us destructive, ravenously, disproportionately, madly, ungovernably hungry, afflicted with a hunger that may be a sort of uncomprehended mourning. This behaviour is met by love for place, by being entered by the accommodating beauty or idiosyncratic strangeness of that river, that hill or neighbourhood or garden, met by this sweet, comprehending erotic passivity. This violence to land is met by the self enlarged by affection and gratitude for particular places, for places that seem to look at us and take us in.

2

The Start of Real Thinking

IN THE LATE WINTER AND EARLY SPRING of 1971,
it became completely clear to me I couldn't continue as I had been living.
I had been hospitalized in the Munroe Wing, the psychiatric ward of the
Regina General Hospital, eighteen months earlier. My razor was taken from
me, and I was kept under a twenty-four-hour watch, initially in a segregated
room. When I eventually requested a release, I went into therapy with a
young, sympathetic British psychologist and began to attend, as well, a group
he ran for youth. I was told I was lucky to be admitted to this gathering, but
I could see, after a few months, I was getting nowhere in it; nothing seemed
able to budge what I had taken to thinking of my likely permanent state.
Mostly this was bottomless, constant, tendrilling anxiety, "free floating," since,
though certain incidents could cause it to spike, it didn't seem connected to
any particular issue or event. This anxiety grew from a mood or condition
of disgust, terror and hopelessness.

It seemed to me that this relatively recent state of mind was passing slowly over my identity like a planet's shadow over a moon, so that it was becoming impossible to tell the two apart. And no way of dislodging it presented itself. Everything I knew the way to now seemed heavy, incapable of rising and worn, the assortment of drugs I took, the complaining, conniving transcendence of Colin Wilson's *The Outsider,* which I had been reading; even Bob Dylan's *Blonde on Blonde* genius, with its knowing, social critique, a previous touchstone, seemed more or less flat and unwakening. None of these things had the pneumatic force to lift the anxiety; if anything, their inertness added weight to it. As I considered my options, I realized I had no way out. Therapy didn't work; hanging around with others as disaffected as I made the enervation seem deeper. I was having suicidal thoughts and was acting out aggressive, violent impulses—thus the hospitalization. One friend, schizophrenic, decided that since he was dead, he might as well collect the benefits of the heir and was trying to talk a prominent Regina lawyer into representing him. He enlisted me in this enterprise, and we discussed his plans endlessly; they were as complicated as fourth-century Christologies; they were part desperate earnestness and part theatre, and gave me vertigo. Everything quaked on a thin foundation.

With my best friend, John Woods, I took up nightly residence in the famous basement beer parlour of the Hotel Saskatchewan, drinking successive drafts and yammering about Nietzsche and Gurdjieff, both of us vogueing as whacked out philosophy students, which we more or less were, for the visual artists, who were always located near the shuffleboard table and practiced an impeccable cool which involved paying no attention to us. But my friend was running out of money and planning to look for work in coal mines at Fernie and Sparwood, and he left town at the beginning of the summer. I enjoyed the beery handball of philosophical argument, and the occasional hit of acid shared with him, but neither got below the turmoil in me.

I had a faint hunch that the way out for me was somehow religious, a sort of overdrive of emotion, but I knew I had come too far in the project of pushing away from my family to return to services at Rosemont United Church. A move like that—impossible—would strangle me even quicker than what I was up to. My Colin Wilson, Nietzsche friend had once spent a few days at a Buddhist monastery in California and was reading P.D. Ouspensky's *In Search of the Miraculous*, which he urged me to look at as well. Gurdjieff, with his ferociously certain claims and theatrical eyes, puzzled and spooked me, but Ouspensky mentioned the master had studied for a short time on Mt. Athos, the Christian monastic island off the Greek coast. I didn't know there was such a place as this or such a thing as Christian contemplative practice. I'd thought the whole tradition was emotional blandness, misplaced certainty and rectitude. I began to say the Jesus Prayer, which I'd picked up, I think, in the Ouspensky book, as I drove a wreck of a truck for a private company contracted to the Post Office, on rounds collecting mail from various postal outlets and boxes in north Regina each day in the late afternoon and early evening.

My reading shifted; while still ploughing through Ouspensky, I also was looking into Thomas Merton's *The Seven Story Mountain*, John of the Cross' *Dark Night of the Soul*, *The Cloud of Unknowing*. One book led to another—Thomas à Kempis' *The Imitation of Christ*, the mystical theologies of Ruusbroec, Tauler, Margery Kempe, Julian of Norwich, Walter Hilton. My mind, for a time, seemed stuck in the swooping spiritual imagination of the northern European fourteenth century. It was an extraordinary couple of months. I worked a split shift, finishing around nine at night, when I went home, ate and slept, so much of this reading must have taken place in the late morning and early afternoon. I imagine myself lying on the bed in the north bedroom, sifting through the books. I must have come across some overview of Christian mystical theology to get into all these corners so quickly, but I can't recall what it was. I got some ideas from Merton—John of the Cross and Teresa of Avila came from him—but the other authors I must have ferreted out on my own. The Regina Public Library was thin on this sort of material, but I chewed whatever was on the bone. I can't say, Merton aside, that I understood even a quarter of what I read, but I knew I was into a rich vein, that others had been there before me, a form of thinking and feeling that surprised and somehow welcomed me. Here was something that had heft, both emotional and philosophical, that accommodated an interior stretch I'd not imagined but desired, though I was confused about where I fit in it.

Later that summer, toward the end of June, I had an extraordinary experience while I was part way through my late afternoon route, a visit from some rushing form of beauty that filled me and filled me with rising surges of love that went on so long and at such a pitch, that, weeping, saying thank you, thank you, I almost asked it to end. I got out of the truck at my parents' house fifteen minutes later for a coffee, reeling, hardly believing my amazing luck. I told no one what had occurred, but started skipping lunch after that day, wore heavy shirts buttoned to the collar in the hammering prairie heat, slept on the floor with a thick belt tied tightly around my chest. I look at pictures of me then, and I see a bit of a wild look between the long sideburns, but there are signs of a still joy in the face too. I thought I'd found something not wholly identifiable, doubtlessly Christian, and, for me, perfect. Nothing that beautiful had ever come my way: I couldn't even have imagined this with anything approaching sufficiency so I could hope for it. There were further experiences through the last weeks of the summer.

Merton had remarked in one of his books that a Cistercian abbey had been established south of Winnipeg years ago, but he did not name the town. I wrote to every community in south central Manitoba below the Number One Highway that had what I supposed to be a Catholic name, St. Agathe, St. Malo, St. Norbert, addressing each letter "Abbot, Trappist Monastery," and received one reply from Our Lady of the Prairies Abbey, the abbot telling me they had a certain number of monks and ran a dairy. I believe he told me the size of the herd the community owned. I was free to pay them a visit. I hitchhiked to St. Norbert at the end of the August, arriving late at night, having walked from downtown Winnipeg, and slept in local park in the sand box, which held some heat from the day, taking in the Persieds meteor shower, convinced it was some sort of sign.

The first monk I met after the gatekeeper was Fr. Ambrose Davidson, the guestmaster, and his brilliant, gentle, expansive listening was a pool I dove into. He told me the worth of what I had experienced; he advised me, as well, to patch up things with my father and finish my degree. I had little sense of what these instructions meant, being in a sense drunk on the elongated experience and just generally ignorant. He let me hang around the monastery for about a week, getting me to do this and that, then sent me on my way. At one point, he dressed me in the Trappist habit and photographed me in the guest-house kitchen; this photograph, he said, would be for promotional purposes, but, looking back, it's clear the act was intended as a psychagogic event. He sent it to me and, in a fit of fierce humility, I tore it up. I had been agog at everything in the abbey and loved especially the singing of Compline; in those days the community had a particularly good cantor. I still remember his reaching voice, its glitter and rich sobriety.

I hitchhiked back at Christmas, again arriving at night (the distance between Regina and St. Norbert around four hundred miles), near midnight, the sky clear, bright with stars. I knew I'd be in trouble if I tried to stay out in that thirty below cold, so let myself into the barn, planning to sleep beside one of the gigantic Holsteins, but found instead a warm room where the milk tank was kept. The 4:30 AM bells woke me, and I met monks coming out for early milking. They asked me what I wanted, then turned me over to Fr. Ambrose. I had been reading Dante and Milton that term at university, those poems themselves revelations, and felt I was happy. I was received into the church the next Easter. Beyond that event, there was the world, awaiting my comprehension. Being a Catholic has always struck me as a form of realism. The few minutes that June gave me everything, an extraordinary economy.

I was incapable at the time of seeing my emotional difficulties, indeed much of my mental unease was, in large part, the result of the emptiness and subterfuge arising from being a beneficiary of a colonial condition. Nor could I have imagined that one way of treating my distress was a return to my culture's sapiential tradition. But in fact, without knowing it, I was now on this path.

3
On Scholem, Ruusbroec and Exegesis

GERSHOM SCHOLEM wrote to his friend Walter Benjamin on
June 28, 1935, giving an account of his recent work. It was to be a "textbook"
offering "an extract of the last fifteen years" (Alter xi) of his writing. In this
enterprise, which would contribute substantially to his masterful *Major
Trends in Jewish Mysticism*, Scholem predicted that "the element of proof
will be totally eliminated" and boasted that the prospective reader would
find "no lack of amazing things, and the historical observer is guaranteed to
get his money's worth. The whole thing is conceived of as an announcement
of a stock-taking, if one which is also fairly voluminous."

Scholem had been living in Palestine for over a decade, immersed in
his retrieval of the lineage of Jewish esoteric thought, working often from
mere manuscript scraps, his purpose exegetical, formational and polemical.
Benjamin was then residing in Paris, in exile from National Socialism, at
work on *The Arcades Project*, a compilation which amounted to a "phantasmagoria of the nineteenth century" (Wolin 174), or a "pre-history of the

modern," which was also meant to be a fully restorative practice of true naming, a form of sacerdotal ascesis, the sole artifact of which was to be a gathering of fragments. Both writers, though their concerns appeared to diverge, sensed their projects were complementary. Each was skeptical of hegemonic rationalism and the politics it brought. Each pursued a re-visioning of the past to which he felt himself particularly joined, Jewish intellectual history and the apex of the Enlightenment; each felt a keen confidence in exegesis, convinced that re-expression of previous texts and dispositions was orientingly worthwhile. Both harboured a hunch about the sufficiency of tesseraic understanding.

Little resembling Scholem's mammoth hermeneutical endeavour, an undertaking at once popular, scholarly and daemonic, has occurred since. There was nothing in twentieth-century Christianity matching the breadth of Scholemian retrieval, Merton's circumscribed yet excellent efforts only a kind of beginning, which in the end has yielded little. The resulting absence of the esoteric in philosophical ontology, in ethics and in politics, both within the Christian churches and, for similar reasons, outside them, has been a continuing source of disaster. This has been not merely an absence in scholarship, but in the range of available intentions that may go into the formation of a life. This absence of the interior is also the root of an occluded and roughly delimited prehension of the world and a reduced, often violent, way of being in it.

|| Scholem was repeatedly struck by what he saw as the provincial and the amateur nature of the various Kabbalistic writings he rescued from near complete neglect and sought to transport into the light of interpretation. In his first Stroock Lecture, delivered at the Jewish Institute of Religion in New York in 1938, which was to become the first chapter of *Major Trends*, he admitted, "one seldom fails to be torn between alternate admiration and disgust" (Alter xvii) while reading the great Kabbalists. "Again and again one is struck by the simultaneous presence of crudely primitive modes of thought and feeling, and of ideas whose profound contemplative mysticism is transparent." It was this farouche roughness that led Kabbalist thought

and scholarship to be silenced, "closed as it was to the rationalism prevailing in the Judaism of the nineteenth century," its few experts, as a result, "never published or their observations recorded" (Scholem 2).

Scholem was an authentic exegete like Origen or Evagrius, unqualified in his commitment, more than merely professional, attuned to the realization one must change his life in order to understand. It is clear to me, similarly, that to consider the Christian mystical tradition, perhaps not quite as recessed as Kabbalistic writings in the early twentieth century, as simply a scholar is never to fully receive it. Here an awkward, amorphous, intense, relentless engagement, which may seem naivete, is as necessary a dispositional basis to a true reading as it was in esoteric Judaism. Thomas Merton, Ernesto Cardenal and Raïssa Maritain are quite different examples of this spirit at work in twentieth-century Christian mystical hermeneutics. Understanding can only be an altered life, caught and savoured sporadically in self-reflection; an account of this interrupted grasp will be various enactments of what it urges.

The philosophical eros instigating the appearance of these new subjectivities is often marked by sadness, in part because the shape of this turning, its teleology, is difficult to discern, and the forms of life it urges can seem oxymoronic, or so contrary as to be invisible, within modernity. Scholem, for instance, found in his research into the Kabbalah, at all stages of its development, a tone that was "deeply conservative and intensely revolutionary" (Alter xxi), this amalgam resembling elements of Benjamin's early millenarian Marxism, but it was something more besides. A similar peculiar fusion of preservation and cataclysmic transformation awaits any careful and persistent reader of Christian mystical thought. Modernity accommodates, even sponsors, reactionary nostalgia and aggressively progressive hopefulness, but not the peculiar fusion Scholem found in his virtually forgotten texts. Nor are the two terms of interiority's immanent politics in Scholem's fusion, with the particular shades he discerns, matched by anything in the modern world. But it must be admitted that the primary reason for the sadness of philosophical eros is the immeasurability of beauty.

|| There have been at least six foundational features to my own committed reading practice over the last thirty or so years. I long ago accepted their inevitable presence in my ingestion of a certain sort of writing, and, over time, have also come to choose them as ways of making my reading as true, or efficacious, as it could be. These rudiments have been: my ignorance; my panic; my eros; my amateurism and provinciality; my sense of acute cultural poverty in the glaciated, arid plain left by capitalism's advances and retreats, and, standing next to this insight into poverty, a persistent appetite for buoying, partial, emergent coherence, which I anticipate—I admit almost groundlessly—will possess theurgical powers. There is a sixth feature, which I do not choose at the moment: my isolation: I speak to no one, except, it seems to me, the angel as this figure appears or is constituted in the understanding of Ibn 'Arabi, the active intelligence or the creative imagination, which is, through besottedness and courage, the sole source of being. I cringe to think of how this claim would sound to certain friends and plead for a generous, patient hearing on this point. The solitary, particular and necessary nature of this interlocutor is an essential component of burgeoning contemplative understanding, as we will see later when we consider the epistemology of St. Teresa of Avila.

I confess I know next to nothing, in a background sense, of medieval Islam and little of early Christian monastic theology, little of Neoplatonism— I am not a scholar of antiquity—but these places are where the thought of Plato, that residue of Neolithic cosmological and introspective comprehension, went after the end of the golden age of Greek philosophical thought. So I read in these areas with a kind of senseless belief in the seemingly chaotic, happenstance efficacy of *lectio divina*. I have particularly chosen such a questionable belief, thinking it was allied to some economy that would lead to truth. My panic—grounded in the view that I had nothing available to me which could tell me how to live or what properly to hope for or how to be vivified by the geographical location where I found myself—also, I believed, was a heuristic instrument; my panic came to me without effort.

My amateurism has made me a little more credulous, and likely less orthodox, than others, scholars and poets, and as a result I have soaked in all sorts of glimmerings from a range of sources, from Christian monasticism to Islamic esotericism and phenomenology. My eros has meant that I have wanted everything. My poverty convinced me I *must* read, *must* think, *must* canvas others on how things seemed to them. My appetite has felt like prophecy: the transformative coherence I wanted was there and would reveal itself by inches over time. So I read and read. My practice of "saying again" is integral to the larger practice of theurgical reading. The mere re-utterance unfailingly releases some part of the power of the text. Then there is the conviction that such reading is elementally political, and that there is an urgent current political need that it be done.

|| Reading of the kind I require and attempt often demands a change in one's life, while it triggers further changes once this reading is fully undergone. Examples of such alterations, provoked by daemonic inquiry and serving as antechambers to deeper textual engagements, initiations into interpretation, can be found in the lives of such spiritual exegetes as Gershom Scholem and Ibn 'Arabi. Scholem grew up in a German Jewish middle-class milieu in the early years of the twentieth century. It was rather unusual, it seems, that a young man from such a background, at that time, should devote himself to Talmudic studies and "seek a way to Jewish substance" (10), as he reports he did in his book *Walter Benjamin: The Story of a Friendship*; and his father vigorously opposed his initial interest in this project. At school, he began by studying mathematics and traditional philosophy, but in 1919, he decided to turn to Kabbalistic literature and complete a thesis on linguistic theory in the ancient mystical texts. Virtually no one then had such concerns in German academic circles. In 1923, he emigrated to Israel, which had no university and, in those days, no hope of one in the near future, still in pursuit of a Zionism that he agreed later was adequately characterized as a "religious-mystical quest for a regeneration of Judaism" (171). He changed his name and remarried.

Scholem's pursuit of foundational understanding in Judaism involved him, at least at the outset, in ever deepening instability. All of these shifts inevitably went with him into his further reading of Kabbalistic manuscripts. This unsettling experience seems to have intensified even after his emigration. Looking back on his relations with Walter Benjamin in the early 1920s, he was struck by the difference in their situation.

> When I left Benjamin in 1923, I took with me the image of a man driven
> by a beeline impulse to fashion an intellectual world of his own, a man who
> unswervingly followed his genius and who knew where he was headed, no
> matter what the external entanglements of his life might be. I was heading
> for a world in which everything still seemed disorganized and confused, in
> which amid severe internal struggles I was seeking a stable position where
> my efforts to understand Judaism would more clearly fit together into a
> integral whole. (133)

Ibn 'Arabi's initial change under the power of deep reading was even more dramatic than Gershom Scholem's. He was born in Murcia in the southeast of Spain in 1165 into a noble family and was sent to Seville to study. He married at a relatively early age, his new wife encouraging him in his movement to Sufism. At the beginning of his Sufi studies, however, he fell ill and seemed near death; a pervasive lethargy spread over him, and he slipped into a semi-conscious fever state in which he saw himself menaced by a diabolic crowd. Then a beautiful being appeared in his delirium and drove the demons off. "Who are you?" Ibn 'Arabi asked (Corbin, *Creative Imagination* 39). The figure replied it was the Sura Yasin, the sura for the dying his father had been reciting at his bedside, the text now assuming physicality to stand in proximity to him and address him as friend. This episode played a significant role in instigating Ibn 'Arabi's peregrination that led him to Mecca and to further theophanic visions. His *divina afflictio* and exile from the legalism of Spain were propadeutic to even deeper subsequent readings. One must be changed in order to read: by means of this change, the text grows a body, substance and the animation of affectivity.

|| I must be changed in order to read. The fourteenth-century Flemish mystic John Ruusbroec observes in his *A Mirror of Eternal Blessedness* that there are three forms of goodness. There is the kind found in "virtuous persons of good will who are always overcoming sin and dying to it" (Russbroec 189). There is the goodness which is a full and rich interiority. Then there is "dying in love and coming to nought," which is a unitary activity with divinity. In all these interior dispositions, Ruusbroec insists it is crucial that the heart be left "empty and undisturbed," so that "you may see him whom you love as often as you wish" (191). This state is particularly essential, says Ruusbroec, in reading, singing and praying, where it makes these acts numinous service a sort of activism. ("In addition, whenever you are reading, singing or praying, if you are able to understand the words, then pay attention to their sense and meaning, for you are serving in God's presence" [192].)

A feature of this service is the appearance of a faultlessly sufficient economy of love, a non-satiating, polyform excess, where eros always makes for more, even as it satisfies its earlier, more modest, while true, aspirations. "Moreover, you should know," Ruusbroec further remarks, "that everything you can desire—and more besides—will be given to you without your having to do anything, for if you truly have divine love, you have all that you can desire" (191). You float in a boat resembling Osip Mandelstam's "Egyptian boat" (*Selected Essays* 79), a craft of eros made of motility and emergent shapes of sense, which are equally surprising and apt. This desire-magnifying yielding, a kind of helpless, yet keen, readiness to saturatingly hear, is the ascesis that makes fuller readings of theurgical works possible and more potent; indeed, it activates the exegesis existentiating the theurgy latent in a remarkable variety of books.

|| Scholem had extensive conversations with Benjamin and his wife Dora in the spring of 1918 in Bern, where the Benjamins were temporarily living to

get relief from the war. Scholem joined them once he'd been released from a military psychiatric hospital, with a diagnosis of dementia praecox and a document declaring him unfit for military service. These talks ranged widely, but always included Judaism and Scholem's growing interest in its mystical sources.

> Right from the start we spoke a great deal about his [Benjamin's] "Programm der Kommenden Philosophie." Benjamin discussed the scope of the concept of experience that was meant here; according to him, it encompassed man's intellectual and psychological connection with the world, which takes place in the realms not yet penetrated by cognition. When I mentioned that consequently it was legitimate to include the mantic disciplines in this conception of experience, Benjamin responded with an extreme formulation: "A philosophy that does not include the possibility of soothsaying from coffee grounds and cannot explicate it cannot be a true philosophy." (Walter Benjamin 59)

While Scholem objected to the wildness coming at the end of this remark, he agreed readily with Benjamin that Kant had "motivated an inferior experience," which had captivated philosophy in the years since.

Benjamin's provocatively casual mapping of the proper extent of philosophical inquiry recalls Henry Corbin's remark, in his *Creative Imagination in the Sufism of Ibn 'Arabi*, on the danger of the exclusion of the mantic—that the human community "must offer a structure in which esoterism is an organic component; or else it will suffer all the consequences implied by a rejection of esoterism" (15). The chief consequence is the variety of violences—the reductions, erasures, autocracies—inherent in all literalisms, realisms and materialisms. The mystical scotoma of modernity does not mean, as rationalist rectitude imagines, the happy absence of ornate supernatural effects or excesses of subjectivity, but the extirpation of interior quiet and alertness, the very rudiments of decorum and ethics.

|| There is more to be drawn out from Ruusbroec's contemplative phenom-
enology. The interior life, once one is born in "God's spirit," is marked by
absorption, de-individuation and autonomy. In his alertness, the contemplative's "will becomes free, for it is then one with the free will of God,"
and in this being taken over, he "is raised up in love above his own nature"
(Ruusbroec 199). While absorbed completely in God, one is extruded, separate in an intensifying "spiritual hunger and thirst which makes us want to
savor him eternally" (209). This savouring, Ruusbroec assures us, is mutual.
In a reversal of Eucharistic imagery, he describes the fierce appetite of
divinity itself: "His hunger is incomparably great: He consumes us right to
the depths of our being, for he is a voracious glutton suffering from bulimia
and consuming the very marrow of our bones" (208). This total consump-
tion is the root of human appetite and daemonic sensuality, as well as the
experience of becoming other than oneself. Affective union, Eucharistic or
otherwise, however, Ruusbroec insists, is emphatically not identity, even
though it involves such annihilation and great intimacy, and in drawing
this distinction between union and the sharing of substance, he makes love
possible, a necessity even, and creates a beginning for an inevitable, vivifying,
utterly non-imperial ethics. The distinction also outlines an extraordinary
form of individuation. The true apokatastasis of interiority is essentially
flawed, that is, it is asymptotic—we approach identity with being's ground,
but always fail to achieve it. Apokatastasis' proper operation depends on the
perpetual existence of this flaw. Ruusbroec's insistence on the distinction
between union and identity presents an effective block to Romanticism and
its possible amoralism.

While the results of interiority may seem remarkable, Ruusbroec repeatedly shows they are also ordinary. His philosophical anthropology reveals
that the imperfect return human innerness effects is nothing more than
nature naturing.

We all possess this image as an eternal life—apart from ourselves, prior to
our creation—while in our created being this image is the super-essential

being of our essential being and eternal life. From this, the substance of our
soul has three attributes, which are but one in nature. The soul's first attri-
bute is an essential bareness devoid of images. Through it we are like the
Father and are also united with him and with his divine nature. (214)

Along with this unification is "mirrorlike resplendence," the soul's higher
reason, the noetic practice of the Son. Thirdly, there is innerness' "spark," its
natural tendency to return to its source. The substance of the organism of the
self in contemplation, then, is awe, followed by phronesis and eros.

|| Our times, in their danger, require from us, operating in our actual esoteric
and political incompetence, an undisciplined, yet phronetic, hermeneutics of
desperation, which is founded on a state of maximum availability, in which
one is reduced—dilated—by the mere, truthful recognition of the poverty
of one's condition, the historically implanted inability in each of us to understand. Each of us, in these perilous days, must wage a politics of the interior:
the mantic books will come toward us with their alarming appetite and
disquieting, deracinating regard; often they will be unbeautiful; they will
always be providentially demanding. Our poverty, our hopelessness, a true
state available to us, will allow us this approach. The true ascesis, which is
genuine political practice, is being honestly and deeply what we actually are.
    Among other things, Scholem's utopian program of interpretation is an
activity we could take up in our circumstances. This program, in its most
hopeful political form, was proposed by Walter Benjamin in discussions with
representatives from the nascent Hebrew University in Paris in 1927, at meetings which Scholem had helped make possible and which, he had hoped,
would facilitate Benjamin's emigration to Palestine. It was to be an undertaking, which Benjamin did not attempt in the end, of approaching "the
great texts of Jewish literature" in Hebrew "not as a philologist but as a metaphysician" (Scholem, *Walter Benjamin* 137). Such a reading of certain texts,
varying from person to person, but all of a similar sort—revelatory or Platonic,
erotic, philosophical—constituting the elemental writings of the West's

wisdom tradition, can only be grounding, individuating and millenarian—apokatastatic—in its political potency, given a shaken life preceding a full encounter with the texts in reading's pre-reading life.

This discipline of daemonic interpretation, or "listening" to works, an exigent *lectio divina*, is a spiritual practice contingent on a particular methodology, outlined earlier, a methodology of transformative helplessness, and the turning to works written "on the back and on the front" (Ezekial 2.10). Both the methodology and the reading it engenders are a discernment of spirits. This interpretive discipline achieves individuation of particularly formed readers, permitting a recovery of a foundational, deeper identity and the return of the play of the esoteric in one's life. It has this power because it is an acute philosophical introspection from the outside. It is potently political because, if interiority is readable as ontology, as Ibn 'Arabi and others claim, transformed eros amounts to an altering of the polis. An element of this altering will be an open and tentative regard to things—Douglas fir, streams, camas fields.

Contemplative interiority, that alert, erotic freedom, is also one of the few sources of skepticism before the power of ideology (imperial, class, romantic) that does not corrupt the one who doubts, damaging her capacity to savour and discern.

4

Imagination, Psychagogy
and Ontology

Turtle Mountain
June 2008

EVAGRIUS PONTICUS, in his book *Praktikos*, urges imageless-
ness in deeper forms of prayer, so that the self's limitless ambition to care for
itself might be disabled, and the entire solipsistic cycle in interior reaching
might be blocked. Catechetically sanctioned religious imagination is included
in this suppression of images, as is the imagination fostered by a non-metaphorical biblical hermeneutic, which conceives, for example, divinity as bodied,
emotioned. Even the sense of suppression itself must be cancelled. In Evagrian,
imageless prayer, any fundamental encounter, if only with silence, will be
authentic.

Henry Corbin, mid-twentieth-century Islamist and Persian scholar, in
his reading of the "Spiritualists" Ibn 'Arabi and Suhrawardi, is equally antago-
nistic to systematic theology as deep, interior comprehension as Evagrius.
Corbin, however, takes a different reconstituted epistemological starting
point than the ascetically formed, alacritous emptiness of Evagrius. For Ibn
'Arabi and Suhrawardi, thirteenth-century Sufis, Corbin observes, "the world

is 'objectively' and actually threefold: between the world that can be apprehended by pure intellectual perception (the universe of the Cherubic
Intelligences) and the universe perceptible to the senses, there is an intermediate world, the world of the Idea-Images, of archetypal figures, of subtile
substances, of 'immaterial matter'" (*Creative Imagination* 3–4). This intermediate world, Corbin argues in *Creative Imagination in the Sufism of Ibn
'Arabi*, is objective, genuinely real—even though access to it now in Western
modernity is boarded up, so that if it is noted now at all, it appears as a
curious ruin, superceded, overgrown, picturesque. This world is "where the
spiritual takes body and the body become spiritual," says Corbin, where the
directing, enabling organ is "the active Imagination…the *place* of theophanic
visions, the scene on which visionary events *appear* in their true reality" (4).

Corbin's Sufic imagination clearly is not unfortunate Romantic imagination, not, that is, a phantasmagoric reach steered by ego-transfixion, the vital
thrust of male, bourgeois liberation and the interior fuel of its republicanism;
nor is it fantasy. The imagination in Ibn 'Arabi has ontological standing; it is
not the accomplishment of creativity, but is something apparently apart from
us, muscularly creative itself, though requiring cooperation from its subject. It
has political, as well as extraordinary psychic import, is an interior state that
is a terrain, a "nation." This is imagination on the other side of the achievement of discernment and permeability, resembling, perhaps, John Cassian's
"prayer of fire," though in it one is not solely receptor.

|| What to think of the sort of popular contemporary poetry that is itself
strictly, devotedly non-Romantic, that is, indeed, entirely ironic, Dean Young's
poetry, for instance, featured in the *American Poetry Review*?

Such poetry intends—and achieves—the end of Romantic "agony," that
emotional falseness, that (usually male) simulacrum for deep feeling and
alertness; and this achievement stands vastly to its credit. But Young's poetry
also is the perfect poetic for globalism, since it signals the end of meaning
and moral absorption in these imperial days—because there cannot be a
situation where one is arrested in moral matters when empire is enjoyed

and sometimes celebrated, if only obliquely. The poetic ironist—the neo-formalist, as well—strikes himself as deeply "moral"—this accounts for the pervasiveness, the rigor, the superior tone of his irony—but this morality, while it imagines it disables the tyranny of metaphysics and thus frees, is that of Plato's Thrasymachus, a tacit and inevitable alignment with power that holds in contempt any speaking of a moral or psychagogic word, tacitly loving might's ethos at the seedy end of the era of American economic hegemony. Speech that betrays no sense of elemental psychagogic meaning, that in fact softly ridicules such possibilities, is a mark of acuity and liberal revolution in this poetry. Here we see the extent of capitalism's ideological deracination. Its great achievement is a dramatic and vicious narrowing of reading. There isn't enough in Dean Young's poetry to sustain any sort of citizenship that would lift and name one. This poetry will lighten us to an illness that at the moment has no name.

‖ In the traditional Western account of Islamic philosophy, the Neoplatonism of Avicenna was dispatched by Averroes' vigorous Aristotelianism in the twelfth century. Before this version of events became the orthodoxy of sanctioned philosophical history, it was wishful thinking in the scholasticism of the twelfth and thirteenth centuries. The active Intelligence is central to Avicenna's philosophical anthropology; here is the confluence of epistemology and cosmology in Avicennism, for this intelligence is only partly a human power. It is human, that is, in the act of passive reception and the preparation making way for this; as an active force, it is angelic. In the Avicennan cosmology, "Angel-Souls," *animae coelestes*, "communicate to the Heavens the movement of their desire," so that "the orbits of the heavenly bodies are characterized by an aspiration of love forever renewed and forever unstilled" (Corbin, *Creative Imagination* 11).

Avicennism, rather than vanishing under the correction of Averroes, moved east in the eleventh and twelfth centuries, where it mingled with nascent Sufism in Syria and Iran. Avicenna, and later Ibn 'Arabi and Suhrawardi, associated the perpetual dynamizing, ordering and cohering power of the angel, according to Corbin, with the Holy Spirit, and identified it with the highest form of human understanding. The world of the angel, the intermediate world, is purely symbolic, constituted entirely by analogy and homology; in it, understanding is transformative, and does not yield to explanation; like metaphor, it vanishes with explanation. Pneumatic epistemology *is* angelology in Ibn 'Arabi's Sufism and Avicenna's Neoplatonism— mystical thought is "meeting the angel" (Corbin, *Avicenna* 20–21), that particular homecoming and ravishment. The active Intelligence is also the source of human individuation, since desire, unlike dogmatic assent, is always specific, singular; fully engaged, it is particularizing, distinguishing. This form of knowing, its source in active Intelligence, is also cosmically restorative, for here understanding is a matter of taking on the interiority of the angel, its epektatic yearning.

It is not surprising that Western European scholasticism possessed "a fear of the angel" (Corbin, *Creative Imagination* 11), a trepidation concerning Avicennan angelology, for in Avicenna's account of cognition, understanding does not require the ministrations of dogma as discipline, nor indeed the mediation of the sacraments. Comprehension and becoming oneself were political, paradisial acts: apokatastasis was not a perpetually deferred state, nor initially a public one. Scholasticism's fear of Avicennan angelology is ontological, then, and strategic, rising from concerns about the vulnerability of ecclesiastical government, and perhaps from a contesting depiction of the eschaton. Rationalism, before such claims as Avicennan angelologists make, is simply or ironically incredulous; but it should be remembered that analogic expression—the "it-is-as-if"—is the most eloquent means of spiritual phenomenology, the most penetrating. I do not wish to diminish analogy philosophically by this remark. In the epistemology of the "Spiritualists," ontology is mediated by—uncovered solely in—interior practice, which in its upper ranges is reportable only by analogy and metaphor; these, as well, in Avicennan philosophy, are the substance of the angelic mind and the machinery of the intermediate world. Metaphor, if it is fine, operates only in the alternate, intermediate domain. Movements of the angel are not caught by the clarity of dogmatic definitions but in the puzzled scenting of phenom-enology. The angel is less a being than an interior state—or: the two, being and state, virtually merge in the experience of the meeting, so the "it-is-as-if" and "this-is-exactly-what-happened" stand phenomenologically quite close in any interior savouring, each amplifying the other.

|| Hegemonic realism in literature through the last six decades may testify in part to our post-war unease concerning the link between fascism and a hyperbolic, Romantic mythology in the 1930s and 1940s, the inflation coming from the second figure in this union, mythologizing's capacity to elevate its devotees beyond morality. A coeval intellectual anxiety has centered on reason's messianism in the long era of the ideology of the new science; this disquiet has manifested itself in a courting of the irrational in comprehension. Martin Heidegger's interest in the manner in which understanding unfolds in the arts, particularly in painting and poetry, is a well-known example of this mid- to late-twentieth-century philosophical enthusiasm.

Heidegger saw the *technē* found in the artisanal crafts and in the fine arts as a mode of "unlocking" (322), a revealing of sequestered truth. Modern technology, on the other hand, committed to massive production and the stockpiling of goods, in contrast, Heidegger charged, is a "setting-upon" (321), a "challenging-forth" (322), an obliteration of objects in their separate-ness as they are converted into "standing reserve." The root of this particular denial of the reality of the world was not the prodigious machine power of the last half of the twentieth century, Heidegger observed, but a style of comprehension that appeared much earlier, in the revolutionary physics of the seventeenth century. There the term of inquiry was not the representa-tion of what is but the requirement "that nature report itself in some way or other that is identifiable through calculation and that it remain orderable as a system of information" (328), as Heidegger says in his essay "The Question Concerning Technology." In this form of knowledge, the essence of nature is gathered, warehoused, for continued use in mathematicized theorems.

Heidegger calls this impulse at the center of the new science "en-framing," an insistence "in which the actual reveals itself as standing reserve" (329). This violence to the autonomous reality of things bites into human character as well, through its endless, solipsistic repetitions, shaping our ethics, as it deepens our boredom.

> As soon as what is unconcealed no longer concerns man even as object, but exclusively as standing reserve, and man in the midst of objectlessness is nothing but the orderer of standing reserve, then he comes to the very brink of a precipitous fall; that is, he comes to the point where he himself will have to be taken as standing-reserve. Meanwhile, man, precisely as the one so threatened, exhalts himself and postures as lord of the earth....In this way, the illusion comes to prevail that everything man encounters exists insofar as it is his construct. This illusion gives rise in turn to one final delusion: it seems as though man everywhere and always encounters only himself. (332)

The power to extricate human beings from this impacted error lies close at hand, Heidegger assures, within the nature of technology itself. "But where danger is, grows / The saving power also" (333), he quotes Holderlin. The impulse to enframe does not exhaust *technē*'s essence, but skews it: it is a later abbreviation of technology's authentic purpose. Far more foundational is *technē*'s identity as *poeisis*, the revealing, the "shining-forth," of "presence" in things, a showing "of the gods and the dialogue of divine and human destinings" (340). "The poetical," Heidegger concludes, "thoroughly pervades every art, every revealing of essential unfolding into the beautiful."

Heidegger gives no detailed phenomenological description of poetic intuition either in this essay or in the earlier and much longer essay "The Origin of the Work of Art," even as he writes optimistically of this form of knowing as a saving "passageway" (166), drawing forth the beautiful, and as a rescuing alternative to the thought impelling large, destructive industry and resource extraction. He makes no comment, in particular, on any sort of ascetical preparation, no mention of interior exercise, to wean the understanding of the poet from the ingrained, pandemic practice of enframing; knowing this way appears to be simply what poets, and artists of all sorts, do. Or perhaps we are to suppose that there is something in the writing of poetry (all forms of poetry?) itself—a mechanism unnamed by Heidegger—that inevitably provokes this noesis. Without ascesis, this saving intuition is likely itself to be Romanticism, a belief in the special intuitive powers of the "beautiful soul," an undefended privileging of "fine" discrimination and judgment, the sort that Heidegger himself appears to exhibit when, in response to Karl Jasper's complaints in a conversation about the brutality of Hitler's rule, he remarked on the beauty of the dictator's hands.

If you hold to dissidence within rationalism's hegemony, you do not automatically become a Heideggerian fantasist—there is the authentically mystical, the comprehensive vitalism of, say, an Ibn 'Arabi. Suspicion on the matter of the nature of the idealized, privileged Heideggerian subject may spread, undermining the nature of the known object as "presence." In Ibn 'Arabi's mystical theology, the world indeed is not object, nor is it an occult revelation to the special few: it is the self of the kenotic individual.

|| Scholasticism is doubly removed from the individual. The essence of particular objects, what makes them what they are, in Thomism, is classical form, shared by all members of a particular group; difference is a matter of accidents, hair and eye colour, length of stalk and leaf shape, and therefore inconsequential. Reason alone is held to be sufficient in the identification of this common form: the scholastic "fear of the Angel" was calmed, in part, by the claim that understanding did not require a force beyond ordinary human powers. Knowing was not an individuating event because no extraordinary intervention was involved in its operation; cognition, as a result, was non-erotic, as was ritual; divine regard was conceived, both in act and in potency, as general; worship, then, was properly generic and non-mystical. The individual saskatoon bush was not known in its haecceity. The recognition of the bush as a saskatoon did not individuate, particularize, the recognizer. The richer reality of specificity lay unnamed, unnoted beneath the taxonomic name.

In Ibn 'Arabi's epistemology, passion is both individuation and thought. With him, as with Isaac of Nineveh, the seventh-century contemplative of the Syriac church, one's particular eros was an initial form of prayer, elemental, unsupercedable, formational, a "stirring," in Isaac's phenomenology of prayer (Isaac of Nineveh 249). Passion, therefore, was identity, individuation, and preceded choice; though encouraged by introspection, its existence was not dependent upon it.

Passion, or one's singular, marking, gathering desire, in Ibn 'Arabi's mystical epistemology, which is also an ontology and theology, is in fact a divine Name, or attribute—an interest in certain forms of beauty, for instance, or an appetite for justice, and a responsiveness to justice or beauty or land or love or a particular form of language—brought out of virtuality, from the "sadness" (Corbin, *Creative Imagination* 184), of divine unknowability wishing to be known. In the Sufism of Ibn 'Arabi, the kataphatic and apophatic complementarily and simultaneously co-exist. Divinity is known in introspection and through the courage of enacting one's inescapable exigence before one's own eyes. Passion as individuation is the *only* source of knowing what is in its unknowability, the sole source, then, of ontology and theology—for Ibn 'Arabi the two share an identity—and this desire is the single origin of compassion. It is also, then, necessarily the root of the one true politics. A deep savouring of one name—one self, one introspection—makes an individual alert to, hungry for, the comprehension of all divine Names, all selves.

|| "Either the human community must offer a structure in which esoterism is an organic component," observes Henry Corbin, "or else it must suffer all the consequences implied by a rejection of esoterism" (15). Chief among these consequences are the abandonment of the individual and the loss of the world both as a gathering of haecceities and as divine presence. Any politics, any desire, any knowing, under these circumstances, would be simulated, crafted, will-steered, beauty-less. In a world refusing the esoteric, there would be an enervation of sacrality, together with an increase in religious

theatricality and in ecclesiastical magisteriality. "In his radical answer to the problem of the intellects," says Corbin,

> St. Thomas grants the individual an "active intellect," but not a separate intellect; the intellect of the individual is no longer a transcendent or celestial Intelligence. This seemingly technical solution implies a fundamental decision, the decision to do away with the transcendental dimension of the individual as such, that is, his immediate and personal relationship with the Angel of Knowledge and of Revelation. (17)

Access to divinity is then mediated by the magisterium; all one sees is authority. Without a place for esoterism, a culture, as a result, witnesses the degenerative transformation of individuation into liberal individualism, a collapsing of the emergence of the individual into socialized, homogenized narcissism.

|| Philosophy and the intensified while broadened subjectivity of mystical theology join in both Ibn 'Arabi's angelology and in Suhrawardi's "oriental wisdom." The latter is a merging of Avicennan Neoplatonism, Islamic philosophy and the traditional thought of Persia. In Suhrawardi's "oriental philosophy," an ontology not ending in "a metaphysic of ecstasy" (20), is purposeless speculation, complicit with secular or curial power, while interiority not founded on a philosophical diaresis, he warns, inevitably breaks down, veering into aberrant, unstable vitalisms.

The key philosophical instrument in Suhrawardi's oriental wisdom was the linguistic theurgy of the "visionary recital," a device he discovered in Avicenna, in such symbolic dramas as *Hayy ibn Yaqzan* and the "Recital of the Birds," where imagination gives an account of and inducts one into the intermediate theophanic world. The highest knowing is such dramaturgy. The quest throughout these narratives, the object of all poetic ecstasy, was encounter with the Angel, Holy Spirit, the active Intelligence, tasting this presence, being tasted by it, and the sort of comprehension this meeting could quicken.

While Suhrawardi developed his philosophy of light in twelfth-century Iran, a workmanlike Aristotelianism stole over the philosophic worldview of Western Europe. This presented no capacity to recognize individuality in objects, since this worldview refused a philosophical basis for idiosyncratic form, and no way to undergo the experience of individuality in the self through an encounter with the active Imagination in the moment of understanding; such experiences were shifted to one side, making no appearance on the ledger sheet of cognition. The anatomy of thought in Suhrawardi's illuminationism resembles what an amalgam of Aquinas, Jacob Boehme, Marguerite Porete and Emmanuel Swendenborg might be, a synthesis inconceivable in the Latin West.

One met the angel, in the spirit of this world-feeling, and, with the interior sensorium invigorated by introspection and the practice of one's desire, tasted what the Angel saw. All this takes place within unnerving autonomy, which nevertheless lies within *phronesis*; the range of one's judgment, however, is joltingly stretched. The encounter, which is the embodiment of the Name, and thus no more than self-aproppriation, occurs within a generously, ingeniously considered autobiography, one, that is, which excises nothing and offers symbolic standing freely: nothing, in principle, is insignificant, nothing, while ordinary, not numinal. Becoming one's forming desire is the meeting with the "Gabriel of your being," the "invisible master" (34). The encounter in part is reading one's life from the vantage of one's eros; in such a reading one is more alive than one is usually thought to be and relations exist more than among only the living or between the living and the dead: one is addressed by the daemonic in history, in literature, in the animal world. Many things walk toward a knower, with formational and impelling intent, in such a clear reading of a life.

|| Ibn 'Arabi was seriously ill in the first years after his marriage. He lay comatose for weeks with a profound fever; within, he reported later, an

extraordinary drama unfolded: in the theatre of his interiority, he was overrun by what he took to be a mass of demons. Suddenly a beautiful being appeared, sweet smelling, powerful, and drove off what threatened him. "Who are you?" Ibn 'Arabi asked the figure. "I am the Sura Yasin" (39), he replied. At that moment, Ibn 'Arabi's father had been reciting this sura, a section of the Koran reserved for the dying, at his son's bedside. Writing grew a body, walked forward, and corrected and retrieved.

Later Ibn 'Arabi befriended two female Sufis, one of whom, Fatima of Cordova, became his "spiritual mother" (40). Ibn 'Arabi records that this woman retained a compelling beauty, the beauty of a young woman, into great age. Later still, while in Mecca, following his attendance at the funeral of Averroes and in flight from the legalism in Andalusia, Ibn 'Arabi stayed at the home of an Iranian sage whose daughter was both beautiful and wise. The angel appeared often and in numerous forms. The guide, as in Plato, shows an interior and often exterior attractiveness, revealed in *phronesis* (Socrates, Diotima). The beauty and severity of such figures flawlessly hold the attention of the student. Ibn 'Arabi's life, Corbin claims, was a psychagogic text, primarily for himself, but also useful to others, particular, but within the phenomenological range of the *fedele d'amore*.

A comparable visionary experience, a residence in the intermediate world, took place in the *divina afflictio* of the Christian mystic Julian of Norwich. At thirty years of age, she prayed for three states: a deep knowledge of Christ's passion; physical suffering while young; and "to have as God's gift three wounds." She happened to fall ill in the spring of 1373 and soon appeared to be at the point of death. The height of her illness stretched through the day of May 8.

> My parish priest was sent for to be at my end, and by the time he came my eyes were fixed, and I could no longer speak. He set the cross before my face and said, "I have brought you the image of your Maker and Saviour. Look at it and be strengthened."
>
> I thought indeed that what I was doing good enough, for my eyes were fixed heavenwards where by the mercy of God I trusted to go. But I agreed

none the less to fix my eyes on the face of the crucifix if I could. And this I was able to do. I thought that perhaps I could look straight ahead longer than I could look up.

Then my sight began to fail, and the room became dark about me, as if it were night, except for the image of the cross which somehow was lighted up; but how was beyond my comprehension. Apart from the cross everything else seemed horrible as if it were occupied by fiends.

Then the rest of my body began to die, and I could hardly feel a thing, As my breathing became shorter and shorter I knew for certain that I was passing away.

Suddenly all my pain was taken away, and I was fit and well as I had ever been; and this was especially true of the lower part of my body. I was amazed at this sudden change, for I thought it must have been a special miracle of God....

Then it came to mind that I should ask for the second wound of our Lord's gracious gift, that I might in my own body fully experience and understand his blessed passion. I wanted his pain to be my pain: a true compassion producing a longing for God....

And at once I saw the red blood trickling down from under the garland, hot, fresh and plentiful, just as it did at the time of his passion....And I had a strong, deep conviction that it was he himself and none other that showed me this vision. (Julian of Norwich 65–66)

With both Julian and Ibn ʿArabi, the sensible and phantasmagoric subjective worlds are undivided in illness and vision. This fusion is not the result of sickness' effacement of judgment, but the undermining of a restricted judgment underwritten by health. With these two meetings of the angel and all like them, interior truth, confirmed by the phenomenologies of others who have discernment—insight with the sharpest, most rooting taste—is pitchedly idiosyncratic—this particularity is an essential mark of its authenticity—yet is not relativistic. Phronetic subjectivity is deeper, less contestable, than objectivity, and losses less of what it reports. It is more useful than psychology or systematic theology in matters of interiority: it reports more deeply and in a more liberating manner to others, without losing its form as a purely personal truth. Its report also carries propulsive power for the auditor.

And, as the biting interior theatres of Ibn 'Arabi and Julian show, such comprehension encourages a belonging to what one knows. There is no "standing reserve" (Heidegger 322) with this knowledge. These visions are introspection from a place outside the self, drawing out an ontic, embedded, pre-existent individuality: truth is the awakening, the unfolding of this particular and particularizing passion; identity and understanding are simultaneous.

|| Saruddin Qunyawi became Ibn 'Arabi's student in Anatolia; he later became his chief interpreter and son-in-law. Sadruddin was also an intimate friend of Mawlana Jalaluddin Rumi. For both Rumi and Ibn 'Arabi, the aesthetic of interiority is the most compelling, and most efficient, philosophy.

> Leap, leap from the world, that you may be king of the world;
> seize the sugar tray that you may be a sugar plantation.
> Leap, leap like a meteor to slay the div; when you leap out of
> stardom, you will be the pole of heaven.
> When Noah sets out for the sea, you will be his ship; when the
> Messiah goes to heaven, you will be the ladder.
> Now like Jesus of Mary you become the soul's physician; and
> now like Moses of 'Emran you will go forth to be a shepherd.
> There is a spiritual fire for the sake of cooking you; if you leap
> back..., you will be a raw cuckold.
> If you do not flee from the fire, and become wholly cooked
> like well-baked bread, you will be a master and lord of the table.
> When you come to the table and the brethren receive you, like
> bread you will be the sustenance of the soul and you will be the soul.
> Though you are the mine of pain, by patience you will become the treasure;
> though you are a flawed house, you will be
> knower of the unseen.

I said this, and a call came from heaven to my spirit's ear, saying,
"If you become like this, you will be like that." (Rumi 144–45)

Such a theology is marked by a convergence of the beloved and the lover, and by a theandrism in daemonic events: the creativity, drama and resusicitative power of divinity requires human participation: "when the Messiah goes to heaven, you will be the ladder."

|| Ibn 'Arabi arrived in Mecca in 1201 at the age of thirty-six and, soon after, began a meditation practice of circling the Ka 'aba, because visionary events, Corbin insists, always occur in the "center" (*Creative Imagination* 324), of the world. Ibn 'Arabi relates his central encounter and understanding, which occurred one night, early in his Meccan stay, as he was performing his ritual circumnambulations.

> *My spirit savored a profound peace; a gentle emotion of which I was perfectly*
> *aware had taken hold of me. I left the paved surface because of the pressing*
> *crowd and continued to circulate on the sand. Suddenly a few lines came to*
> *my mind; I recited them loudly enough to be heard not only by myself but*
> *by someone following me if there had been anyone following me.*
>   *Ah! To know if they know what heart they have possessed!*
>   *How my heart would like to know what mountain paths they have taken!*
>   *Ought you to suppose them safe and sound, or to suppose they have*
> *perished?*
>   *The* fedeli d'amore *remain perplexed in love, exposed to every peril.*
>   *No sooner had I recited these verses than I felt on my shoulder the touch*
> *of a hand softer than silk. I turned around and found myself in the presence*
> *of a young girl, a princess from among the daughters of the Greeks. Never had*
> *I seen a woman more beautiful of face, softer of speech, more tender of heart,*
> *more spiritual in her ideas more subtle in her symbolic allusions....She surpassed*
> *all the people of her time in refinement of mind and cultivation, in beauty*
> *and in knowledge. (140)*

Ibn 'Arabi identifies the sophianic figure as "the interpreter of ardent desires" (141); she faces and admonishes the circumambulating Sufi, who is eager, pressing and perhaps somewhat unstable in his interior exercises:

> How can a fedele d'amore *retain a residue of perplexity and hesitation when*
> *the very condition of adoration is that it fills the soul entirely? It puts the*
> *senses to sleep, ravishes the intelligences, does away with thoughts and carries*
> *away its fedele in the stream of those who vanish. Where then is there room*
> *for perplexity? It is unworthy of you to say such things. (144)*

Ibn 'Arabi's thought flourished as he circled the Ka 'aba, the center of the world; the repetitive gesture continued as a mental practice after it had been an actual exercise, the work flavoured by the encounter with the angel in one of his earliest circlings. Like Isaac of Nineveh's hesychasm, this non-comprehending, reiterative discipline was methodology, an important noetic device, both somatic and psychic, in the genuine philosophy that is always individual without yielding its universal utility. Yet another such device in this philosophy is the esoteric hermeneutic of *ta' wil*, which rests on the confidence that behind every appearance is an innerness, which has it its own story to tell. Yet another method in this psychagoguery is meditation on the Names of divinity as "lords" (121): these Names, it should be once more noted, are not most accurately seen as theological propositions, but as human passions—for this reason, Hafiz conducted his theology only in the winehouse.

The Names "are essentially relative to the beings who name them, since these beings discover and experience them in their own mode of being," Corbin remarks. The Names, appearing as desires in the "oriental philosopher," are "nothing other than nostalgia of the divine Names" latent in the divine essence from the beginning, "yearning to be revealed. And this nostalgia of the divine Names is nothing other than the sadness of the unrevealed God, the anguish He experiences in His unknownness and occultation" (115). As Ibn 'Arabi observed, "The divine suzerainity has a secret, and it is *thou—*

this *thou* is the being to whom one speaks; if (this thou) should disappear, this suzeraintity would also cease to be" (121). Also: "By knowing Him, I give Him being" (124)—the remarks not meant to pertain to the divinity beyond names, but to the "God created in the faiths" (266), partial in its report of divine essence, yet piercingly true.

The chief philosophical act in this theosophy, however, involves "feeding the Angel," providing a domestic situation for introspective power with an external source, a cognition modeled by Abraham ("God's intimate") in Genesis 18.1–12.

> *The Lord appeared to Abraham by the oaks of Mamre, as he sat at the entrance of his tent in the heat of the day. He looked up and saw three men standing near him. When he saw them, he ran from the tent entrance to meet them, and bowed down to the ground. He said, "My lord, if I find favour with you, do not pass by your servant. Let a little water be brought, and wash your feet, and rest yourself under the tree.*
>
> *Let me bring a little bread, that you may refresh yourselves, and after that you may pass on—since you have come to your servant." So they said, "Do as you have said." And Abraham hastened into the tent to Sarah, and said, "make ready quickly three measures of choice flour, knead it, and make cakes." Abraham ran to the herd and took a calf, tender and good, and gave it to the servant, who hastened to prepare it. Then he took curds and milk and the calf that he had prepared, and set it before them; and he stood by them under the tree while they ate.*
>
> *They said to him, "Where is your wife Sarah?" And he said, "There, in the tent." Then one said, "I will surely return to you in due season and your wife Sarah shall have s son." And Sarah was listening at the tent entrance behind him. Now Abraham and Sarah were old, advanced in age.*

Abraham's feeding of the angel bestows exoteric being on the hidden divinity; the act is also self-confirmation: these are I and by feeding them, I actualize what in their predictive power is potency, but which when I feed them becomes my life.

|| The moment of awakening in metaphor is a provocation to the Sufi religious imagination, converting it into active Intelligence, Imagination: this stirring provides a wedding to a particular world, which is provident, an "it-is-for-the-beholder" world. This world, the true one now, appears in the lover's plucked desire as the larger form of this desire. This realization is another instance of feeding the Angel. While such conviction is not a human achievement, it requires a readiness on the part of an individual, what Ibn 'Arabi called *himma*, creativity of the heart, a capacity for polyform homological intuition.

Woken subjectivity and a true account of reality meet in Imagination. A proof of the veracity of the successive forms in active Intelligence as ontology is that they correct and still the subject, bring the individual home. "Indeed," Corbin says, "revealed being (*zahir*) is theophanic imagination, and its true, hidden (*batin*) reality is Divine Being. It is because revealed being is Imagination that we require a hermeneutics of the forms manifested in it, that is to say, a *ta 'wil* that carries them back (as the etymology of the word *ta 'wil* indicates) to their true reality" (*Creative Imagination* 208). This "carrying back" leads to a recognition of oneself and significant compassionate regard: from others come further Names. There is, incidentally, then, no generosity, no condescension, in this compassion, no sanctity; here is mere truthfulness: the feeling of compassion is simply a fuller ontology, a more complete kataphatic theology. You are helped by this insight; you extend no help.

|| Ibn 'Arabi's erotic kataphaticism, Corbin points out, works efficiently against the tendency to totalitarianism latent in monotheism: there are many Names or passions or Attributes. Only the one who is a holy book herself, who has *himma*, and enjoys the manifestation of many Names as Names, does not mistake her own formational transfixity for an exhaustive identification of

divinity—it is impossible for the person with *himma*, then, to be unyielding, exhaustively definitional in speech, though she indeed may find a provisional home within a particular creed. While this kataphaticism is only phenomenology, it is always pro-actively political.

A similar oblique political effect lies in the difficulty of the language in particular poetry, in, say, César Vallejo's *The Black Heralds*, as this book has been translated by Rebecca Seiferle, where the text is filled with neologisms formed from roots in Vallejo's native Quechua. The politics sped by Vallejo's language and by the oddness of the poems, too, is progressive as it unravels an earlier hegemonic, colonial speech. The language is intended to set itself against and to disable reason, as this power is construed as a European artifact, to do this as well to an imported common sense and to a confidence about the coherence, the sufficiency, of the status quo spreading from the metropolis. A way is cleared for the insight: I live in empire, I live in the wealth of an earlier imperial theft.

Vallejo's difficulty is a theurgic and revolutionary power, a "visionary recital." It shows a love for the mind as a place of theogonic imagination; it harbours a belief that the mind can be well only in a new world, or in the act of constructing one, or in the deep confession of the old one. The mind is in trouble precisely because it does not reside in this world. Residence can begin at any moment.

AUTOCHTHONIC TERCET

I

The labourer's fist becomes velvet,
and on each lip is traced a cross.
It's fiesta! The plow's rhythm flies,
and each cowbell's a bronze church bell

What is dull is whetted. The pouch speaks...
In the indigenous veins shines

a yaravi of blood that is strained
by the pupil in nostalgias of sun.

As in rare secular prints, the pallas,
fluting themselves into deep sighs
rosary a symbol with their whirling.

Then the Apostle shines on his throne;
and amid incense, candles and songs is
the modern Sungod of the peasant.

...

III

Daybreak. The chicha finally explodes
into sobs, lusts, fistfights;
amid the odors of pepper and urine,
a drunk traces a thousand scribbles.

"Tomorrow when I go away," a rural
Romeo wails, singing erratically.
Now there's morning soup for sale;
and an apertif of plates clinking loudly.

Three women go by...a vagabond whistles...Far away,
the river travels drunk and sings and cries
prehistories of water, ancient times.

And when a caja fromTayanga sounds,
Dawn, as if beginning to dance a blue huaino,
unfurls her saffron calves. (Vallejo 72–75)

|| Knowledge of the divinity and daemonic, in the thought of Ibn 'Arabi, has no limit; it is a series of theophanies that are theophanic forms, these being individuals or passions, or, if misconstrued, "faiths." To be a "Koran," in Ibn 'Arabi's unusual use of the term, is to be perfect in the vision of the accumulated Divine Names, the ubiquitous presence of the Attributes. Without loss of individuality, all distinctions in this state of understanding are annulled; this discriminating, yet not distinguishing emptiness is *fana'* (annihilation), a non-monistic, oxymoronic apprehension of the necessary co-existence of the extremest particularity and the most comprehensive unity. This impossible fusion of individuals and divinity in *fana'*, indeed, precedes this epiphanic non-distinguishing insight. "It is not you who cast the dart when you cast it, but Allah who casts it" (Koran VIII: 17). In Corbin's gloss of this text, we find a plausible account of the intent, individualizing availability that is the source of the ferality and uncanny reach in a poet like Vallejo: "When you create, it is not you who create and that is why your creation is true" (*Creative Imagination* 215). As you hear, you and your language become the only conceivable things they could be.

Himma, the heart's (*qalb*) genius, does not create *ex nihilo*, but draws from virtuality what is latent in "another place," in, say, the withinness of things, their melancholia, or in the ghost layer, the history of hurt, epiphany, courage, backing all events. Someone with interior vision will note such novel realities, when they appear in art, as "presence," "depth," "resonance," "nourishment," "home," or the daemonic, and when they appear in behaviour, will see them as authentic inspiration or the appearance of the miraculous, which startlingly deepens and extends integrity. In both art and ethics, these creations will be disarmingly beautiful, but only to those who already possess an optical heart; for those who are non-metaphorical, or who are claimed by ontological or dogmatic conviction, for those drawn solely by aesthetic form or by decorum in behaviour, or who are impressed by the sufficiency of common sense or reason, these achievements will be invisible and the industry surrounding them will seem affectation or the sign of delusion.

Vallejo's poetry, in Seiferle's translation, is thick with such new things, which to those not previously drawn, indeed may appear as capricious difficulty, artistic discourtesy or self-absorbed eccentricity. Poetry and non-representational or iconographic art has a special facility to subsist from this second world, drawing its powers into arresting being in the ordinary world. Here these powers vivify, abrade and form unlike anything else. Behind every object and event is a higher one: a spiritual hermeneutic, therefore, is perpetually appropriate; it provides a citizenship in both worlds, which is health.

‖ When creature and divinity are taken to be irredeemably separated, as is the case in dogmatic monotheism, prayer inevitably becomes petitionatory. Such piety is noxious in Ibn 'Arabi's theandric cosmology, where true prayer is a causing to exist, a constituting of being by offering palpable life to the God beyond knowing. A similar cosmological cooperativism exists in St. Maximus the Confessor, and even more boldly in Angelus Silesius, who said, "I know that without me, the life of God were lost." The one who prays correctly achieves this sustaining of divine life by being the Name that forms him, by fully inhabiting his powers. The Name is the one who prays, that is his individuating passion, and it is not invention; by occupying the Name and enacting it, being is, divinity is, the inter-dependence that forms an aligned, vitalizing world.

The "vassal of this Lord," says Corbin, similarly is the "the secret of his suzerainty" (125). Such reciprocity, while benefiting from negative theology's insistence that divinity lies beyond all human accounts, supercedes the *via negativa*, while sublating it, as it does the *via positiva*. In the place of these, this theology proposes a prayer of intimate conversation—in which both participants are stripped, one by apophasis, the other by eros' ascesis—an exchange that exposes, existentiates, the hidden God, and makes the individual into her Angel, her longstanding, latent identity and divinity's previously hidden one.

A true poetry, true because metaphor commands belief in a second world, is theophanic, as is a true politics. The nature of the aesthetic in César Vallejo's

The Black Heralds, linguistically hybrid, densely imagistic, made his later commitment to a millenarian Marxism sweetly inevitable. Vallejo's Marxism, devoted and activistic though it was, did not cause a loss of his poetic helplessness: *himma* makes what is unwarranted to appear, first psychically, then politically, the unlike vivifyingly joined, human desire here becoming the creativity of being, not as will to power, but as luminous acquiescence.

5

Mostly on Prayer

I hear a voice I had not known.

—PSALM 81.5

MORAL IMPERATIVES do not usually grasp attention as panic does; I do not have an ethics as much as a polyform desperation, together with a pressing sense that the various therapies I am in need of are implausible, in fact quite possibly inconceivable. Three febrile despairs now work in me. Two are famous, artifacts in the museum of early modern thought. One of these is Kantian—how to know the essence of things, not just my thoughts about them? My being home seems to rest upon such an unlikely achievement. How to know things as they might seem, given self-reflective consciousness, to themselves? This is an old worry, a perpetual failure and despair in Western philosophy, studied routinely in first-year philosophy classes, no longer remotely controversial. Nor is it particularly provoking—a comfortable placidity on this matter appears to have liberated ontological judgment from a variety of vexing, irresolvable questions. It is, for me, however, oddly, an ache, a thrashing about. This is like suffering a disease for which immunity has long existed, a peculiar state of affairs.

Another despair or feverishness is more Cartesian. How to conduct the search for foundational certitude when all seems in cultural flux, therefore doubtable? The third despair or anxiety is harder to describe, in part because it makes no appearance in the European philosophical tradition. It concerns a disarming sense that my life is taking place within, is shaped by, a long, unacknowledged colonial war in Western Canada that is both psychic and murderous, a mythopoetic, multi-generational total war. This seemingly endless confrontation goes on around us; few speak of it in the white population, though many of its apparently separate outrages receive shocked coverage in mainstream media.

In all of these urgencies, as I try to manage their exigencies and sort through their complexities, I feel I am doing highstakes hobbyist medicine. This essay is a confession, then, an apologia for what whips within, and I recognize something hopeless in this gesture. I will try to unpack these panics—haul out their rags and contraptions and lay them out separately on the floor—and then attempt to describe my hapless, homemade remedies. I do this with trepidation because I have found no sure way around the fear that what I complain of may be hypochondria, and my treatments, right up to the kitchen table self-administered surgeries on the self-in-the-world may be monstrous follies of self-dramatization. I have no pressing sense this is the case, but can't deny that these are plausible doubts. Edmund Husserl, who appears in these pages both in this essay and, more extensively, in a later one, was struck by the need to risk all in doing "radical philosophy" (2); he was convinced the initial content of such philosophy would be transcendental phenomenology, his stripped, yet conceivably universal, account of the basic acts of comprehension. I believe a truer, richer way to a securing first philosophy is even more primitive than elemental Husserlian phenomenology; it is what I attempt here, mere confession, helpless, unthematized, volcanic, incapable of imagining its consolation.

Some rough recent biography is in order. This sketch will involve further admissions of confusion. In my fifties, I moved from the prairies to the base of a ridge near the bottom of a mountain that faces, on its south slope, the

Pacific Ocean. This sounds more of a wilderness situation than it actually is. I occupy a house at the southeast edge of a crescent that presses into a small mountain, all of which is a park. Behind the house is a cliff and below this is a swath of blackberries. Few people, as a result, come to this part of the mountain; the cliff seems just too dangerous; the canes threaten; there are only deer trails here. The lower edges of the slope are crowded with oaks; camas lilies, if the winter has been particularly wet, reach thickly to the top. A narrow avenue, with a modest traffic flow, lies at the end of the crescent. I sit and read in a 12 × 12 shed at the back of the property, beside a diseased pear tree.

I was quite ill when I moved here, chronically sick for the first time in my life—previous health trouble suddenly seemed a different species of occurrence—and remained in this illness for four years. During this period I had numerous surgeries and ingested what seemed handfuls of pills in disconcerting dosages. (When will the bill for all this swallowing come in?) Now as I stagger from this period of illness, it seems time to take stock, to try to get a sense of where I've ended up. It feels as if the illness, and to a lesser extent the move, took off the first couple of feet of soil in me. Everything now seems more urgent.

I've already mentioned three points of disquiet that have been alive in me, as a kind of fretful, intentionality splintering intensity; they have been with me, in fact, for over a decade. There are two others that seem at times to branch from these and sometimes appear to force them. In the void of having been ill, these and the previous three conundra float with less constraint in awareness. Part of the effort of this essay will be to see how some of these cathected vectors connect. These latter two preoccupations feel as if they have become the actual core of my life, and since I appear to share them with virtually no one, they have come to seem to me, at my least secure, to be definitive marks of a kind of aspirational marginality. The first preoccupation is that the European mind, the shape of this longing, which is the shape of my longing and the longing of those like me, has not settled in North America during the extended period of colonial occupation, nor can it ever, unless an unimaginable amount of interior or philosophical work is done. It is impossible, as I've said, to conceive, with absolute clarity, of the sort and the extent of this corrective, erotic work. This unsettledness causes many problems—diseases of innerness, destruction of biotas, domestic violence, systemic injustice against those who appeared not to suffer this estrangement, that is, First Nation and Métis communities.

The second preoccupation is with prayer, especially as it's understood in the Christian contemplative tradition, specifically that part of the tradition which is monastic. The two fixations, equally compelling, have seemed merely contiguous in the past, but now I wonder about possible therapeutic or causal links. One difficulty in thinking this thought is that it is clear a source of this chthonic estrangement of the colonist from his spoils has been the non-syncretism of doctrinal Christianity, especially in its missionary forms, and this is not the sort of causality I now wish to explore.

Beneath the smoothness, the relative fine running of late capitalism, I imagine a disturbingly vast inchoate hunger, unpleasantly savourable, attendable. I imagine we are all floating, moaning with loss, pining, without being able to name this telos, for self-completing beauty and home. No matter how we spend our days, no matter what sentences we form at work, what acts we fashion, this is where we truly live; this floating hunger holds the names that are our names beneath our public names. (Think of decades of German nights crowded with Holocaust dreams, often unremembered at daybreak.) We are floating in the places where we live, as we work the thin living that comes with squatter rights on the crust of global commercial culture. How can I be sure this conviction is not an ill mirage itself? I ask myself on certain days. At other times I think that if the main impetus in the contemplative life is thirst, we are either on the verge of or are actually in one of the great contemplative ages, rivaling the advent of eremites in the Egyptian desert in the fourth century or the great Cistercian revival in the twelfth century—and it has been the convulsive iconoclasm of capitalism that has, in part, brought us here. Looking at such interior phenomena, I feel I live largely on the other side of the tapestry of imperial commerce, where it does not look like itself, but—a fall of differently coloured threads—where its presence and nature are illuminatingly inferable. There is, I've discovered, no spiritual director, friend, therapist who can assure me that I am not deluded in these worries and hunches. My own hunger persists; I even dream of it.

A person has to sit somewhere, even if there is no sure place of settling, so I have chosen to sit, doubt-shaken, with prayer. I have come to believe I do this for political, psychagogic-political, reasons, as well as for self-preservational ones. I am also interested in prayer for what could only be called reasons of deep pleasure. I experience prayer as a delight, a home, a large room in which my feet have been miraculously set. I am sure I would not feel this had I not read many masters on prayer and had my appetite, my entire interior sensorial apparatus, sharpened by their acuity. There are so many of these guides, brilliant, deep, generous—St. Teresa of Avila, her *Interior Castle*; St. John of the Cross; Evagrius; John Cassian; the author of *The Cloud of Unknowing*; Thomas Merton on contemplative prayer; Julian of Norwich, her *Revelations of Divine Love*; Pseudo-Dionysius; John Scotus Eriugena. These books, uncannily, happily intimate, seem to know the reader better than he can know himself. For years I have been going into libraries, even monastic libraries, and retrieving volumes last taken out in, say, 1958, some even with uncut pages. I sometimes have seen these visits, their frequency, relentlessness even, as a kind of stupidity, an arcane obsession, an inattention to a protocol of ignoring such texts in modernity, puzzling even to me who feels fully the push of the necessity of these visits. These books have a particular smell that I suppose has got even into my clothes. It certainly has got into the room where I work. I am not an antiquarian or a patristics scholar. I am, however, desperate, as I've said, and unsteady, tippy, because I am never sure I am not wrong in my eros. Lately I have been spending time with contemplative masters from the seventh century Syrian Church of the East, like Isaac of Nineveh.

|| My anxieties, considered psychagogically, find a plausible, coherent description in Isaac's philosophy of prayer as corrective "stirrings," an estranged, multi-vectored intelligence that, in offering no account of itself, appears feral, unlike, an eroto-cognition that thinks ahead of one, nosing out the telos of one's unrevealed, primal longing; their whirling, their refusal of pattern, resemble, as well, the "stirring up sparks" of divinity that lies at the heart of Proclan theurgy. Confession is the lighting, the magnification of anomalous energies, a nurturance and acceleration of them, these motions a higher form of knowing, the building possibility in one of identity and ethics. Their peculiarity, the feeling they foster of one being alone, idiosyncratic, singular, is a mark of the interior, momentumed authenticity, if Isaac is to be believed, of "true prayer."

The shape this essay strives for is a cross between al-Ghazali's *Deliverance from Error* and Slavoj Zizek's *The Fragile Absolute*—an attempt at discernment, a reading of daemonic structure in one's life and a sort of Hegelian pneumatic tracing the grain of the times.

|| During the metal fatigue of systems—Descartes' early seventeenth century, Edmund Husserl's early twentieth century—the desire to become nothing is strong. We must start again. We have invested far too much in labouring along a false trail. We must renounce this way of proceeding, find a new way into things. But the nothingness Descartes and Husserl accomplish, I sense, is a false nullity, the result of theatrical reductions of the self that mask the assertion of certain ambitions, Descartes' for a hegemonic role for geometry in discursive thought, the revivification of Enlightenment utopianism with Husserl. Each ply the hope that a new architectonic will rise from this collapse of a particular, complex, wrongly-founded subjectivity.

Over the last century, meanwhile, late capitalism, the anarchy of the market, its deracinations, its relativizations, evaporations, has worked us down, unintended spirit of ascesis, to an atomic self. In reality TV and low-end blogs, the remnant is on view, the bare asserted self, no aides, no add-ons, no net of metaphysics. Unquieted by structure, the volume of this self's assertion seems as if, in fact, it might serve as substance and force its own sustaining context, and, though the insistence of this granular self is often, of course, mistaken for weight, it is aesthetically obvious, in time, that this identification is an error. Yes, perhaps nothing, one may feel, but not this nothing. The appetite for nothingness may be psycho-cultural gain and inevitable, in any case, as Marx thought. The discernment of false emptiness must itself be seen as a saving aesthetical-moral insight.

Over all this and through this has been a culture-wide longing for placed-ness. The yearning for the attachment to land has a similar shape, an echoic emotional shape, as longing for contemplative fixity, for what Syrian mystical authors like Aphrahat and Isaac called *ihidaya*, that interior quality of being "singular, individual, unique, singleminded, undivided in heart: single, celibate, Only-Begotten" (Brock xxii). It is possible that the first puzzling, masked, disconcerting hunger for chthonic home, anachronistic in capitalism's time of stripping, and therefore, it seems, impossible to satisfy, unless one is wealthy enough to buy apparent immunity from the stripping, is most readily, though strangely, met by addressing the second hunger for prayer.

|| What is the nature of the attention that by deflection or obliquity may assuage this appetite for place? The mystics of the Church of the East have much to say about this fixity. Isaac of Nineveh was a contemplative and theologian, born in Qatar, on the Persian Gulf, at that time an important center of Christian thought. A monk and teacher in his home region until schismatic pressures drove him to seek refuge in the mountains of Khuzistan, in what is now eastern Iran, he was later ordained bishop of Nineveh at the great monastery of Beth Abe in present-day northern Iraq, though he occupied this post for only a short period in 676–677, before retiring to the Khuzistan mountains as an anchorite, moving as he aged to the monastery of Rabbun Shabur. Writings of his on prayer and ascetical formation were collected by Theophan the Recluse in the Russian *Dobrotolubiye*, that nineteenth-century *Philokalia*, but most of Isaac's works had been lost much earlier, perhaps as early as the ninth century.

The influence of Evagrius, in particular his notion of *apatheia*, is apparent in Isaac's thinking on prayer, but Evagrian impassivity appears there as a counter ideal, or, better, as a perfection that has been popularly misunderstood, disastrously romanticized, and so is in need of retrieval. Pure prayer is the acme of the interior life, the true end of intelligence for Isaac, but it is not effaced emptiness, "not a matter of some being totally without thought or reflection or movement," but rather it is clarification of vision, consisting in "the heart being purified of all evil, and in gazing favourably on everything and considering it from God's point of view" (Isaac of Nineveh 294). He insists on the importance of trustworthy phenomenologies of this particular state, so that one might "first learn how and what it is" (293). Without this knowledge, distortion is likely, specifically the grotesquery of rectitudinous quietism.

The student of prayer, moreover, deprived of such phenomenologies, "when the acquisition of it [pure prayer] is actually within his grasp...may easily let it slip away through having failed to recognize it," because "his expectations may be set upon things that are impossible, rather than upon the reality of the matter in hand, which is quite possible to attain" (293). Do not "require of the mind motionlessness," Isaac counsels, "...for this cannot be asked of human nature." Prayer is closer to the touch, a realignment to ordinariness. The contemplative, instead, should strive to discover "stirrings" in prayer and receive what power they offer. He should go further and bind himself to these liftings and so become a person of God (I Timothy 6.11), "near" to spiritual things and "close, too, to finding that for which you yearn without your being aware of it, namely, the apperception of God, the wonderment of mind that is free of all images, and the spiritual silence of which the fathers speak" (Isaac of Nineveh 297).

Imagelessness, then, can only be the result of a deep, identifying, affect-rich appropriation of images that are "good" in prayer, a consequent mute dilation of attention to these pressings. This opening is an angelic wakefulness seen as the point of Christian practice in the Antiochene Church of the East: "Be wakeful and praying continually" (Matthew 26.41).

|| For Evagrius, in his *Chapters on Prayer* and elsewhere, interiority of a central sort, the approach to *apatheia*, is simply joy expressing itself in thanksgiving, this with the potential to be a perpetual state. "Once a person knows this," Isaac remarks, "he will have acquired prayer as a treasure within himself" (249). Again, the resolving matter is close at hand. Evagrian prayer, matured further as deep practice, as unconsidered, unconsoled fluidity, Isaac of Nineveh calls "pure prayer" and "wonderment." It is prayer of thanksgiving that is non-anthropomorphic, prayerless and labourless, alert though unstriving; it is nothing other than the world stepping forward as it is— coherent, spiky with individuality, unconniving, gratis, mammoth wealth on view as breathtaking unexceptionality, a display that appears to be carelessness yet is a preserving. But such prayerless prayer does not appear without stillness, and "stillness comes from the stripping away of the self" (250). There is no suspicion, nothing punitive in this stripping; it is, rather, recognition of the nature of conditions that obtain, together with delight. As the author of the anonymous fourth-century *Book of Steps*, yet another foundational Christian document from the Persian Gulf, declares, "Let us abandon everything and proceed with our Lord's humility and self-emptying" (Brock xxxi–xxxii). This kenosis, the *msarrquta* of the Syriac church, is largely the retraction of the self that is eros' ekstasis, the "hidden self-emptying," building, as Joseph the Visionary says, from "a love of God burning in the heart" (xxxi), transfixity by divinity as Reality, then, simply what is. Mercy is possible, one of the richer forms of desire, under these conditions, appearing with repentance, "a broken heart," and "a voluntary mortification with regard to everything" (Isaac of Nineveh 251). "And what is a merciful heart?" Isaac asks in what is likely an imaginary apothegmata of an unnamed elder in *Discourse LXXIV*.

> He replied, "The heart's burning for all creation, for human beings, for birds and animals, and for demons and everything there is. At the recollection of them and at the sight of them his eyes gush forth with tears owing to the force of the compassion which constrains his heart, so that, as a result of

his abundant sense of mercy, the heart shrinks and cannot bear to hear or
examine any harm or small suffering of anything in creation. For this reason
he offers up prayer with tears at all times, even for irrational animals, and
for the enemies of the truth, and for those who harm him, for their preserva-
tion and being forgiven. As a result of the immense compassion infused in
his heart without measure—like God's—he even does this for reptiles [which
were part of the evil creation in Zoroasterian cosmologies]. (251)

This is Isaac's "vale of limpidity," "a luminous heart"; it is *shafyuta*, which
has no exact English equivalent, but which connotes "limpidity, lucidity, lumi-
nousity, clarity, purity, transparency, serenity or sincerity of heart" (Brock
xxviii). These qualities provide re-entry to the world that reconstitutes it as
ingenious sufficiency, meeting even unearthed yearnings, an address and
overture that formatively surprise the heart, aligning cosmology so that the
cosmos seems suddenly restored; this limpidity, affective, epistemological, is
quintessential homecoming.

‖ Isaac disqualifies himself as a source of a reliable phenomenological
account of prayer, claiming not to have experienced "a thousandth part" of
what must be detailed. Nevertheless, he endeavours to depict a complete
range of prayer "for the purpose of illuminating and goading our own soul"
(Isaac of Nineveh 253), his soul, that is, "awakened" by "its own desire." His
writing—repetition, reportage of the daemonic states of others, attention to
his own eros—is self-correction, re-configuration, a speeding.

The emptiness, which is higher prayer's essence, is a perduring disposition, or at least a familiar one that is returned to with relief, an availability
identifiable by its flavours of readiness, attentiveness, preparedness, "impelling and fervent intensity." Before it is a "dwelling in wonder," however, this
prayer is "groans, prostrations, heartfelt requests and supplications, sweet
tears" (254); it is, as well, continuous interior, as well as external utterance, the
"keys" providing "actual entry into the treasury." The latter form of prayer is
hesychasm, repetition as cooling, truing of the febrile self; it is a rendering, as

well, into truthfulness of the cosmos; indeed, it is the origin of the cosmos as cosmos, as all that is as ordered, beautiful.

|| The effects of the highest prayer are evident at all stages of prayer. What Isaac locates in pure prayer, then, appears also in hesychastic interiority. Hesychasm, a form of attention found in Cassian and favoured in mystical Orthodoxy, is the practice of leading "the mind within" (Kadloubovsky and Palmer 405). It is also described as attending to oneself in silence and holding the "mind within the body" and "singleness of contemplation." St. Gregory of Palamas (1296–1359), Archbishop of Thessalonica, leading defender of this form of prayer, recommended its efforts even to beginners in the contemplative life.

> In those who have not undertaken this work [of building unitary focus], the mind, when collected within, often jumps out, so that, just as often, they have at once to bring it back; but in those who are not practiced in this work, the mind again slips away, since it is extremely mobile and hard to hold by attention to singleness of contemplation. Hence some advise them to refrain from breathing fast, but to restrain their breath somewhat, so that, together with their breath, they may also hold the mind inside, until, with God's help, through training, they accustom the mind not to go out into its surroundings and mingle with them, and make it strong enough to concentrate upon one thing. (405)

In his "On the Blessed Hesychasts," Gregory describes this innerness as "keeping spiritual Sabbath" (405); control of breath and audible or interior repetition of brief scriptural passages, Cassian's "versicle" (Psalm 70.1) or "the publican's prayer" ("Lord, have mercy upon me, a sinner"), instill the practice of settling and holding the mind at home in the heart. They reduce, gather, compose, dignify, sober ("holy sobriety") and feed the mind, are a setting of roots within what one is and a consequent true seeing of things.

For Gregory, the advantage of the exercises is the avoidance of the mind's dispersal among the multiplicity of things seen, but it is also a way of restoring those things to their private and providential suchness. They become what they are by not being the object of an appeal to found a life. In their freedom, they then become an unintended source of perfectly sustaining wealth. Hesychasm holds the self back so that it becomes clear that the self's estrangement from satisfaction is the result of its own interventions. The retraction of self, which is continuous prayer, is cosmos-forming struck emptiness. This is more than philosophically fundamental. It is the origin of the autonomous world itself as it truly is.

|| The Church and Christendom have collapsed as a source of coherence; philosophy, as it is professionally practiced, has nothing foundational to contribute, exhausted after its disassembling of the Pythagorean-Orphic-Platonic tradition (another mythopoetic war with colonial overtones); the hope of a liberal-utilitarian apotheosis, the universal homogeneous state, no longer offers erotic teleological momentum; Marx's historical inexorability has lost its force, though it is clear he was right about the psychagogically destructive vigor of the bourgouisie. But the nothing we are left with as a result of this pandemic superstructural breakdown places us in a position of sapiential privilege, if only we can find the courageous musicality to yield to it, with an appetite for construing its negative depth.

Psychology can't do anything politically, or sapientially, foundational; it is not deep or smart enough, too removed from its own roots in philosophy. We are left with the inconsequence of prayer, then, with, however, Christendom, philosophy, liberalism and Marxist acuity sublated in this deposit. Surely this fecund poverty, structurally if not in its details, is the meaning of Plato's Allegory of the Cave. In the rigor and transparency of prayer, says Isaac, we live in the "New World," where "the intellect has been swallowed up in the spirit" (258), its brilliance deepening, the hiddenness of things stepping forth. A new politics requires new epistemologies, and there is little in our current ways of knowing that can assist us. We must look elsewhere for our paradigms of comprehension, attention, feeling, while not, however, straying, with or without imperial entitlement, from what is ours.

6
Seeing into Things

Suhrawardi and Mandelstam

I

Suhrawardi, Persian philosopher and mystic, died in 1191 at the age of thirty-eight in the northern Syrian city of Aleppo. He was a charismatic teacher and the author of more than fifty books; these included treatments on logic, commentaries on Aristotle, translations of similar, earlier commentaries, visionary recitals (mystical narratives or novels with a theurgical power) and phenomenologies of interiority. He was born in the village of Suhraward in northwestern Iran and, after an initial philosophical training in Aristotelean Avicennism in various locations in Persia, including Isfahan, the great center of Iranian learning, he wandered in Asia Minor and Syria, attaching himself to a series of Sufi teachers. When he arrived in Aleppo in 1183, he was taken for a donkey driver because of his dress; soon, however, his eloquence, learning, conviviality and prowess in magic secured him access to the court of Malik Zahir, the adolescent son of Saladin, and Aleppo's newly appointed regent.

While Suhrawardi was adept in the Peripateticism of Avicenna, which had provided the philosophical undergirding to Islam for many years, he devoted the most productive period of his life to undermining its spirit of hegemonic rationalism by introducing Dionysian elements from Plato, Empedocles, Pythagoras and the Egyptian hermetic tradition, as well as insights from the Persian wisdom tradition to Shi'ite thought.

Above all, Suhrawardi wished to give personal mystical and ascetical experience the highest philosophical standing. This did not mean he renounced Avicennan rationalism and exegesis, but broadened both, as he believed Avicenna himself, in his later years, unsuccessfully had attempted to do. Taxonomic, non-phenomenological Aritotleleanism exercised a far greater influence in Latin scholasticism than it did in Mediterranean and Western Asian Islam in the Middle Ages in part because of the success of the new Suhrawardian synthesis.

Suhrawardi ran afoul of powerful jurists and systematic theologians also connected to the court of Malik Zahir shortly after the ruler fell under the spell of the wandering scholar and theosophist, the orthodox thinkers complaining to Saladin of the sway Suhrawardi had over his son. Saladin, who had taken Aleppo from the Chrisitan armies only in 1187, and who was about to face the Third Crusade under Richard the Lionhearted of England and Philip Augustus of France, needed the support of traditional Muslim leaders in his defence of his conquered territories, so repeatedly pressed his son to murder his teacher. Eventually, Malik Zahir obeyed his father, leaving the imprisoned Suhrawardi, some say, to die of starvation. He is sometimes called al-Maqtul, "he who was killed."

Suhrawardi wrote his most important book, *Ḥikmat al-Ishrāq* (*The Philosophy of Illumination*), over a few months in 1186. The day it was completed, he noted, an extraordinary planetary conjunction occurred in the constellation of Libra. The book is an unusual amalgam of logic and mystical metaphysics intended to provoke discernment, phronesis, in its readers. But perhaps its form is not really all that strange. Its combination of philosophical rigor and spiritual phenomenology has a medieval equivalent in the meticulous philosophical cosmology of John Scotus Eriugena in his *Periphyseon,* though perhaps resembles more closely the style of such modern thinkers as Ludwig Wittgenstein, Simone Weil and Jan Zwicky.

|| Suhrawardi's cosmology is a full articulation of cognitional theory; and, for him, epistemology is chiefly a study of subjectivities. What is most real, quintessentially existent? This, Suhrawardi would reply, is what understands its essence immediately, without the lens of definition, without the need to comprehend unassimilated parts; this is the most real: that which accommodates, in other words, the most penetrating, effortless intuition of itself as it is known. The most real is what is most clear, what most stands forth.

> Since this apprehension cannot be by a form or by something superadded,
> you need nothing to apprehend your essence save that essence, which is
> evident in itself and not absent from itself....If you examine this matter
> closely, you will find that that by which you are you is only a thing that
> apprehends its own essence—your "ego." (par. 116)

This sort of impressive, doubt-blocking insight of and into self bears a rough resemblance to Descartes' initial and unique experience in the *cogito,* an intuitive, self-confirming perception. Its force is individualizing—it gives identity—and forms the basis of subsequent thought: "Thus anything that apprehends its own essence is a pure light, and every pure light is evident to itself and apprehends its own essence. This is one of the methods of proof [i.e., that a thing is evident and light and most real]" (par. 118).

The true life of a thing is its residual light.

> Light is divided into light of itself and in itself and light of itself but in
> another. You know that accidental light is light in another. Thus it is not a
> light in itself although it is a light of itself, since its existence is in another.
> The dusky substance is not evident of itself or to itself according to what you
> know. Life is a thing's being evident to itself, and a living thing is percipient

and active. You know about perception, and the attribution of activity to light
is clear, since light emanates by essence. Thus pure light is alive and every
living thing is a pure light. (par. 121)

It appears sometimes that things listen and respond to us, or, to put this
differently, that the effect of seeing something deeply can be the same as
when one sees oneself: you are poured into yourself with force and preci-
sion. There is a degree of self-recognition in the moment of viewing objects
deeply; thus there seems a subjectivity in things, or something which aids
the formation of human subjectivity—which could only be a form of subjectivity, or something closely related to it—and here is where contemplative
comprehension rests.

The radiator shop in Bellevue, Alberta. The brown rising river, the
Crowsnest, at the moment it turns east. The semen smell of cottonwood
poplar buds. The lip red, scarred flowers of cottonwoods. Dippers burrowing
under water. Harlequin ducks in pairs, casually riding the hillocks of fast
water. The blond ponytail of the cop talking to the middle-aged, male
speeder hauling a boat through the 60 kph zone at Frank. The biker run rad
shop in the Pass. Old paint in opened tins, white, with dust mixed in, dust
borne as seeds, behind the abandoned house. Tubers or iris bulbs of what
looks like faces in-skinned in this and that. The moose-browsed low willow,
this piece of limestone that dribbled and cartwheeled a hundred years ago
from that mountain onto a coal town, killing seventy people.

|| The self comprehending the self freshly, orientingly, extensively, resonantly,
that noetic instant, is Suhrawardi's template for knowledge, the ground, indeed
the nature, of philosophy. But one may have this experience of recognition,
of the self coming to the self, from things other than the self as well—an old
coffee pot, the shape of a mountain, the face of a friend. Individuality comes
from such recognition of objects, and the recognition, like the self seeing the
self, is exigent, irrational, beneath usual knowledge, convicted. By this sort of
attention, the seer and the thing seen are individualized, the comprehended,

freed, it seems, from a dross of opinion, habit, language, the reductive force of shared form, so that it stands forth, bright, startling, unlike anything, yet leagued to the viewer, who himself is individuated in this taking in of the unlike thing. He becomes the one who knows at some depth and is joined to this thing. He carries its smell.

This intuition of self, objects, or Light Itself breeds or is loneliness because you are claimed, elsewhere, unavailable but to it, that which draws disarmingly and names. The land, all forms of otherness, accommodates our attention, soaks us up and, in its clarity, comes nearer, and assuages our thirst for coherence. Objects appear to listen to us and respond. Suhrawardi's critique of Avicennan Aristoteleanism was an assertion of the primacy of quiddity, the Platonic Forms and an epistemology of presence. The form of cognition in this epistemology is badly or skimpily translated as "intuition," if that word suggests privileged, apodictic insight: it is a contemplative state of savouring, dwelling with something; its actual word, *dhawaq*, means "tasting." Suhrawardi's epistemology, then, is a fusion of physics, theology and formation; you see with the eye that sees you, and are shaped by this seeing, which is itself formed by the presence of light in what is viewed, the one who comprehends now lightened, clarified, located, understood in the act of knowing. This recognition is *opus Dei*, the work of God. It takes priority over theological speculation.

|| The Suhrawardian synthesis is a broad retrieval—conservative, innovative, aligning.

> The most evil age is the one in which the carpet of striving has been rolled up, in which the movement of thought is interrupted, the door of revelation bolted, the path of visions blocked. (par. 2)

> This science is the very intuition of the inspired and illumined Plato, the guide and master of philosophy, and of those who came before him, from the time of Hermes, "the father of the philosophers," up to Plato's time, including such mighty pillars of philosophy as Empedocles, Pythagoras and others. (par. 4)

Do not imagine that philosophy has existed only in these recent times. The
world has never been without philosophy or without a person possessing
proofs and clear evidences to champion it. He is God's vice-regent on His
earth....Even though the First Teacher [Aristotle] was very great, profound and
insightful, one ought not exaggerate about him so as to disparage his masters.
Among them are the messengers and lawgivers such as Agathadaemon [Seth],
Hermes, Asclepius and others. (par. 4)

Suhrawardian sensibility is not a rejection of taxonomic rationality and
an embrace of irrationality or occult vitalism, but a re-statement of reason's
traditional range. The Illuminationist synthesis combines physics, logic and
metaphysics; philosophy and theology (this in a particularly intimate, personal
way); exegesis and original insight; ascesis, understanding and erotic passivity
(the mind of the "messengers"). Doubt on the matter of these joinings, or on
claims made within this synthesis, can be met, urged Suhrawardi, only by
astute, unmediated, and protean introspection, "by climbing the ladder of
the soul."

|| Suhrawardi's mature thought began with a dream in which Aristotle
appeared. In the dream, Suhrawardi complained to the master, "Helper of
Souls, Imam of Wisdom, Primus Magister," about his intense, disabling confusion concerning the nature of knowledge. Do we know things by understanding
their essences, which we capture in definitions? Do names tell us anything of
natures or are they purely conventional? Can certain names not only identify but cause things to come to their fullest state of existence? The Helper of
Souls, Imam of Wisdom, drew the dreamer to consider the experience of self-
recognition.

"Come back to yourself," he said to me, "and your problem will be solved."
"How so?" I asked.
"Is the knowledge which you have of yourself a direct perception of your-
self, or do you get it from something else...?" (Corbin, Spiritual Body 118–19)

Knowledge can concern only what is savourable, delectable to the interior person—that is, that which is individual, and therefore remarkable, beautiful, and that object's or person's relations. Such entities are "lights." Suhrawardi rejected the essential definitions of the Peripatetics as meaningless; one knows solely by direct acquaintance, and only luminosity possesses the conviviality necessary to allow such acquaintance. Only contemplative knowledge can be understanding.

|| It is possible to grasp a number of things without self-recognition: but this is an understanding without a proper valuation of objects, persons or events, and, as a result, these are held within misshapen affective auras. Such "understanding" amounts to dangerous and damaging ignorance: when it forms social "truths," these incubate what Bernard Lonergan calls the "surd," a pandemic, cultural incoherence. A man for whom therapy has not been successful is in possession of roughly the same set of facts as the one for whom it has been successful. But there is another self-recognition, religious and more deeply existential than therapy's. It reports too little to say the self seeing truly the self is a paradigm for all knowing; it is the source of all real knowing, the proper alignment of all things, their true valuation. You are known by yourself with intuitive, savouring clarity, and the world for you re-achieves its order and sufficiency.

|| Suhrawardi's *ishraq* philosophy sublates Avicennism, remodeling its Peripatetic rationalism, under the inspiration of a part of Avicenna's own writings, his visionary recitals, in particular *The Recital of Hayy ibn Yaqzan*. Henry Corbin calls these performances, not uncommon in medieval Islam (Suhrawardi wrote two), "spiritual romances" and "mental dramaturgy." They are the highest form of utterance in both the Illuminationist and, in Suhrawardi's view, the Avicennan schools. Avicenna's *Recital of Hayy ibn Yaqzan*, like the *Divine Comedy*, like the palinode in the *Phaedrus*, the world system in the *Timaeus*, Socrates' cities in the *Republic*, Augustine's cosmology appearing at the end of the *Confessions*, is a spiritual geography

in which an interlocutor is led through a series of terrains, visualizing them, their topographies, imagining the lives possible in them. The recital leads to more acute introspection, provides a guide to striving and, by broadening the interior imagination, fosters a desire for anagogic ascent.

The Recital of Hayy ibn Yaqzan (Corbin, Avicenna 137–50) is an "initiation into the Orient" in the words of Corbin (Avicenna 44). Like Plato's Allegory of the Cave, the nature of the Orient, the lit land, its graceful return to order, is announced by a daemonic stranger who suddenly appears; he is the guide to this new terrain, its insights, its politics. He instructs the neophyte, reveals the challenging regions, prepares him, in a manner that nearly overwhelms him, for the journey. At the beginning of the rectial, the narrator-philosopher glimpses the Sage as he, the narrator, and his companions visit the "pleasure places" of the city, that is, as an early Persian commentary suggests, as they enter into their souls, suspended from distractions, in the sweetness of a contemplative state. The Sage is beautiful, "had tasted of years" though has "the freshness proper to a young man" (137), is a puer aeternalis. When asked what he does, he replies he travels in order to know all the configurations of things. "My profession is to be forever journeying, to travel about the universe so that I may know all its conditions. My face is turned toward my father, and my father is Vigilans."

The narrator asks him about the science of physiogamy. This seems a puzzling initial question, but as the Sage describes it, physiogamy is a "science" of phronesis or discernment, "the profit of which is paid cash down and whose benefit is immediate for it reveals to thee what every man conceals in his nature, so that thou canst proportion thine attitude of freedom or reserve toward each man" (138). This lesson marks the beginning of critical introspection for the narrator-auditor, since it fosters in him alertness toward interiority and begins the exercise of an acuity in the reading of others that will lead him deeper into himself. It also will aid importantly in his selection of future interlocutors and teachers. One's own insight, then, takes on the powers of the Socratic midwife, facilitator of philosophy.

The narrator of the recital now asks the Sage to guide him, only to be told he is told he is not ready to be taken to the various places in the journey. His abysmal companions, self-deception and violent anger, stand in his path. He is offered two ways of dealing with these blocks. "As for the stratagems and effectual means to which you have recourse in respect to these companions, there is one that consists in subduing the slack and gluttonous companion by the help of the one who is violent and malicious, and in forcing the former to retreat" (140). But the only sure way to overcome his particular passions, the disastrous intimacies, is "expatriation" (139). However, though he burns with desire, such a move, except for infrequent excursions, is impossible for him.

This rebuff acts psychagogically to heighten the narrator's desire and sharpen his self-awareness. He recognizes that his attention is too sporadic for him to place himself in the hands of his daemonic co-conversationalist. He asks him then for a different account: What places have you travelled to? He aspires correctly to the theatre and the pedagogy of the journey, the travels in imagination; by this, his mind and desire are formed by the enactment of other, perceived-to-be-extraordinary possibilities. The Sage now describes a geography which includes physical features, but also embodies spiritual and moral states, much as the landscape in Indigenous stories holds and reveals the deeds of heroes. He is presented with a spiritual topography germane to him. It begins with an account of the lower reaches of the Occident, the places of sophistry and attachment.

> At the outermost edge of the Occident there is a vast sea, which in the Book of God is called the Hot (and Muddy) Sea. It is in those parts that the Sun sets. The streams that fall into that sea come from an uninhabited country whose vastness none can circumscribe. No inhabitant peoples it; save for strangers who arrive there unexpectedly, coming from other regions. Perpetual darkness reigns in that country. Those who emigrate there obtain a flash of light each time that the sun sinks to its setting. It soil is a desert of salt. (142)

The Recital of Hayy ibn Yaqzan is a directed meditation like the one uttered by Socrates for Glaucon of the city of the tyrant in the *Republic*. We occupy, enact and sublate what we imagine. We try on names until the proper name presents itself. But the drama works only if it is a phenomenology of one who has discernment, is an account of a genuine traveller.

After the stark initial region is one like it, the narrator is told, another desert, filled with other strangers who do not travel or war. Then comes a "climate" of smaller people, who make quick movements; then there is a region of even smaller people (is the body disappearing?) who "passionately love the arts of the writer, the sciences of the stars, theurgy, magic; they have a taste for subtle occupations and deep works" (143). There are ten cities in this region.

Then there is a terrain inhabited by people who are extremely beautiful. The narrator throughout is being led through a geoterium of all possible states of desire, as Socrates draws Glaucon through a succession of imaginary cities, encouraging him to see and taste the various life states in them. The intent of this theatre, as with the spiritual exercises in the *Republic*, is to teach a taxonomy of souls, so that the narrator, who has initially only enthusiasm, achieves the capacity to read and evaluate them and himself, as he incoherently shifts allegiances. But more than training in phronetic introspection, *The Recital* works as a final cause on transcendental eros, exactly as Diotima's account of the Higher Mysteries in the *Symposium* does on the young Socrates. A woman reigns over this last clime, one peopled by the beautiful, says the Sage. "A natural disposition inclines them to the good and the beautiful" (144), in their behaviour. There are nine cities in this realm.

Next there is a people who love to wound and kill; a "red personage" rules there but is sometime overcome by the fair faced queen and drawn into passionate love. Then there is a region where the people are temperate, just, wise, pious, then a country inhabited by cerebral evil-doers ("However if they tend to goodness they go to its utmost extreme."). Then there is a region of angels. "From it the divine imperative and destiny descend on all those who occupy the degrees below" (145). At this point, the two speakers leave the

Occident, a domain of will and calculation, and begin to set out for the east, the Orient, the land of *cognitio matutina*, the pure knowledge of morning.

"Then, cutting straight across toward the Orient, thou wilt come upon the sun rising between two troops [i.e. two horns] of the Demon" (146). These two troops are beasts of prey, on the left side of the Orient, and birds of prey on the right. These creatures, in fact, have mixed, multiple natures, one a flying man, another a viper with a boar's head. Visitors who manage to disentangle themselves from the demons make their way to a climate inhabited by "terrestrial angels," who now undertake to lead them. These are called *jinn*, daemons. Leaving this terrain or clime, the traveller enters the region of higher angelic presences, who are divided into two groups: "One occupies the right side: they are the angels who know and order. Opposite them a group occupies the left side: they are the angels who obey and act" (148). Two angels are assigned to each person, one who orders, the other who obeys; to the latter, "it falls to write." Just as with Platonic formational narratives, we are not here reading ontologies or even psychologies, but are engaging in a labour of alteration of interiority, which is possible when the hopeless desire of an interlocutor and a narrativized, genuine phenomenology of one who has actually crossed over meet. The story places a compelling charge around the account and provides it with a sort of docking mechanism by which it can penetrate and link with the auditor. The narrative, or even the choice of story as a vehicle, is a way of roughly individualizing and daemonizing the exchange.

What follows the meeting with the angel sounds much like the ascent of the chariot in the *Phaedrus*. "He who is taught a certain road leading out of this clime and who is helped to accomplish this exodus, such a one will find an egress to what is beyond the celestial spheres. Then in a fugitive glimpse, he descries the posterity of the Primordial Creation (the Forms?), over whom rules as king the One, the Obeyed" (148). Of this king, Avicenna says, "His beauty is the veil of his beauty....His manifestation is the cause of His occultation....His epiphany is the cause of his Hiddenness" (150). Nevertheless "[w]hoever perceives a trace of His beauty fixes his contemplation on it forever." Occasionally solitaries will go farther and return from his palace, homesick, laden with gifts.

So concludes the Phaedrusean journey: one descends to a crepuscular place, then with difficulty ascends to a vision of a stable, complete world. This movement along the *axis mundi* is echoed in the *Republic* and the *Divine Comedy*. None of these theurgical dramas is cosmology or metaphysics, but pedagogy, the turning of the soul; each is a visionary recital, capable of transformation with particular, disposed individuals, the apex of philosophy.

|| If you see correctly after the ascesis worked by these athletic dramas of innerness, how and what do you see? The simple answer is that you comprehend the world in such a way that the world is understood as it is; the phantasmagoria of the recital provokes a surprisingly penetrating realism. Suhrawardi's doctrine of presence says we truly know a thing when see it with the same immediacy as when we see ourselves, and the coursing narratives train the auditor in this immediacy and reach in self-recognition. A thirteenth-century commentator, Shams al-Din Shahrazuri, described the philosophy of illumination as based on "illumination which is unveiling (*kashf*), or the philosophy of the easterners...the Persians" (Wallbridge and Ziai xvii), a cognition with Zoroastrian and Gnostic elements. This illumination "is the manifestation of the intelligible lights, of their first principles, and their emanation of illuminations upon the perfected souls when they are abstracted from bodily matter," a perfection of Forms in disparate individuals taking full shape in the noetic states of completely formed souls.

This "tasting" of things is both sensorial and a mystical perception of more-than-sensory presences, which Suhrawardi calls "immaterial lights," present in what is available to the senses, that which is most evident and insistent there. There are different degrees of intensity to this insight depending on the rank of philosopher one is: a divine philosopher proficient in intuitive philosophy (*ta'alluh*, deification) but lacking discursive philosophical skills; a discursive philosopher without intuitive philosophy

(a Peripetetic); a divine philosopher skilled in both intuitive and discursive
philosophy; a divine philosopher proficient in intuition but possessing only
average skill in discursive thought; a student of both discursive and intuitive
philosophy; a student of only either intuitive or discursive philosophy. For
some of these types any sort of contemplative acuity is impossible.

Intuitive philosophy, a direct delectation first of the self by the self, then
of all mental acts including the imagination, including one's body, then
indeed everything, facilitates union, friendship between the knower and
what is known. A kind of living epistemic tissue forms: it seems impossible
to lose this knowledge, which feels non-volitional, inevitable, necessary.
The knowledge is not self-aware: the knower has no sense of acquiring
knowledge; you are "always and unceasingly aware of your own essence"
(Suhrawardi par. 116), and of the world insofar as it presses with the force of
self-knowledge.

All things have a "general word" and an "individualizing word," and while
we speak of essences, a quality designated by the general words, these are
not objects that can be known since they are not anything; only what the
individualizing word signifies is an object of knowledge: "the universal is not
existent outside the mind" (par. 11).

II

Osip Mandelstam was not a reader of Suhrawardi, nor, as far as I
can tell, was he a Platonist, though he revered Dante, who, in his *Comedia*,
performs the paradigmatic Platonic orphic itinerary. Mandelstam was born in
Warsaw in 1891, growing up in St. Petersburg, moving to Moscow in the early
1920s with his wife, Nadezhda. He was one of the shining poets of the pre-
Revolutionary scene, a member of the Acmeist movement, a group including
Anna Akhmatova and Nikolai Gumilev. Arrested in the spring of 1934 because
of a literary transgression, the rectial of a poem insulting Stalin ("The Kremlin
Mountaineer"), he was tortured, a horror from which he never fully recovered. He underwent periods of exile, dying in 1938 near Vladivostock in
transit to one of the more extreme labour camps in the Russian far east.

His Acemeism made him a qualified, corrupted nominalist in his poetics. Certain words were purely conventional, even calculated, illusions with possible utilitarian applications, while others seemed vital, though help-less, pining for objects and objects for them. As Mandelstam put it in an unpublished poem from 1909, "Like women yearning for a caress, objects / Yearn for cherished names" (Freidin 39). But words for Mandelstam not only exist, "cherished," apart from things, uncommanded by them, lost from the point of view of objects, teloi of the object's nostalgia, they, as individu-ating powers, exist apart from and before their particular speakers. "Maybe before there were lips, there was already a whisper" (Osip Mandelstam, *Poems* 35). Language, as in the Prologue to the Gospel of St. John, is an engine antedating things and their relations, and it seems to generate both. But Mandelstam's creationist poetics is not intellectualist (the word "thinks" things thus causing them to be), nor emanationist (objects pulse from the procreative power of language), but romantic or erotic: while not within the power of things and speakers, words are in a relation of love, of maintaining essential compassion, with each. And words do not create non-human and human entities from nothing but call things and speakers out of some blurred, savourless, seemingly inert ontic state into vivacity, simply by bright-ening them, by making them distinct.

Yet Mandelstam is keen that the link between words and things be extremely loose, even to the point of a sort of nominalism, in part so that the words may be admired as physical objects. "But we worry about *things* and forget / that only the *word* glows and shines" (Osip Mandelstam, *Selected Essays* 65), as fellow Acemeist Nikolai Gumilev wrote. Nevertheless, it is a fatal error to insist upon the inviolable autonomy of language, for such an apartness corrupts. Gumilev continues, "We've surrounded it [the engen-dering Logos] with a wall / ... / and like bees in a deserted hive / the dead words rots and stink." The procreative word must be in act, lighting things, or it decays. Its unparalleled power and degree of dependency is disturbing. Language in its autonomy is vivified by an unrequited, Aristophanic love for things and things for their words. "Is the thing the master of the word?" Mandelstam asks in the 1921 essay "The Word and Culture."

The word is a Psyche. The living word does not signify an object, but freely
chooses, as though for a dwelling place, this or that objective significance,
materiality, some beloved body. And around the thing the word hovers freely,
like a soul around a body that has been abandoned but not forgotten. (52)

Love and autonomy, but the latter is key, prior, for in it lies creative, embodying,
life-calling force. Language requires this solitude because it must perform
politico-theurgical wonders.

A heroic era has begun in the life of the word. The word is flesh and bread. It
shares the fate of bread and flesh: suffering. People are hungry. Still hungrier
is the state. But there is something even hungrier: time. Time wants to devour
the state....Whoever will raise high the word and show it to time, as the priest
does the Eucharist, will be a second Joshua, son of Nun. There is nothing
hungrier than the contemporary state, and a hungry state is more terrible
than a hungry man. To show compassion for the state which denies the word
is the contemporary poet's civic "way," the heroic feat that awaits him.

As physical objects, unsubsumed in use to anything, individual words have
the independence, the self-possessed substantiality of theurgical objects in
the penetrating therapies of Iamblichus and Proclus, and like these objects,
upon which Neoplatonic philosophical ritual rests, they maintain an affective individualizing link with things, while not encapsulating them within an
exhaustive name or, to speak more accurately, the theatre of such a putative
name. Essential names, words attached to universal traits, say nothing, as
Suhrawardi argued, while the names of individual things share the singular
reality of those things. For Mandelstam, this sharing is symbiotic, dialogical:
the word transfers the weight of logoi into its object, ballast, a living root; the
object returns substantiality and current to the name.

In certain societies—Western, Roman or totalitarian—the mechanism
is broken as language is locked in "from the outside," in ecclesiastical or govern-
mental walls, and there becomes saturated with the odours and flavours of
this enclausteration; there it is adored with an easily offended reverence.

The mutual erotic pull disappears, the gravitas of yearning evaporates. Mandelstamian affect-drenched linguistic autonomy in this context is an intensely pious heterodoxy, a chthonic nationalism which is revolutionary. "Russian nominalism, that is, a doctrine of the reality of the word as such," he writes in "About the Nature of the Word," "animates the spirit of our language and links it with Hellenic philological culture, not etymologically and not literarily but through a principle of inner freedom that is equally inherent in them both" (69). The language was both formal and final cause of the real country, template, repository, refresher. The country's real, secret names brought it to being. The hero of this vital, political, land-allied life through words, in Mandelstam's view, was Velimir Khlebnikov, who "busies himself with words, like a mole, and he provides for the future by burrowing through passageways in the earth to last for a whole century" (70). Indeed, such a use of language—or so it seemed in 1921, in the early decadence of the October Revolution, before the terror—was the only national treasure.

> We have no Acropolis. Our culture has been wandering until now and has not found its walls. But to make up for it, every word of Dal's dictionary is a kernel of Acropolis, a small castle, a winged fortress of nominalism, equipped with the Hellenic spirit for incessant struggle with the formless element, with the non-being that threatens our history on all sides. (73)

Russia's undeterminedness resembles Canada's in nature if not in scale; our language, though, requires the more thorough disarrangement of some yet unimagined process of decolonization.

|| Walt Whitman invented for Americans and for their local things a new, primitive Adamic nomenclature, and this came at the very last moment, since they'd used up the philology they had drawn across the ocean from Europe, and which had endured with them the shock of the newness of this continent. His language helped create a new imaginal state, which the newcomers then more completely occupied with verve and ruthlessness—a

true Johanine event, the world bubbling out from words. For Mandelstam, such a gesture would be quintessentially "Hellenistic." "Hellenism means consciously surrounding man with utensils instead of indifferent objects... the humanization of the surrounding world; the environment heated with the most delicate teleological warmth" (75). Language may achieve this result by means of an elegiac eros for things. Hellenism and lonely, hopeless, transfixed speech, in yet another Mandelstamian image for language's sustaining work in a period of political travail, is an Egyptian funeral boat "in which everything is stored that is needed for continuation of a man's earthly wanderings, including even an aromatic jar, a hand mirror and a comb" (75).

ǁ In 1933, Osip and Nadezhda Mandelstam were permitted to travel to the Crimea, where they were given space at the writers' rest home in Koktebel, then crammed with refugees from the Ukrainian famine. After a long battle to find paper in the impoverished town, Mandelstam began to dictate "Conversation about Dante," his longest and most sustained prose composition, to his wife. He was oppressed by a sense of what he took to be the classical Greek roots of Russian culture falling under a monolithic night. "Assyrian captives swarm like chickens under the feet of the immense king" (154). He finished the essay the following year. He completed "The Stalin Epigram," the poem ridiculing the dictator, and the source of all his subsequent trouble, in November, 1933, and, at some point in the winter, recited the piece to a group of friends. While the poem complains, "Our lives no longer feel ground under them / At ten paces you can't hear your words" (*Selected Poems* 69), news of the poem soon reached "the Kremlin mountaineer," and Mandelstam was arrested in May 1934. He was interrogated at the Lubyanka prison, then delivered to his wife, who hardly recognized him, at one of Moscow's train stations to be sent into exile, first to Cherdyn, where he attempted suicide, then to Voronezh in the Ural Mountains.

"Conversation about Dante" is in part a meditation on language's infiltration of the body—Mandelstam describes the place of the Italian vowels in the mouth, the movements of the muscles they cause, the shape they make the mouth take as they issue from it. But the somatic roots of language also interested Mandelstam. It pleased him to guess how many pairs of sandals Dante wore out as he wrote the *Divine Comedy*, since he believed its rhythms were produced by walking. Language is in the body, working on it; the body is on the land, which works itself into the shapes of language. His reverence for Hellenism and for Dante, who was inseparable from the residual Platonism in the *Comedy*, and his own Acmeism, gave Mandelstam a theurgist's interest—a Proclan keenness—in language. Yet before they formed worlds, words and the ground speaking through them, shaped the poet's body. Poetry grows from the body of nature, gesturally isomorphic to it.

> *Poetic speech is a crossbred process, and it consists of two sonorities. The first of these is the change that we hear and sense in the very instruments of poetic speech, which arise in the process of its impulse. The second sonority is the speech proper, that is, the intonational and phonetic work performed by the said instruments.*
>
> *Understood thus, poetry is not a part of nature, not even the best or choicest part. Still less is it a reflection of nature, which would lead to a mockery of the law of identity; but it is something that, with astonishing independence, settles down in a new extraspatial field of action, not so much narrating nature as acting it out by means of its instruments, which are commonly called images.* (Selected Essays 3)

Mandelstam underscores the precarity of meaning formation in poetic speech by an image that underscores the relative freedom of poetry from the command of the author: achieving coherence in poetic utterance is like running across the width of a river that is filled with mobile Chinese junks sailing in different directions. This is a process marked by "rapidity and decisiveness" (4), yet which also feels "instrumentless," purely qualitative and instant in its discernments. "Its route cannot be reconstructed by interrogating the boatmen: they will not tell how and why they are leaping from junk to junk."

Aside from image and precariously made, yet decisively and rapidly made, meaning in poetry, there is rhythm. This clearly comes from our bodies, an anticipation or expectation of undulant shape in our muscles, joints, lungs, patterns of breath, placed there by the many millennia our species has been walking, African savannahs, stretches of central and north east Asia, Beringia. A friend who was attempting to learn Neolithic Cree songs, would play them on his Walkman as he made his way to work on foot; he reported their beat fit exactly an easy, relaxed stride. Mandelstam declares that an early reading of Dante requires a pair of "indestructible Swiss boots with hobnails," but once a way in the text has been found, you fall into the author's lope. "The *Inferno* and especially the *Purgatorio* glorify the human gait, the measure and rhythm of walking, the foot and its shape. The step, linked to the breathing and saturated with thought: this Dante understands as the beginning of prosody" (6).

Mandelstam was struck by what he took to be the social awkwardness of Dante, this a sort of twin of the linguistic instability pressed on all strong poets. Without his *dolce padre*, Virgil, he wouldn't know how to act or speak; scandal and "the most grotesque buffoonery" (11) would mark his passage through Hell and Purgatory, the poet throughout the plaything of a huge oscillation in the self from cravenness to "marvelous fits of self-esteem" and back. Mandelstam's Dante is poor biography, but superb autobiography; his Dante is "a poor man...an internal *raznochinets*," an intellectual without noble birth, dithering, ingenious, like Mandelstam himself, undermined by the forces of language and thought while carried forward on their wave. In this state, the strange, perfect words arrive on the tongue.

|| A similar awkwardness marks such a word, the bright word, as if it too were both masterfully decisive and toppling.

Every word is a bundle and the meaning sticks out of it in various directions, not striving toward any one official point. When we pronounce "sun" we are, as it were, making an immense journey which has become so familiar to us that we move along in our sleep. What distinguishes poetry from automatic speech is that it rouses us and shakes us awake in the middle of a word. Then the word turns out to be far longer than we thought, and we remember that to speak means to be forever on the road. (13)

Suhrawardian "lights" are the one thing knowable, for only they can be known as the self is known, and these, as with self-recognition, are always singular and individuating both for the knower and the object of knowledge, as they are apprehended, all this because "lights," individuals, particularities, are the one manner of thing savourable, the sole object with formational powers. Divinity, it is true, is an object for contemplation, but only under some apparently individualizing aspect, person, symbol, icon, gesture, sacrament. Apophatic theology, in other words, is not knowing without an interiorly delectable object—this is the error of quietism—but a form of kataphatic knowing that yearns past all doubts about the sufficiency of the individual-izing power, person, symbol, image and so forth.

What does Suhrawardi's "individualizing word" and Mandelstam's mourning, elegiac word do but render a thing fresh, vital, by placing it in a revealing relation to other things, effecting a novel shape, thus making it delectable, contemplatible, offering it a green aspect? Often such a "word" is a metaphor; a proper name (Rex, Heather, Peter), a nickname ("Night-train" Lane, a great corner linebacker with the Detroit Lions in the 1960s) are also such freshening, creative words, and themselves have the structure of meta-phor. Often there is an appropriate playfulness in names and images. They don't exhaust their subjects; they seek no "official point," but brighten them and reinforce relationship.

It's not just apophaticism that is insatiable and endless; so is naming—insatiable, endless, endearing, a perpetual well of affection. Necessary, exigent excess in names is ascesis. Naming, the urge to name, thus, is a stable source of genius and decorum toward the attended thing.

|| Nadezhda Mandelstam's last letter to her husband never reached him. After the couple had returned to Moscow from their previous Voronezh exile in May 1937, they discovered they had lost the right of "living space" in the capital and, as illegal residents, barred from work, they began a year-long wandering from place to place, the threat of future detainment hanging over them as the wave of additional arrests built momentum. Mandelstam had two heart attacks during this period. Finally in May 1938, he was charged with counter-revolutionary activities, imprisoned, then sent east on one of the countless prison trains in the autumn. Nadezhda Mandelstam's letter begins with a cry of his name and ends, "I could never tell you how much I love you. I cannot tell you even now. I speak to you, only to you....It's me, Nadia. Where are you?" (Nadezhda Mandelstam 621). The word longs for its object, the true word yearns for the company of another true, vitalizing name.

II

7

A Mandelstamian Generation
in China

I MADE A NUMBER OF TRIPS to China in the mid- to late-1990s, and on each of them I visited with poets in Beijing. I was seeing a journalist in the city whom I'd met when we were both graduate students at McMaster University. She previously had gone to Beijing University, China's top school ("the soul of the nation," as one small farmer in hills north of the capital once surprisingly put it to me), and knew many of the people in the robust contemporary poetry scene which had grown up on the campus in the 1980s. These friends passed me on to others. We'd have conversations in dimly lit *danwei* apartments that went on through the night, great food spread across the tables and lots of beer. There was a huge energy for poetry among these young writers; everyone I'd read—Transtromer, Celan, Holub, Herbert—they had too, and discussed in rapid fire Mandarin, which was translated in bits and pieces to me. And they kept talking about the extremely active and innovative poetry community in the city. I felt I'd known one or two of the poets for most of my life after a couple of those epic eight-hour talks.

Xiangzi (Acorn), the poet to whom I'd grown closest, suggested one day that I might like to meet Xi Chuan (West Stream)—"he's the best of us," Xiangzi told me. A few days later I was introduced to Xi Chuan in his small *hutong* apartment not far from the center of the city, and Xiangzi, Xi Chuan, Huaizhao, my girlfriend, and I walked to a nearby restaurant, where we ate at a long sidewalk table. A conversation began there that's lasted nearly twenty years. I felt I'd stumbled onto one of the great poetic generations, comparable to the one that grew up around The Stray Dog cabaret in St. Petersburg in the early 1900s, Mandelstam, Akhmatova, Gumilev and the others. The group in Beijing had grown out of the Cultural Revolution and various states of socialism following it, and its existence, then, in the 1990s, seemed to be more or less unknown in the West.

A selection of Xi Chuan's poetry, *Notes on the Mosquito*, translated by Lucas Klein, published in 2012 by New Directions, now brings his work to a wider audience outside China. The book covers around thirty years of writing. The early poetry, especially the work done at Beida, leans toward the lyrical, Romantic, but the writing completely changes after the Tiananmen Square events in June, 1989. In fact, Xi Chuan passed through a period in the early 1990s when it was as if he'd forgotten how to write entirely. He came out of this period of silence with a commitment to what he calls "bad poetry."

China now is in a peculiar situation—a rapidly developing market economy, fueled by cheap labour supplied often by unprotected itinerant workers from the west of the country, is fused with a Leninist control of mainstream media. All this amounts to what some call "a second Cultural Revolution." Many poets I talked to in the late 1990s worried that the country's new money obsession meant there was no longer a philosophical or idealistic core functioning within Chinese culture, and as a result a weird interior entropy was gathering with the growth. This wasn't the result of just capitalist anarchism. Maoist suppression had eliminated or pushed to the far fringes the traditional cultural stabilizers, Taoism, Buddhism and Confucianism, though vestiges of these remained—I once encountered a community of three Taoist nuns, dressed in traditional nineteenth-century costumes, living halfway up a mountain on a ledge at a bend in the trail, with their big black dog, north of Xining, close to the barrens of Qinghai. Other possible cultural centers didn't seem appropriate or were no longer operational. Liberal Western political ideals then appeared impossible to translate into the contemporary Mandarin of the Chinese mainland or perhaps not worth the effort, and the socialist millenarianism of the early 1950s had degenerated long ago into a hundred thousand "princelings," children of current or previous cadres, trying to become rich through *guanxi* (their Party connections). There was a sense I got from talking to the poets that they felt it might be the work of intellectuals to somehow fill this void—but with what? And how welcome would these contributions be?

The first time I heard Xi Chuan talk about his attachment to "bad poetry" was at a 2008 gathering of the Pamirs Poetry Journey that drew poets from across China, Europe and North America, including Robert Hass, Anne Waldman and Tomaz Salamun, to a small resort in Anhui province to discuss poetics and translation. Dropping his commitment to "good poetry," which he'd pursued through the 1980s, he felt he was more in tune with the times, or that the times, with their rupture and speed, had replaced his early poetics entirely. In an interview he gave to the CBC's Eleanor Wachtel around the opening of the Beijing Olympics in the summer of 2008, he said that the Chinese ruling elite post-1949 "always tell us that we may have a bright future, [so] we need to have a bright way of living, and we have been told of all the socialist values, without the dark side." But after the Tiananmen Massacre, he "tried to think of the dark side of our lives."

The year 1989 was a triply traumatic one for Xi Chuan. His fellow poet and friend Hai Zi committed suicide in March, and in May, Luo Yihe, another poet and ally, died from a cerebral hemmorrhage while protesting before the gigantic painting of Mao at the front gate of the Forbidden City. A sizeable portion of the Beida poetry explosion and much of his cohort of friends were gone. Then came the mass killing of students in the square on June 4. "I am surrounded by the dead," he told me at our first meeting. His post-Tiananmen turn-around—and a subsequent discovery that difficulty and a

refusal of lyric beauty were a form of non-compliance—was his version of
Neruda's "I am not Theocritus" moment.

> I am not Theocritus: I took life
> and I faced her and kissed her,
> and then I went through the tunnels of the mines
> to see how other men live
> and when I came out, my hands stained with garbage
> and sadness
> I held my hands up and showed them to the generals
> and said: "I am not part of this crime." (Neruda, Neruda and Vallejo 121)

But Xi Chuan, like Neruda, never really was Theocritus, though clearly an
idealized nature preoccupation stands near the center of his earliest work.
The last poem from this period included in *Notes on the Mosquito*, "Send
Your Flock to the Sea," begins

> Send your flock to the sea, shepherd,
> leave the world to stones—
> stones of night, the sky's
> resplendent stars, which you will not see. (19)

There's something other than a weak version of Wordsworthian sublime
here; Xi Chuan's shepherds are as ironized as Pessoa's, and there is a sense—
one that gets even more pronounced in the later poems—that the language
is a bit of a code and something else, the actual point of the poem, is being
discussed at a slant. It's not really allegory that's at work but a kind of
eloquent obliquity—which could be easily deciphered if you were equally
steeped in the conditions Xi Chuan is describing.

> Fierce gale. Salt on your face.
> The great sun in the shipwreck abyss
> The lighthouse walks to the sea, flames rise on the water. (19)

You'd need the mind of a late-1980s Beijing intellectual to say exactly what is going on in this poem, to read this stanza as a daring hint, but patriotic songs of the Cultural Revolution often referred to Mao as the great sun of the peoples' hearts. Now Xi Chuan in conversation says, "I am a hotel of persons. A hotel of persons, ghosts and evils." We are a long way from shepherds and the sea coast.

There has been a tendency in North America and Europe to imagine Chinese writers, poets especially perhaps, as inevitably and necessarily political, dissidents in a way that flatters the West. This was true for writers in the old Soviet Union too, which made it difficult, for example, to appreciate the complete range of someone like Joseph Brodsky once he first became known outside of Russia. Taking Xi Chuan this way, or any in his generation, would bring on similar reductive distortions. It is true that in China's current state of cultural undefinition, some intellectuals, as Xi Chuan told Wachtel, "are trying to rethink or reflect on history, not only ancient history but also on modern history, revolutionary history," in order to imagine a possible, more coherent China. It's also true that traditionally poets, like scholars, in the Confucian scheme of things, have seen themselves as serving the state by helping to shape its notion of itself, either by speaking directly to the masses or by educating the ruler. But the West is chiefly keen to identify dissidents wherever it can, because these, it supposes, are warriors for its own cause within an opposing power, who work utterly at their own risk. It's hard to believe that any of the major Chinese poets I spoke to seeks to fulfill the role of furthering Western cultural expansion. As Xi Chuan said in the Wachtel interview, "I don't think China will one day become, for instance, Canada, America, England or France." Nor, it seems, does he think precisely that it should. When I asked the Chinese poets in 2008 gathered at White Stone Town in Anhui province how they thought of being seen by the West as dissidents, Ouyang Jianghe, one of the most fiery of the group, exploded that he had no wish to be regarded as a writer who was professionally a disaffected Chinese intellectual. Such a vocation was far too soft and besides was a self-serving invention from elsewhere.

Xi Chuan's poetry from the 1990s on puzzled many of his readers, unable to see the point of this largely disjointed, non-imagistic voice. This response is not restricted to China—Rachel Blau DuPlessis reported a similar reaction to Xi Chuan's reading at the Modern Language Association meeting in Seattle in January 2012. What his readers didn't take in was that his new work had no point if you considered it solely from the perspective of style. In the essay "Style Comes as a Reward," published in 2012 in the online journal *Almost Island*, Xi Chuan spoke of form and voice in poetry as an incidental result of a quite different project.

> *Although each writer has a dream or ambition of acquiring his or her own style, he or she may find that a true style has its own will—whether it will come or not, who knows? And another's style is not yours, although sometimes we mix them up. We may only get a weak style if we haven't understood that a true style is part of creativity. The buds of style hide themselves in human sufferings, weaknesses, the brightness and darkness of the nature, the shadows of philosophy, social changes. During the last three decades, China has changed a lot. Before that, there was the Cultural Revolution. I grew up in and after the revolution and was thrown into its mayhems and turbulences. And after the revolution, I find myself peddling a kind of self-coloured socialism. The way in front of me is not from A to B, but from A to X. It makes me need new ideas, new images and new syntaxes. By and by, what I have learned from previous writers and poets, their schools and isms, regardless of whether they are Chinese or not, is not sufficient anymore.*

Most of the post-1989 poems in *Mosquito* are the result of an attempt to read and somehow replicate, while not completely interpreting, the era in which he lives. The newer poems can be essay-like or aphoristic in the fashion of Confucius' *Analects*, or they can be straightforward conversation or fragmented cultural fieldnotes. They follow a playful, extreme zigzag pattern of sense, forming heterogeneous assemblages, making one think of private cultural museums, the poems co-opted to house shards of what has caught the poet's eye, like living rooms turned into eccentric art galleries by their owners. Everywhere Xi Chuan's current interest in fakery and frauds, false histories, facts and philosophies is on display.

> It seems to me that history and reality are themselves inventing a kind of literature. To be honest to oneself means to be loyal to your sense of reality. You don't need to mirror the reality, but you need to be symmetrical to the vigor of history and reality. Style comes as reward. And now I can say that I don't care about it.

Instead of writing directly about the volcanic events of 1989 and after, he's learned to react to their tearing power. He makes an attempt, though, at a mapping in the long poem "Ill Fortune," which he told me was "about Tiananmen" when he gave me a copy of a typescript of it in 2008. Now he qualifies this description by saying it chronicles the "hard experiences" from the Cultural Revolution onward, including the Tiananmen protests. Unaccountably, Klein translates only sections of this major work; a complete version, translated by Wang Ping and Alex Lemon, appears in *Grain* 37.1 (2009). Here is the poem's third section in the Klein translation.

ILL FORTUNE C 00024

> There is a lotus floating in the sky. There is a splotch of birdshit caught
>   by the ground. There is a fist that has penetrated his ear. On
>   Sunlight Avenue he will be transparent.
> The fire in the sky has already been put out, how many lives in this dust
>   on the ground? He hears his childhood nickname called, a boy who
>   constantly walks into his heart.
> In the dawn stockade of his heart there is only one chair.
> On the bloody battlefield of his heart a chessboard is waiting.
> He has been submitted to nine times, been resisted ten, been killed
>   three times, and killed four.

Moonlight cast on the scum-covered river, dew washes clean the romantic spirits.

In a carnival, a spirit stepped on his heel. Ill fortune beginning, a guy
   with revolutionary eyes shoved him out of line.

Many years later he lit his first match. "Just like that," he whispered to
   the butterfly.

On both sides of the street swept by butterflies, on both sides of the
   street that had been a field, each compound looks like the family
   he betrayed, every magpie is falling.

The old world demolished right up to his feet, he feels himself becoming
   transparent.

Grief rushes into his temples like the Big Dipper rushing out of rooftops...
   a cough, a dizzy spell, and he utterly forgets the script of his life. (173)

Xi Chuan translated two lectures given at Beijing Normal University in 2008 by visiting poets, one from a former communist country and another from North America, and he was struck, as he says in "Style Comes as a Reward," by how each had matched his language, his music and structure, to the conditions and possible futures of their countries—"The two poets left me with lots of questions. I too have my difficulties and conditions." The decaying socialist state, the goods-becalmed, soporific West—this is China today, plus the regime's capacity for violence. I noticed everybody always seemed to have an eye out for the possibility of a display of naked power each time I visited the country. An all-China art exhibition had been set up at the National Gallery during one of my later trips, only to be torn down the day after its installation. No one was really shocked by this—it was theatre, a kind of performance art staged by the government, to remind everyone of what it could do.

|| Xi Chuan, Hai Zi and their contemporaries are all post-Misty poets—or New Generation or New Tide: they have been given various names both in China and in the Chinese diaspora. The Misties, members of the *Menglongshi* school, the name orthodox Marxist literary critics used to defame their often

obscure work, came into existence in the late 1970s around the newly established literary magazine *Jintian* (*Today*) and poetry readings in Beijing and
other parts of the country that drew huge crowds. Readings given by Allen
Ginsberg on campuses in the capital in the mid-1980s, which people still talk
about, also gave impetus. The group that included Bei Dao, Duo Duo, Meng
Ke and Gu Cheng, among others, was one of the first to speak out after the
end of the Cultural Revolution, in the early days of Deng Xiaoping.

Zhai Yongming was born in 1955, eight years before Xi Chuan, and is old
enough to have experienced the Cultural Revolution as a "sent down youth,"
an experience that must surely live in the cells—even though, as she says in
her poem "The Language of the 50s," those tumultuous times are now only
"the stuff of stand-up" (155), and material for dinner party one-liners. Her first
book *Nuren* (*Women*) appeared in 1984, so her career straddles the end of
the Misty era and the beginning of the late 1980s Beijing University poetry
scene that fostered Hai Zi and Xi Chuan. Since 1998, she's owned a bar, White
Night, in Chengdu in Sichuan, which is one of the cultural centers of the city.
She's also helped write a film, *24 City*, with filmmaker Jia Zhangke, and worked
as an installation artist, giving her poetry a visual art form. A volume of selected
poems in English, *The Changing Room*, published by Zephyr Press / the
Chinese University Press, appeared in 2011. The translator is Andrea Lingenfelter,
and the book contains a penetrating introduction by Wang Ping, who herself
experienced many of the cultural shifts that shaped Zhai Yongming and
her poetry.

The Changing Room stands to *Notes on the Mosquito* as Akhmatova
might to Khlebnikov, especially if you focus on selections from *Nuren* and
later poems like "Report on a Child Prostitute" and "The Testament of Hu
Huishan," concerned with the death of school children in the 2008 Sichuan
earthquake in buildings made from inferior concrete. Such poems, humane,
attentive, have a Philip Larkin ("Whitsun Weddings") or Robert Frost feel—
curious about particular others, compassionate without being sentimental,
rueful—but with an edge of outrage that carries this work beyond a fascinated report.

Her early work established her as a confessional and feminist poet, one of the first in China, heavily influenced by Sylvia Plath in the minds of many North American critics. She herself sees the *Nuren* poems as acts of obedience to a particular mental state, which she calls "Black Night Consciousness," describing this as an "individual and universal consciousness" (Lingenfelter xiii), which "has ordained that I be the bearer of female (*nuxing*) consciousness, beliefs, feelings." In relation to this vocation, she has declared, "I will directly take that charge upon myself, and put it into what I see as the best work I can do on behalf of that consciousness. Namely poetry." The communication of this female consciousness involves an exploration of, among other things, "a psychology of private resistance."

A woman dressed in black arrives in the dead of night
Just one secretive glance leaves me spent
I realize with a start: this is the season when all fish die
And every road is criss-crossed with traces of birds in flight

A corpse-like chain of mountain ranges dragged off by the darkness
The heartbeats of nearby thickets barely audible
Enormous birds peer down at me from the sky
With human eyes
In a barbarous atmosphere that keeps its secrets
Winter lets its brutally male consciousness rise and fall

I've always been uncommonly serene
Like the blind, I see night's darkness in the light of day. (Zhai 3)

The phantasmagoria in these early lines and their penetrating spiritual and political psychology are qualities that appear as well in her later work, and are not usually associated with early American confessional writing. Her poetry immediately goes into a generalized, floating ghost world, which is also a kind of vigorous introspection and a version of the actual world, or at least the world of the person under pressure of obeying "black night consciousness" (Lingenfelter xiii).

The towering achievements in *The Changing Room* are Zhai Yongming's long and mid-length sequences—"The Tranquil Village," "Fourteen Plainsongs," "The Changing Room," or the continuous poem "My Younger Brother Under Water."

> *Water it's a room filled with waves*
> *it's a little bit sad*
> *poured down from the sky into the perfume vial inside the body (Zhai 93)*

The voice in these longer pieces is interior, sensuous, chagrined, alert to public woe—it contains a full range of phenomenological flavours. One of these is a draining nostalgia, often associated with the author's mother and her mother's experience in the war and revolution of the 1940s and 1950s. Both Zhai Yongming and Xi Chuan come from military families, their parents caught, in varying degrees, in the exhilarating labour of establishing a new China, one that, in the very early 1950s at least, seemed to be ruled from the bottom up. As Mao Zedong said in his speech just prior to launching the new government on October 1, 1949, "The...people of China have now stood up." The lives of that revolutionary generation as a result could possess a substance that mesmerized and sapped their children. "Mother busy with nation building," writes Zhai Yongming, "is the prettiest girl by the Yellow River," and so solid a figure she stands up better even to time—"My forty years went by more quickly than my mother's" (45). The implacable, gorgeous mother, "her expression as keen as an eagle's / She was married in a military uniform / my skinny father at her side" (41), keeps her daughter company through disturbed nights, which are filled with unappeasable presences.

1 INSOMNIAC SONG

> *On a sleepless night*
> *on so many sleepless nights*

I hear my restless mother
busy at the stove in the next room
washing my clothes before dawn

In the dark thinking of the past
its immense bulk   its unmeasurable
significance: it stares into the future (41)

The night, its unshiftable stasis, like the stare of the past, both weaken her.
Even the rescuing face of the mother brings another sort of immobility and
dimishment: "Thinking of the past blindly / my mother's beautiful young
face" (41).

"The Changing Room," the tour de force occupying the middle of the
book, initially appears to channel the Song Dynasty poet Li Qingzhao into
the urban Beijing twenty-first century. Again and again, we find ourselves
in a contemporary version of Li Qingzhao's twelfth-century bed chamber,
where she sits "Saddened by the dying spring,...too weary / to arrange my
hair... / The cherry-red bed-curtain is drawn closed / concealing its tassels"
(Li Qingzhao 124). But in Zhai Yongming's "little changing room" grisly,
desperate transformations are underway.

In my little changing room
I alter my come-hither glances, downy skin and scent
someone is reading a children's book in the dark (89)

In my little changing room
I change my hairstyle, lingerie and blood type (91)

The creepy excerpts from "a children's book," read by the poem's speaker
or anonymous men, quiver with menace: "One winter morning there was a
great fire... / acetylene racing and slapping the wind / Scarlet on the snow
wounded me" or "The weeping emergency room the terror of flames / takes
root in my skin   the shriek of the radio" (89).

Outside "the changing room," upheaval is the norm—"The constantly moving household changes like seasons / My classmates abandon grammar sowing disorder / with sets of metal teeth" (91). We are inside an autobiography of multiple deprivals and queasy accommodations—"In my little changing room / I change my gender, bones and hair" (89).

|| There are several other remarkable poets in the group following the Bei Dao, Duo Duo generation—Ouyang Jianghe, whose own selected poems, *Double Shadows*, appeared from Zephyr Press / the Chinese University Press at the same time as Zhai Yongming's book; Wang Jiaxin, translator of Yeats and Celan and a poet of luminous, reaching control; Yu Jian, from Kuming, whose *Flash Cards* was published in the United States in 2011; Lan Lan; Song Lin; Chen Dongdong and many others. Most of them have appeared in English with only the odd poem in journals and anthologies.

Poetry isn't as popular in China now as it was in the 1980s, when it was seen as the primary means of personal and political expression after years of imposed silence, and hundreds turned out to poetry readings across the nation. Some of the poet-heroes of the 1980s have "plunged into the sea," to make money in the hot economy, while a few others have switched to being visual artists in order to make truly big money. The Mandelstamian generation of Xi Chuan, Zhai Yongming and their friends may well represent the end of the Misty poetry explosion. It's difficult to see what this will mean in terms of a vital poetry culture in the nationalism of China's socialist market economy, "where the sanctification of tradition" in popularized, truncated forms "has become both power and fashion" (243), as Xi Chuan writes in an eloquent and brave afterword to *Mosquito*, "This Tradition This Instant." He seems to favour an energetic and critical form of Straussian retrieval of the past—that adds up to much more than a reciting of a few couplets from the poets of the T'ang Dynasty. This disinterring may be, he suggests, a basic condition for Chinese cultural survival.

The Beijing skyline, the most futuristic imaginable, changes yearly; the city has grown nearly to the base of the Great Wall; no one seems to know

how many people live in it. The air monitoring system at the American
Embassy gives hourly cautions about pollution levels, its measurements
disagreeing wildly with official readings; several thousand new cars enter
the endless traffic streams on Beijing's six ring roads, though the government
tries to limit the issuing of new licenses. China is entering, as Xi Chuan says,
a big bend in its river.

8

Poetry as
Pneumatic Force

Lecture at Beijing Normal University
October 2008

MY SUBJECT IS what poetry can do in a society or culture,
what sort of political engine it might be. I am not interested in making poetry
useful, of course, because part of poetry's energy comes from imagining itself
to be useless, but I wish to attempt to describe something of poetry's nature.
But first I must tell you about where I come from, the society where these
thoughts arise.

Canada is quite a young country, independent from Britain only in 1867,
but mentally and culturally attached to that country, the former colonial
center, well into the twentieth century. Not until 1967 was there a new nation-
alist, autonomous thinking, and this did not go very far. In 1869, the new
Dominion of Canada purchased an extremely large tract of land from one of
the world's first multinational corporations, the Hudson's Bay Company, which
had been founded in 1670 and called itself "The Company of Adventurers."
The company had called this new region Rupert's Land, after a British prince;
it included all the territory drained by rivers emptying into Hudson Bay, the

Arctic Ocean and the Pacific Ocean, north of the 49th parallel, the border with the United States. The company received 300,000 pounds sterling for this breadth of land—just about what you would pay now for a couple of upscale houses in Vancouver—and three million acres of farm land scattered throughout Western Canada. The Canadian government gained with this purchase all surface, water and subsurface rights; and the region has proved to be extraordinarily rich in oil, natural gas, uranium, potash and a range of agricultural products. The government and its licensees have extracted many trillions of dollars from the area.

The British North America Act, a piece of English legislation, is the earliest form of the Canadian constitution, and, among other things, it recognizes what it calls "aboriginal title"; that is, it declares a land's original occupiers and users—those who hunted, trapped and fished for thousands of years on it—to be its owners by virtue of this early subsistence labour. This has meant that the Dominion of Canada entered into nation-to-nation trea- ties with the numerous original Indigenous nations in eastern and western Canada, the Cree, the Blackfoot, the Ojibway, Dene, Chipeweyan and many others, in which aboriginal title was believed, by the colonists, to be extin- guished in exchange for parcels of land, called reservations, and certain rights and benefits like health care assistance and particular tax exemptions. The alternative to signing was homelessness, starvation and the likelihood of war. Nevertheless, some parts of Western Canada were never part of treaty—all of British Columbia chiefly—and settler culture has built itself on unrelin- quished land and remains in this morally ambiguous state today. The people taking treaty, their descendants, had been on the North American continent for perhaps 20,000 years, longer if you track settlements back to Beringia and northeast Asia.

Canada proceeded to exploit old Rupert's Land much as the Hudson's Bay Company had done, only more extensively and efficiently. Indigenous people, on the whole, were and are marginalized in the Western Canadian culture that has developed over the last hundred and fifty years. European settlers, miners, oil developers have never or almost never deeply rooted themselves in the land of these drainages, never really come to a deep sense of home there—they have been adventurers themselves, mobile labourers, land speculators, roughnecks, truckers, farmers whose land failed after a generation or two, all moving through; the culture itself has been mobile, pursuing caches of natural riches here and there. The diasporic Europeans in North America never really rooted themselves where they were partly because their attitude was chiefly one of conquest—the people, the land, the rivers—but also because of a sense of cultural and racial superiority to the place and to the original inhabitants that lasts until today. Europe, and lately the United States, has provided the cultural norm, and white Canadians, descendants of European settlers, have prostrated themselves repeatedly before what they believe is the cultural value in the metropolitan centers of those places.

All of this creates rather significant social problems, so big they appear to form the nature of reality for us and are therefore seldom acknowledged. The newcomers' culture can never be autochthonous, that is, deeply rooted in the place where it finds itself, and it can never open itself to Indigenous culture in its linguistic, philosophical and literary richness because of this spirit of conquest and superiority, together with an eristic inclination in thought and a nervous momentum brought to it by the pneuma of capitalism. Thus Indigenous people remain largely unacknowledged and impoverished; and descendants of European settlers continue always to feel that they are drifting or floating where they are, unrooted in their place and even in their own bodies. And because they feel small real connection to where they are, their exploitation of resources, like the oil sands of northeastern Alberta, the "dirty oil" from there, will tend to be ruthless. What to do about intractable psycho-political problems like these? It's almost an engineering question: How do you go about lifting such a huge social and cultural weight? Perhaps it can't be done.

I know no more about marine engineering than what I read in newspapers, but I understand that the most efficient way to raise gigantic objects from deep water is to attach floatation devices to these things, sunken ships primarily, and then to inflate these devices. I wish to propose to you that poetry is just such a floatation device for lifting apparently unbudgeable cultural and psycho-political problems. Most people in my country, including most of the poets, would find this claim laughable. Poetry seems far too unimportant, too carefully clever an artifact, to tackle large social problems like this. And some people, even some poets, think poetry is a purely decorative art. But let me try to explain what I mean. China has been a country whose poets (Li Bai, Tu Fu, as well as Xi Chuan, Song Lin and Haizi) and wandering contemplatives have tried to benefit the nation, so perhaps a Chinese audience can better understand this claim.

Poetry is a theurgic power, one of the few perhaps that remain active. "Theurgy" is an unusual word that appears in the Western intellectual tradition in the third century with philosophers like the Syrian Neoplatonist Iamblichus. It means god work and refers to healing, therapeutic transformation through ritual. So poetry as a theurgic power is an anagogic device, something that can transform a person; that is, it has the capacity to transfix a person and reposition him or her. It can lift and turn; it is a pneumatic, a hydraulic instrument. Love can work this way too, so can a certain form of philosophy, so can inspired psychological diagnosis. Poetry can operate this way, can perform its theurgic, transformative, therapeutic work, through its musicality, its repetitions, its attention to detail, its speed. Let me offer as example the work of the Chilean poet Pablo Neruda, though there are many other poets I could have chosen.

Pablo Neruda reached for both the private and the political in his work. His massive *Canto General* stands at the middle of his career like a volcano. The book was written while Neruda was on the run in the late 1940s from Gonzalez Videla, the elected socialist president of Chile who quickly turned right-wing dictator. Neruda had campaigned for this man, so he felt his electoral betrayal with a special pang. Videla, by the way, was the mentor of a young army officer named Augusto Pinochet, whom he put in charge of a large concentration camp for Chilean leftists and others in the dry north of the country, Pinochet, who went on to practice even darker arts twenty-five years later during his own dictatorship following his bombing of the presidential palace and the murder of Salvador Allende, then Chile's president. *Canto General* has two important long poems rooting it, "The Heights of Macchu Picchu" and "Let the Woodcutter Awaken." I'll quote from the second poem at some length to give you a sense of its musical range and the political and affective powers gathered in this range.

West of the Colorado River
there's a place that I love.
I hasten there with every pulsing thing
that transpires in me, with all
that I was, that I am, that I sustain.
There are some high red stones, the wild
thousand-handed air
that made them edified structures:
the blind scarlet rose from the abyss
and became copper, fire and strength in them.
America stretched out like a buffalo skin,
aerial and clear night of the gallop,
there toward the starry heights,
I drink your glass of green dew....

I love the farmer's little house. Recent mothers sleep
scented like tamarind syrup, the linens
freshly ironed. Fire
burns in a thousand homes ringed with onions.
(When the men sing at the riverside they have
a hoarse voice like stones from the riverbed:
tobacco rose from its broad leaves
and reached these homes like a fire sprite.)
Come into Missouri, behold the cheese and wheat,
fragrant boards, red as violins,

man navigating the barley,

the newly mounted blue colt smells

the aroma of bread and alfalfa:

bells, butterflies, blacksmith shops,

and in the dilapidated wild movie houses

love opens its teeth

in the dream born of the earth.

It's your peace we love, not your mask.

Your warrior's face is not beautiful.

...we love

your city, your substance,

your light, your mechanisms, the West's

energy, the peaceful

honey, from hive and hamlet,

the gigantic lad on the tractor,

the oats that you inherited

from Jefferson, the whispering wheel

that measures your earthy ocean,

the factory smoke and a new

colony's thousandth kiss:

we love your laborer's blood:

Your folk hand full of oil. (255–57)

"Let the Woodcutter Awaken" (the "woodcutter" is Lincoln)—indeed the whole epic *Canto General*—is an attempt to conjure an opposition to the threat of an appearance of European fascism in the Western Hemisphere during the 1930s and 1940s; against this ominous possibility it wields a politico-musical weapon. The book was written in the shadow of the Spanish Civil War and in the shadow of Stalingrad. This part of "Let the Woodcutter Awaken"—it goes on at greater length—appears to hover at visiting UFO height and shift quickly from place to place over the continent. You will notice in the Nerudean linguistic tumble, discontinuous images falling on one another, what appears to be a refusal of poetic control. This abnegation of control, however, is not the refusal of craft or the absence of skill, but the adoption of a Dionysian craft and a theurgic skill. You see a similar choice being made in Whitman, whom Neruda loved. Neruda is letting the inner body, the deepest unconsciousness, speak in its unsmooth, associative way.

There are what I believe to be three theurgical or ritually transformative powers in Neruda's poem—its muralism, its interest in individuals and its speed, which gathers together many different things at a run. Neruda learned a great deal from the great muralists Diego Rivera and David Siqueiros while living in exile in Mexico; you can see an approximation of their sweeping historical vision throughout the long poem. In the farm house ringed with onions, with the moon on the ship docked at Manhattan, in the Jeffersonian oats, a great span of history and current economic activity is held in a single look: we are made to feel the surveyors, scrutinizers of history, not its confused victims; we take it in with rumination, are not overrun by it. The great diorama is presented, and we calmly view it. The poem is the moment of empowering Marxist or Hegelian insight, and a certain sense of capacity and even mastery comes with this insight; we see how things are, how they must be, and in this, sense the owl of Minerva, meaning philo-sophical understanding (as Hegel remarks at the end of his Preface to *The Phenomenology of Spirit*), begin its dusky flight across the terrain; we under-stand the inevitability in what is spread before us. And in this sweeping view are nailheads of shining, arresting particularity. The men singing at the river in their tobaccoey voices, the people in rundown film theatres where "love opens its teeth," the carefully rendered details of these scenes, their trans-fixing quality, engender empathy as a kind of spiritual exercise: we are held by these sharply drawn images, glints of experience, and are caused to forget ourselves; we go over to the objects and scenes in ekstasis; we give their people, their action and the aromas of their homes briefly our whole heart.

The last theurgic device operating in the poem is its breakneck enjamb-ment of unlike things. These lists of strange, or strangely paired objects, tractors, rivers, factories, laundry, fields of oats, ships and their smells, the lists moved through at speed, without pause, befuddle and disarm; caricatures of the nature of things are shaken, making space for a new vision—here it is the vision of a commonwealth of random individuals, human, non-human, swept together in a solidarity that at first exists only in the ear. Neruda does not declare these stands, at least not here; he tells us nothing—thus this part of *Canto General* is not particularly didactic—but he enacts them inside the reader. It's like someone filling your basement with gold while you sleep, as Saint John of the Cross said of a somewhat different operation, the work of grace. The importance of the poem, the place of its greatest vitality, is with these theurgic-political effects, the empowering muralism, the inducement to empathy through specificity, the small model of a hyperbolically inclusive community built in the ear, which work below the surface of the poem, but are aided by the music and imagery of this surface. Here the poem acts as a Hermetic psychopomp, as a spiritual guide, shaping a new political vision and new erotic allegiances to things that are unlike and beyond the self. These internal effects make the poem a plausible, wonderful pneumatic device for lifting a great cultural and political weight that offers no handhold to partisan politics. They also nurture an inner life in the reader, working an ascetical practice against a sense of disenfranchisement, against atomism and its despair.

Poems like "Let the Woodcutter Awaken" or, say, Geoffrey Hill's *The Triumph of Love*, aim to achieve a noetic, conceivably transformative muscularity that dogmatic, surface-obsessed realism can't achieve. Poetry, and perhaps, as I say, certain forms of philosophy, certain forms of diagnostic insight and types of love are the only ways we can manage—lift and raise—particular sorts of political problems in my country. Poetry cannot do this efficiently; it inevitably will appear pathetic as it tries, but it is poetry's unforced, uncalculated nature to exercise rescuing, theurgic power.

9
Fresh Coherence

St. John's and Victoria
January–March 2011

An Initial Query

If the harmonic shape of music is formed by the conventions of
dance steps—this the world via kinaesthetic mimesis—the shape of thinking
must surely be in part the result of the skeleton of grammar, which, if it is not
the world, at least is an efficient means for inserting ourselves in it. That is,
thinking falls into categories made by predication, concatenation, adjectival
and adverbial colouration and the action of verbs operating as the energy
tentacles of nouns, perhaps with substantial residue, perhaps without. Added
to choreography and grammar is invention, which may become routinized.

Robert Schumann believed his time wanted freedom from music's traditional four-bar structure and a return to a state of origin or nature. What is
wanted now from thought, or what shape does this time anticipate thought
producing, especially poetic thought or larger analogical thought? It is a
form, I think, that links—makes a coherent whole of—a mass of apparently
heterogeneous things, without reshaping or reducing, even in the slightest
way, the peculiarity of events and objects. This desideratum could be read

as a nostalgia for earlier, sanguine syntheses, but is, more likely, a promising loneliness for things; in fact, it may be a reaching for a phenomenological architectonic, for an understanding of autobiography as cosmology, since things deeply comprehended are savoured in intimate individual conscious-ness; indeed such savouring alone seems able to make singularity evident. The present alternatives to this ambitious project, in poetry in this country at any rate, is irony in both its postmodern and flaneur forms, which tacitly admits the appeal, the draw, of the undertaking, I sense, yet which mocks the scale of the attempt[1]—and an array of self-accommodating subjectivisms, which ceaselessly steer into gaps of disquiet.

Pound's and Duncan's grand forms, the ad hoc or intuited encyclopedia and the symposium of the totality of persons, the marginal crucially, fail to gel or have a credible through-line because both lack a durable, engendering and creative philosophical infrastructure, an interior order which includes intentionality and teleology. Realist narrative, in its present form, is ideologically reductive and of no use in finding a new type of cognitive rebar. Archeologist Steven Mithen, in his writing on paleolinguistics, argues song is prior to gram-maticized speech, and that its lignified rhythms intend particular emotional clarities and politics.[2] In the four song cycles I finished between 1994 and 2008 (*Moosewood Sandhills, To the River, Kill-site* and *Orphic Politics*) and the masque "Assiniboia," completed in 2011, I have attempted to work out a version of the perduring and apt philosophical structure I find absent in various modernisms and their agnosticisms and largely to express it in powers somewhat prior to syntax.

A Few More Questions: Interiority as World

What is hermetic autobiography—private experience of one's life—which is, or is a hermeneutic of, cosmology? What is the coherence of song or rhythmic sound? The latter first: it is a somatic or kinetic "making sense," making personal, the outside or otherwise made individual to one. It is a coherence aside from intelligence or at least its more commonplace artifacts of taxonomy, causality and narrative. It is a making sense like prayer's: that is, it is a proximity; the coherence of song achieves the resolution of intimacy. This intimacy particularizes in a vivifying, resonant way: it amounts to retrieval of what is primary and essential in selfhood and, with luck, a marriage to this foundational existential element. For the Islamic philosopher Ibn 'Arabi, as we will see, such a marriage is an appropriation of a divine Name.

What, then, is autobiography, which is, or is a hermeneutic of, cosmology, autobiography perhaps surfaced by the mood of intimacy sound may create? The traditional reply to this question is that no such thing exists. The most comprehensive ontology, metaphysics, the universal account, is the antipode of psychology, the private story. Even the natures of these truths occupy different taxonomical slots, one marked by invariancy, immutability, the other provisional, perspectival, specific, susceptible to change. Nothing seems more unlike metaphysical abstraction than individuation, from scholasticism to the present. Yet in the thought of mystical, medieval Islam, they overlap exactly, the personal leagued in a non-relativistic way to the ontological. For someone formed by the history of Western philosophy, this will seem initially incomprehensible, a nonsensical fancy. But then she may recall the Prologue to the Gospel of John, the central text in Western philosophical theology, the first three verses specifically, where an isomorphism is asserted between private intelligence, in which its true ground or identity is delectated ("and the Word was God"), and Being; indeed here the interior world of thinking is the place from which the sensible comes into concreteness, so they share an identity.

But this, it will be objected, is a unique case, since the thinking described in John 1.1–3 is divine, therefore comprehensive and unfailingly precise. All other thinking is contingent and enjoys no such necessary isomorphic relation with the world. This objection, concerning the exceptionalism of the Logos, is persuasive in Christian Aristotelianism, but not in Sufi Neoplatonism. There, the identity of Jesus, the Logos, is simply the actualization of one of the divine attributes or relations to being, though an eminent one, "prophethood," of a certain sort. What is described in the Prologue of John is therefore a template of all nature, human and non-human. All names give a specific, yet putatively comprehensive, account of everything.

Similar to the creative action of the Logos, individuation of all sorts, in
Ibn 'Arabi, is the means by which the intelligibility of reality becomes manifest—or, to put this more precisely, successive instantiations of the individual
make the world. No anti-metaphysical, relativistic, utilitarian theory of veracity
should be read into this view. But it should be recognized that if cognition,
like consciousness, is experienced as specific, idiosyncratic, true while partial,
only then is it possible, even essential, to treat conversation as noesis.

Becoming the Name

You appropriate the Name, latent and expectant in Reality, and become it,
and this is an enactment—a bringing into fact—of the world. The nature
of being, indeed, is dependent on this appropriation. The uncovering and
assumption of a Name is, or constitutes, reality. "He is your mirror for your
vision of yourself, and you are His mirror for his vision of His Names—
which are none other than Himself—and the manifestation of their
determinations" (Ibn 'Arabi 26). There is no being aside from successive
instantiations of the self, which is divine being. One becomes haecceity;
further, one discerns, in contemplative availability, haecceity, existentiating it.

What is being proposed here is not, I think, a monism. In fact, Ibn 'Arabi's
claim may not have principally an ontological intent, but may be an epistemological observation or, more accurately, a phenomenological account
of contemplative practice or philosophical introspection. It may, addition-
ally, be a theological observation concerning what Maximus the Confessor
called theandrism, the cooperative creativity of human and divine acts.
Occasionally, in a moment of peaked emotion, of illness or ill fortune, we
will truly see something, a tree, an animal, a neighbourhood, a loved one, in
their idiosyncratic actuality, as we suspect they truly are, and we are overwhelmed, while quieted, housed, by the detail of their being. Before this
moment of recognition, they existed, of course, but now they stand out with
an aching clarity, which seems at once identity and a notion of our relationship to it. The Name is brought out of potency. The distinction between the
tree or field as it always was and as it is in epiphanous, grateful appraisal

may be like Hegel's distinction between existence and actuality. Only what is actual, seen, can make a daemonically sustaining world. The divine names of things are uncovered in acts of recognition, so they carry the presence of the relieved self—they cannot in their actuality be thought outside relationship. Conscious beings also uncover their names through acts of recognition, but they may do so as well through introspective song or prayer.

What is the Name, which is selfhood, which is kataphatic theology? "And now we return to the gifts and say that the gifts are either Essence gifts or Name gifts. Now, as for Essence bestowals, or grants and gifts, they come only from a divine self-disclosure. This self-disclosure of Essence can only take on the form of the preparedness of the object of self-disclosure; it is never otherwise" (Ibn 'Arabi 25). Divine being, being itself, Reality, is nothing other than an unfolding or articulation of something already contained in the essence of the individual, or at least what is allowed by her protean "preparedness," an emergent topology. All this is strange talk, of course, but a talk which the West, for its health, must learn to move in and where it must prepare itself to find nourishment.

What Cannot Be Said

In the Arian controversy of the fourth century, the second person of the Trinity was identified as solely human because this figure was credally categorized as *genitos* (generated), while the Creator was declared to be *agenitos* (ungenerated). Clearly, the two "persons" could not be the same beings, the Arians deduced, since it opposed divine nature to act outside reason. Arianism, in its deepest spirit, was not a revolt within the magisterium, the promotion of a severely truncated Christology, as it is universally depicted, but a subscription to a reductive epistemology, which entailed a suppression of the esoteric, a refusal of interiority—where song speaks and intimacy knows—as gnosis. The Arian cognitive terrain is very much like the modern map of thinking. So much epistemological ground has been blocked out, made not to exist, become unsayable, uninhabitable, by modernity's embargo placed on the esoteric.

Another way of saying what the anti-Arian Nicene Creed declares ("We believe...in the Son of God...begotten not made, one in being with the Father") is that the distinct "flavour" or "scent" of the Second Person is interiorally tastable. Phronetic prayer, non-credulous, while non-skeptical, enters into different relationships, and this is knowing. And intimacy requires individuation. (And vice versa: what the Trinity knows, thus, is conversational.)

Becoming Your Self

In the thought of J.S. Mill, authentic, subsistent identity is the result of insistant self-determination; in Ibn 'Arabi, it appears through annihilation, which arises from "bewilderment," a state of being in which one is "drowned in the sea which the knowledge of God is" (47), the defining condition paradigmaticized by Noah, who *"found no helpers other than God"* (Koran 71:25 quoted in Ibn 'Arabi, 47). "In the case of the Muhammadans," Ibn 'Arabi continues, *"All things perish save His Face* (28:88). And ruin is destruction. Whoever wishes to attain the mysteries of Noah must ascend to the sphere of Noah" (50), which is an aspect of plain human possibility, existentially latent. For Ibn 'Arabi, allegory is a realism of the non-existent but yearnable, accounts of the prophets, Noah, Job, Jesus, Hud and others, sequestered within individual beings as idiosyncratic potency.

"Whoever holds to what is odd (*fard*, which also means individuality or particularity or haecceity) does speak of the One" (40); indeed, this is the only way to speak at all aside from apophasis' probing muteness, all things "tongues" or accurate yet non-exhaustive reports of the Real.

Names are latent individualities and, when uttered in existentiation, a brighter world that is full home, since it is the self. It is the self encountering the self without alienation in a variety of clarifying autonomies. Each haecceity nevertheless is an identification of a single essence, "quintessence as both boundless and quailified" (41). Individuation is ontogenesis, which, without a pause, is apokatastasis and plunging introspection.

Noah, in his wisdom, said unto his people, He will loose heaven upon you
in torrents, *those being the intellectual sciences dealing with meanings and
discursive thought.* And He will succour you with wealth *(Koran 71:12), that
is to say, by means of which He takes you unto Himself, and when He [that
is the "Real"] takes you unto Himself, you will see your own forms in Him.
Whosoever among you imagines that he sees Him knows not, and whosoever
amongst you sees himself is the one who knows." (43–44)*

Song and Individuation

Something must provide the upholding grid for large coherent accounts;
narrative, description, allegory, metaphor as reach for homology are all
possible devices. Poetic music is yet another, even though it is usually seen
as ancillary embellishment. I claimed earlier that the knowledge provoked
by song or rhythm is an understanding resembling prayer's, a knowledge
achieved by means of proximity. This noesis may be described as intimation
amounting to insight; as inaccurate but proprietary recognition of looming
resolution and presence; as burgeoning construal and buoyancy; as meeting
the angel and Abramatically feeding it, as an Ibn 'Arabi or Suhrawardi might say.

As cognition, song is first ascesis: it suspends quotidian self-identification
by dissolving attachment to explanation and story, destabilizing then extir-
pating previous artistic or artifactual individuations. The de-individuation
provided by poetic rhythm thus provides a momentary refuge from ideology
(though sentimental music and formal rhythms in poetry and oratory can
work much mischief) and in this uprooting is an advance on knowledge,
a practice of *scientia* in the phrase of John Burnside. It achieves this effect
through bewilderment and alarm (New Music, *Orphic Politics*), as much as
through enchantment.

Then its swoops, its separations and linkages, particularize newly. How?
The music in poetic speech creates a feeling of dawning nearness or an intimacy. In prayer, in *lectio divina*, say, or *theoria physike*, you are addressed
by texts, the active intelligence, the this-ness of events, persons, objects,
places. The effect of song is different, though something seems to move

toward one. But poetic music gives the *shape* of resolution, an intimation, scent, of protean, spreading telos-like form. And this is a resolution specific to you—otherwise there is no intimacy, no knowing—think of the difference between general advice and spiritual direction—no delectation or resolving understanding. What appears is the shape you may relax into of existential home. And so, by the lever of relief, you become quiddity, with shocked surprise, the queer, unsettling sense of satisfied premonition and gratitude, for the solution "came" to you from a previously unnoted, unsurmized location. Ultimately, the intimacy is of self with self—and with the world, which is the self in its multiple versions.

Apologia

I have never set out to create hermetic or even particularly difficult work, but I am interested in oddness, largely because, when it is apparent in things, they are absolutely, without reservation, remarkable; in this, oddness is indistinguishable from beauty; indeed, particularity is undoubtedly beauty's foundation, the passion of the thing disclosed. A person normally comes to recognition of oddness visually, the arresting sight, but comprehension can also take an aural route, shaping peculiarity, the knower shaping herself toward particularity, through strange, enjambed sound, digging into unlikeness by means of the tornness or smoothness of rhythm.

I have wanted to say the unsayable seven-fold depth of objects and desires, that thin, motile thing, and have gerrybuilt phrase-abutting-and-nudging columns of fragments to try this; these on their own sought speed and elision, since they named and shifted, named, partly erased and reconfigured on the fly, largely out of a courteous tentativeness toward things, and, in this way, they found their coherence, which was their music. And I discovered that music defined things, if you saw them generously, marked with their desire and the eros they provoked.

I have believed this music to be knowing since it sought to hold things with their buzz and tremble of affect, to see them with an empathetic, comprehensive realism, take them in with, in Ibn 'Arabi's language, the angel inside. Only this way of apprehension, I am convinced, decolonizes, builds the nourishing land and makes home.

The most attractive things, in biology, physics and art, have a deep, patterned complexity, pattern laid on or emerging from pattern, suggesting time and labour in their assemblage, suggesting, as well, motion. One way to render this phenomenon is mathematics; another way is rhythm or song.

Notes

1. See Raïssa Maritain in "Sense and Non-Sense in Poetry" in *The Situation of Poetry: Four Essays on the Relations between Poetry, Mysticsim, Magic and Knowledge* (1955) for another version of this state of affairs (9). Maritain writes here about the earliest days of surrealism and the aftermath of this movement in the first quarter of the twentieth century. She sets her remarks on surrealism's ontological ambitions within a meditation on poetic obscurity. It should be noted that her thinking operates from a neo-Thomistic perspective.

   > The principal cause of the obscurity which goes to the point of non-sense is truly, even if the poet is an atheist, of a quality which it is impossible not to call religious. A pathetic cause, and one which in our day has erupted with an unprecedented intensity, it is first of all—in Lautréamont, in Rimbaud—the despair of ever seizing absolute reality, the interior life in its pure liberty; and for others, in the early period of surrealism, it was the hope, that suddenly surged up, for the rediscovery of that river of the spirit which flows under all our customary activity, of that profound, authentic reality, foreign to all formulae, perceived in those "minutes of abandonment to hidden forces" which vivify....They [the poets] overwhelmed poetry with this weight, at first. Later, not having obtained from it what they expected, they undervalued it. And then a new despair pushed them toward other spiritual adventures.

   The form this undervaluation took was an attachment to literary automatism. The cause of the disappointment of the surrealist philosophical program for Maritain was the error of burdening "poetry with the duties of sanctity, which are essentially the giving of the self."

2. Mithen, in *The Singing Neanderthals*, compares hominid proto-language to infant-directed speech, with its soothing and bonding features, including "a higher overall pitch, a wider range of pitch, longer 'hyperactivated' vowels and pauses, shorter phrases and greater repetition" (69). He recognizes such speech as a scoring of emotion, its central

intent being the building of intimacy, so that the lines of community are tightly drawn. Such rhythm-emphasized communication grows from, and is enhanced by, the fluid stride bipedalism makes possible from Homo ergaster on. All music, Mithen continues, quoting from the work of ethnomusicologist John Blacking, begins "as a stirring of the body" (153), which carries political significance since "to feel with the body is probably as close as anyone can ever get to resonating with another person."

10

Turning the

Soul Around

The Ascetical Practice of Philosophy in the Republic

Lecture at the Department of Classics
Dalhousie University, 2011

SOCRATES NOTORIOUSLY ADVANCES no positions: his
interlocutors complain that he says nothing of his own views while quizzing
them repeatedly about theirs (*Republic* 337a); he admits he is "incapable of
giving birth" to ideas (*Theaetetus* 149b); he states he is incompetent to speak
on the natures of things (*Republic* 337a). He is either silent or maddeningly
perverse on ontological matters: "Socrates does injustice, and is meddlesome,
by investigating the things under the earth and the heavenly things and by
making the weaker speech the stronger and by teaching others the same
things," as his final condemnation declares (*Apology* 19b–c). He identifies the
Good as the appropriate end of human desire, yet says almost nothing about
its essential nature (*Symposium* 211a–b); he speaks of gods but articulates no
comprehensive, systematic theology. Philosophy is the art of turning around
the soul (*Republic* 518d; 521c–d), he insists; its point, it seems, is therapeutic,
the transformation of an interior life; and the philosopher is the one who is
so transformed and who assists others in such transformation. In this latter

role, he is a midwife (*Theaetetus* 149b); an "uncanny go-between" joining the right lovers (*Theaetetus* 149d); a corrector of erotic misalignment (*Republic* 403c)—never a metaphysician, ethicist, epistemologist or political theorist.

Philosophy as transformational process has priority over philosophy as a source of pronouncements on reality, the latter an undertaking that Socrates appears to see as a lesser form of intellectual endeavour, not truly philosophy at all (*Theaetetus* 174a–b), but often in fact a place to retreat from the rigors of authentic philosophy. In emphasizing the therapeutic nature of philosophy over system-building, Socrates stands at the head of a diverse tradition which includes such Neoplatonists as Iamblichus and Suhrawardi; apophatic theologians like Pseudo-Dionysius the Areopagite, the author of *The Cloud of Unknowing* and Meister Eckhart; Descartes in *Meditations on First Philosophy*; and Ludwig Wittgenstein,[1] though each understood differently the confusion from which he wished to rescue his interlocutors or readers.

For Socrates the confusion that most contorts an individual is erotic. Those outside philosophy desire in such a way that their inner lives are malformed; the proper quest of longing is thus undermined in them. They must be persuaded to undertake an ascetical journey—which, like the journey in the *Odyssey*, is a long return—conducted largely within the spiritual exercise of dialectical exchange. The transformation of philosophy, this journey, is variously described as a flight (*Phaedrus* 252b); a sea voyage (*Phaedo* 99d); "assimilation to a god" (*Theaetetus* 176b); ascent from darkness into light (*Republic* 514a–516c). Each metaphor, however, illuminates a single thing: philosophy as the correction and proper unfolding of eros.

|| Much inconclusive scholarly discussion has gathered around what the figures of the sun, the divided line and the allegory of the cave in the *Republic*, the leading images of the Good in the dialogue, reveal about Socratic epistemology, ontology, metaphysics and political theory. The controversy inevitably exists, I wish to suggest, because these images are not intended as segments of a system replicating the nature of being and the structure of human knowledge,

though they may appear to be exactly this, but are eikastic images offered to quicken dispositional migration in the Socratic interlocutor. They therefore need to be only sufficiently plausible to beckon desire, while not being precise: they must disarm and arouse, yet not create disciples. Part of their philosophical effectiveness is that they resist the institution of an orthodoxy. It is not that Socrates is an obscurantist—he believes, after all, that the Good itself, a beauty beyond being, is somehow the source of what is and the telos of contemplative attention—but that he's suspicious of preoccupation with ontological clarity: such clarity can easily breed dogmatism, foreclosing philosophic inquiry entirely. Pointing to the severe personal and social consequences of dogmatic thought, thought drawn exclusively from clearly etched hypotheses or ideals, is one way he attempts to lead Glaucon, his primary interlocutor in the *Republic*, into a philosophical life.

Plato himself has struck some commentators as a hopeless solitary, disquieted by ordinary human relations, seeking safe harbour in an imagined transcendence, an intellectualist contemplation of an ineffable ideal replacing, for him, the uncontrollability of human sexual and emotional relations. This view shares features with the somewhat older argument that Plato in the *Republic* shows himself to be a totalitarian thinker: just as he fears the unwieldiness of a liberal democratic state, so he fears the raggedness of human passion, and is keen to jettison it in pursuit of an otherworldly perfection. But this criticism, in fact, comes closer to describing the politics and psychology of Glaucon, whose version of the perfect city is, indeed, intolerant of ordinary human attachment. It is this idealism and the unimaginative deductive thinking that accompanies it from which Socrates wishes to rescue him. Philosophy is the unfolding of eros coming to assimilation to a god (*Theaetetus* 176b), coming to a vision of the Good (*Republic* 508d–509a). One block to such an unfolding is the conviction that philosophy is the erection of abstract systems—metaphysical, epistemological, and political—and their application in human affairs. This conviction, it appears, is the paramount obstacle standing between Glaucon and the philosophical life. His ridicule of the apparent excess of genuine philosophical eros—its insatiability, its hyperbolic nature, its apparent lack of dignity, its seeming risibility—reveals the profound incomprehension and fear of human desire that some attribute to Plato.

The eros of philosophy begins necessarily with pre-philosophical eros, so the *Republic* is preoccupied with political matters in a particular way because Glaucon is so preoccupied. Glaucon's interest in politics, it becomes clear in the course of the dialogue, arises from an Achilles-like thirst for honour, and this nature, defining his character before his encounter with Socrates, we soon see, is based on the particular grip Homer has on him. In particular, he is interested in war and in the sort of state that would be successful in war, because in such a state the Achillean rewards would be greatest. Socrates has gone down at the beginning of the dialogue—he descends, an orphic ritual act—to the port city of Piraeus to view a religious festival—horses ridden hard on the beach by riders carrying blazing torches. Glaucon accompanies him, the katabasis announced in the first sentence of the dialogue—"I went down"—suggesting we are on nothing other than a journey of initiation. The two meet other friends in the course of the day, and a mammoth discussion ensues that carries on through the night, all participants caught in the school of theurgical talk.

Glaucon's long exchange with Socrates begins with his request that Socrates defend justice as the sophist Thrasymachus, in the earliest stages of the dialogue, with extravagant, an almost brutal zeal, has championed the merits of injustice (*Republic* 358d). Socrates, in his account of the conversation, remarks that Glaucon is "always most courageous in everything" (357a), but Glaucon's courage, it soon becomes clear, is untempered by prudence and can be, as a result, on occasion, graceless: here, in the first moments of his conversation with Socrates, it manifests itself as presumption. He turns Socratic method on Socrates at the outset of their conversation, asking him a series of questions in which he sketches a taxonomy of what is good. There is the sort of good we seek for its own sake, such as pleasures that have no deleterious effects; there is the kind of good liked both for its own sake and for its consequences; there is the good, like gymnastic exercise, that is drudgery but whose rewards we cherish. In what category, he asks, does the practice of justice fall? Justice belongs, Socrates replies, to the "finest" kind of good that "the man who is going to be blessed should like both for itself and what comes out of it" (358a). Glaucon fails to see that Socrates' reply subtly alters his taxonomy, adding to it what appears to be a fourth category; he believes Socrates has placed justice in his second category, the kind of good liked both for itself and its consequences. But justice as Socrates describes it has no place in Glaucon's second category: there is no mention of a desire for blessedness in that category; there is no suggestion there that one must learn an attraction to this sort of good: the good of thinking and seeing is self-evident to everyone; Socrates has suggested that the good of justice is not. Socrates is talking about another kind of goodness, the "finest kind," but this is a sort beyond, it seems, the present reach of Glaucon. His own view is that justice is a form of goodness, like submitting to medical treatment when ill, whose practice is unpleasant but whose benefits are worth seeking.

Much of Glaucon's character is already made clear in the first quarter of the dialogue: an aspiration to "blessedness," a sort of transcendent virtue, a virtue perhaps of attentive, phronetic passivity, is incomprehensible to him; whenever Socrates, throughout their exchange, suggests matters beyond the consideration of physical reality or practical statecraft, Glaucon, if he notes them at all, dismisses such remarks as daemonic hyperbole, verging on the laughable (509c). Also it is evident that Glaucon sees justice in terms of ruler-ship, a hard undertaking practiced by the leader that nevertheless rewards those who exercise it with personal honour and wealth (358a). Since he is drawn to honour, he might be interested in finding a way to overcome any resistance to the hard work he suspects justice entails; he perhaps thinks that Socrates' instruction on how justice is "better" will help him surmount this resistance to the drudgery of doing justice and so win him its consid-erable rewards. Besides, the vulgarity of Thrasymachus' self-interested defence of massive injustice is evident to all engaged in the conversation: no real renown will come from rule marked by such thuggish lawlessness and slashing talk. He wonders how one can engage in political life and win a truly good reputation. The terms of Socrates' conversation with his companion are laid down at the outset by the latter's limitations.

|| Often in Plato's dialogues an individual is kept from philosophy simply by the conviction that he already is a philosopher or, what amounts to the same thing, that he bears a profound resemblance to Socrates himself. Theodorus in the *Theaetetus* and Euthyphro in the dialogue that bears his name both labour under this personal misidentification; Phaedrus, in the dialogue named after him, conflates his sophistical lover Lysias and Socrates; Agathon, in the *Symposium*, is presented as a Socratic equal. Glaucon has no awareness of himself as limited; indeed, he seems to hold the belief that he is precisely what Socrates is: he offers a superficial imitation of Socrates, in the early stages of their exchange, engaging in a sham dialectic, proposing a taxonomy and telling a paradigmatic tale—all Socratic psychagogic devices. It quickly becomes evident, however, that Glaucon is not Socrates' double but a caricature, just as Glaucon's story of Gyges' ancestor is an inversion of the story of the cave that Socrates later will tell. Both stories involve descents into the earth and ascents into the world with new authority, but the authority of Gyges' ancestor comes from the mastery of technique—the twisting of a magical ring—rather than abandonment to philosophical eros and a vision of the Good. In Glaucon's tale, a shepherd finds a crack in the earth into which he descends—his action recalling the shamanic endeavour of Odysseus in Calypso's cave, as well as Socrates' descent at the beginning of the dialogue—and discovers a gigantic corpse, naked except for a ring. This he removes and places on his own finger and returns to the earth's surface, where he learns that the ring has extraordinary powers: twisted so that its face is turned to the wearer, it confers invisibility. With this advantage, the shepherd makes love to the queen, kills the king, and has his way with the state. Glaucon's shepherd clearly is not an Odyssean or Socratic ecstatic, and his achievement is not Socrates' transformation through immurement in the earth. He's a trickster who has mastered magical technique, a grave-robber, a tourist to the underworld.

Glaucon oddly imagines himself a philosopher while, at the same time, being repelled by what strikes him as the extreme oddness of the philosophical life (509c; 581d). The *atopos* nature of the philosopher is just as much beyond the scope of his imagination as the man in his tale who practices justice when the license to practice injustice is available to him, a figure he finds "wretched" and "foolish" (360d). We have a foretaste, in these valuations, of the mocking incredulity with which he will greet Socrates' attempt to introduce the "daemonic excess" of the good beyond being later in their conversation.

Socrates is clear that he would prefer to respond to Glaucon's request to disclose the nature of justice by locating his search for it in the soul, but recognizes that such an investigation is beyond the present capacity of his interlocutor who, though courageous, lacks sharp sight and prudence (368d); he relents, then, and proposes to seek justice in the city where what is in the soul is written large (369a). Such a discussion is easily within Glaucon's range; it builds on his political preoccupations; indeed it flushes out the political exaggerations of his malformed erotic ambitions.

Socrates and Adeimantus, Glaucon's brother, begin to construct an imaginary city in which they attempt to identify justice, but they are interrupted by Glaucon who complains that the two have made "a city of sows," yet one "without relishes" (372c–d). Instead of Socrates' "healthy city," he wishes to see a "luxurious city"—what Socrates calls a "feverish city"—described, one that, as Socrates puts it, will be "gorged with a bulky mass of things" (372e–373b). Such a city, Socrates warns, will require more doctors because of its excess and an army to take land from its neighbours in its appetite for more. Glaucon is not disconcerted by the inevitable warlike nature of the feverish city; he, after all, has a strong interest in the art of war, valuing it over commercial endeavours like shoemaking (374b). When Socrates outlines the education of the guardians in Book VII, Glaucon is most keen to hear of the applications of calculation, geometry and astronomy to generalship and the conduct of battle (522c–e; 525b; 526c–d; 527d). The pleonexic city, expansionist, bellicose, is his true home.

Glaucon, however, has an eros that precedes his conversation with Socrates—a desire for personal honour (548d)—that could serve as a prelude to a philosophical life. This desire now leads him to seek renown in a warlike city; but it is not his political ambitions that bar him from the philosophical life into which Socrates is attempting to lead him. Glaucon confuses philosophy with geometrical thinking and is fascinated by the convertibility of this sort of thought into military success. He experiences severe difficulty in imagining a form of reasoning higher than such thinking when Socrates asks him to do so (511b–d), and it is his weddedness to such thought—a being "unable to step above the hypotheses" (511a)—that leads him to dream of a polis that sacrifices human beings and human attachment to towering, meta-human ideals. Socrates attempts to wean him from attachment to such a city and such thinking by showing him the repellently anti-human outcome of both. At the end of Book III, he sketches in an absurdly ascetical regime for the guardians (416d–417b); in Book IV he recommends holding women in common (424a); in Book V, he speaks of the rearing of human beings in pens (460c).

Socrates does not hold the more outrageous political views about Glaucon's city that have made some commentators see Plato as a totalitarian, but Glaucon certainly is capable of holding them; indeed they lie latent in the fundamental, pleonexic desire that shapes his character. By speaking of the inevitable eugenics and militarism of Glaucon's "feverish city," Socrates attempts to provoke his companion to shame, rescuing him from a burgeoning attachment to tyranny, nudging him toward the kenotic pursuit of wisdom. But at the beginning of Book IV it is Adeimantus who is unsettled by the severity of the guardians' lives; Glaucon seems undisturbed by this. It is Polemarchus, another participant in the conversation, who initially raises an objection to the institution of holding women in common (449b); Glaucon adds a weak protest later, merely asking for a clarification. Glaucon seems troublingly unaware of the brutishness that, at his instigation, is being drawn in speech by the creation of the sort of city he insists be constructed. He does not see the oddness of the citizens of his imaginary city, who are the product of calculation, their lack of musicality, their ugliness. However, if Socrates can arouse shame in his interlocutor at any point around the application of geometrical thinking to politics, Glaucon might just be brought to the practice of philosophy.

|| Shame is part of Socrates' psychagogic method; it appears throughout the dialogues as a way of correcting erotic disfigurement; its aftermath is a vacuum in which philosophical desire may appear. Alcibiades reports its surprising appearance in his life in the *Symposium*: Socrates alone provokes it (*Symposium* 216a). Alcibiades is overwhelmed by the speeches of Socrates that appear "utterly ridiculous at first" (222b), concerned with "pack-asses and blacksmiths, cobblers and tanners," but that within appear "almost the talk of a god" containing numberless "representations of ideal excellence" (222c). Alcibiades confesses himself transfixed by such talk; his "heart beats faster than if I were in a religious frenzy and tears run down my face" (216c); he is disarmed, his soul "thrown into confusion and dismay"; he imagines his life little better than a slave's, yet his desire to expose himself to the beauty within the Socratic speeches intensifies so that if he did not block his ears as Odysseus blocked his companions' as they approached the Isle of the Sirens, he would grow old sitting before the man who repeatedly charms him. Thunderstruck by Socrates' words, he is convinced it is impossible for him to remain in his present state (216c); he sees that he "neglects his true interests" in his pursuit of renown in public life, that he is "a mass of imperfections." Dismayed by the building erotic effect Socrates' words have on him and the compunction they arouse in him, he contemplates flight from the one who most draws him. He describes the experience of his encounter with Socrates as being wounded—worse than snake bite, he says—in his soul (219a).

Theodorus, the educator in the *Theaetetus,* is another figure in the dialogues who speaks of shame as part of a brush with Socrates. For Alcibiades, his exposure to Socrates' "representations of ideal excellence," to philosophy, is a confusing experience of erotic intensification, disorientation, humiliation and an overmastering sense of the untenability of his present situation. Theodorus feels none of the erotic tug that Alcibiades reports, yet speaks of conversations with Socrates as a stripping (162b), a being taken "to the mat in speeches" (169b); he shies away from this discomfiting experience throughout the dialogue, remarking that he is "unused to conversations of this sort" and "not of an age to get used to it either" (146b); he wishes to speak only of geometry (169b). Theodorus avoids shame as he avoids the experience of philosophy, but he has been led towards both. Glaucon does not flee the experience of shame as both Alcibiades and Theodorus do, the disassembling of false self-esteem and the prelude of philosophy, since he appears to be impervious to it. He does not see, though Adeimantus, Polemarchus and even Thrasymachus do, that the city in speech fashioned to satisfy his pleonexia creates outrage. Even when Socrates asserts that the vigor of the city requires selective breeding among the guardians, in which the most fit are to be rewarded with "abundant intercourse" (460b), whose offspring will be raised in "pens" by selected nurses, Glaucon does not recognize the barbarity his unexamined desire has initiated. Throughout his account, Socrates uses animal imagery to illustrate the eugenics of Glaucon's city: the best breeders among the guardians will be selected like horses for their fitness (459b–c); the progeny of the fittest are bunched in "flocks." Since most people are likely to object to such political measures concerning procreation, Socrates observes, the "eminent rulers" of the city must use "a throng of lies and deceptions for the benefit of the ruled" (459d). Glaucon misses the irony of these remarks; he agrees to the grotesque conventions Socrates proposes, using the same language from animal breeding that Socrates employs to mock them: all this must be done, Glaucon asserts, if "the guardians' species is to remain pure" (460c). Glaucon is unashamable in his attachment to the pursuit of honour in a society committed to the engineering of human beings, a city which his longing for glory, his longing for a "feverish" luxury, has brought into speech. Shame—catanyxis, in the language of John Chrysostom, the acute awareness one is on the wrong path—is part of the apokatastasis of philosophy, the breaking of old erotic postures and the resetting of the soul so that it loves what it is fit to love. In his immunity to shame, Glaucon, in his encounter with Socrates, comes to a refusal of philosophy.

|| Yet another Socratic psychagogic device is the telling of formational tales. As psychologies, epistemologies and ontologies, images such as the tripartite soul, the sun and the divided line seem failures, as we've noted, crudely imprecise, shifting, contradicted. Socrates locates all longing in the lowest part of the soul in Book IV of the *Republic*; however, in Book IX he claims that all three parts of the soul have appropriate passions (580d–e). Which is it? Just how does the Good create intelligibility? How does it resemble the sun? What is "participation" by which things are and are knowable? A commentator is left with the task of accounting for the apparent philosophical incompetence of Socrates; he contradicts himself; he is vague; he lacks rigor. The difficulty arises, however, only if one assumes that Socrates' philosophical aim is to erect explanatory systems; if one sees his intent as therapeutic, these images are not somewhat clumsy theories, but psychagogic heuristics, "spiritual exercises" by which his interlocutors, in their imaginations, practice different lives, like Stoic meditations on the operation of necessity in physical reality, meant to make human affairs seem of little import against a backdrop of the working of the cosmos. These images and claims need to be suggestive, resonant and true, without being precise. Further, the images used to trigger such exercises in the Socratic interlocutor change as his capacity for philosophy changes over the course of the dialogue.

The term "spiritual exercises" is chiefly associated with *The Spiritual Exercises* of Ignatius of Loyola, though the method used there, in that particular direction of contemplative focus, is ancient. Most of the meditations outlined in the *Exercises* begin with a "representation of place," in which the exercitant is encouraged to visualize an incident from scripture or some other event, and to participate, in imagination, in the scene he presents to himself. In the "Meditation on the Kingdom of Christ," for instance, which appears in the first week of the *Exercises,* one is asked "to see in imagination the synagogues, villages and towns where Christ our Lord preached" (91), while asking "not to be deaf to His call, but prompt and diligent" in accomplishing the divine will. One is further encouraged to imagine himself addressed by an "earthy king" who asks for his support in the conquest of the "infidel" and a "heavenly king" who similarly seeks his support in the conquest of the whole world. In conversation with persons of the Trinity, in "tasting their divinity," the one engaged in the *Exercises* is meant to "draw profit" (107). The purpose of this interior labour, says Ignatius, this training, is "the conquest of self" (21) and the reformation of the soul, so that a kind of connoisseurship of grace is possible.

The stories Socrates tells Glaucon, hedged about with comparable instructions, have a similar intent: they are ways for Glaucon to savour and rehearse a new sort of longing, a new posture for the recessed body; as such, they have the capacity to re-jig the soul. On the surface, such stories are full of "blacksmiths, cobblers and tanners," suns, caves—these initially hold the imagination; on a deeper reading, motivated by analysis in search of meaning, they appear to be awkwardly rendered doctrines on the nature of reality or the structure of innerness. Their true value, however, is psychagogic: in the consideration of them the Socratic interlocutor undergoes an interior realignment as he practices an attraction for things that before did not draw him; he tries out the poses of new dispositions. The three images Socrates uses over the course of the longer way to illuminate "what is greater than justice" (*Republic* 504d), problematically imprecise, "poetic," as philosophical doctrine, thus would be better read as formational tales, exercises by which Glaucon might imaginatively enact a participation in some aspect of the philosophical life. At the beginning of the account of the longer way, Glaucon, as Socrates predicted he would (506e), has found consideration of the good itself beyond his reach: he accuses Socrates of daemonic excess when Socrates speaks of this good that is "beyond being, exceeding it in dignity and power," which is nevertheless the cause of its existence. Socrates then leads Glaucon through the figure of the divided line as a directed meditation: conceive, he bids him, of two things, one the "king of the intelligible class...the other...king of the visible" (509d); he asks Glaucon if he "has" these two forms, that is, if he is able to visualize them interiorly; in doing so, Glaucon enacts them, participates in them. He is then urged to "take a line cut in two unequal segments, one for the class that is seen, the other for the class that is intellected" and then to similarly divide the portions of the line above and below the first cut. The purpose of this exercise is to help Glaucon, who has a pre-philosophical predilection for geometrical figures, enter in his imagination a region previously inaccessible to him, that lying beyond hypothetical thought, where one understands without images drawn from the visible world (510b). Glaucon had just dismissed what is approached by such inquiry as another version of the "smoke and nonsense" of the wisdom-lover. Now he delectates in his imagination a strange sort of investigation difficult for him to "sufficiently understand" (510b); to so contemplate alters him, just as he is corrected by "seeing" (514a) the story of the cave where again he is led to conceive and savour a form of eros, a vocation, utterly new to him. These exercises do not make him a philosopher, but at least they allow him to entertain soberly in imagination what before he could not properly see and therefore mocked.

‖ The psychologies Socrates presents in the *Republic* also have a maiuetic intent. In Books VIII and IX, he lays out a typology of souls and the cities that arise from them—aristocracies, timocracies, oligarchies, democracies and tyrannies. This typology, again, is not a study in political psychology, but an exercise designed to increase Glaucon's interior acuity. Glaucon's natural disposition is in part timocratic, since he loves victories and honour (548d), and in part tyrannic, given the lure that the story of Gyges' ancestor has for him. He has demonstrated his incapacity for the philosophical life; perhaps he might be led to become simply more just, less bewitched in his desires. His procession through the various characters and types of cities is both an examination of conscience and an interior stretching where he tries out various interior dispositions. In the end, he will be asked to make what amounts to a choice of life (the point, as well, of *The Spiritual Exercises*), saying which of the cities is happiest.

Socrates encourages Glaucon to represent the souls and their cities deeply to himself, for "in an argument such as this, one must not just suppose such things but must consider them quite well," since the point of the consideration is "the greatest thing, a good life and a bad one" (578c). With the tyrant, he tells Glaucon to "go in" the tyrant's city, "creeping down into every corner and looking," and then to declare whether the city seems happy or wretched (576e); then "with his thought to creep into a man's disposition and see through it," experiencing the soul of the tyrant intimately (577a). Taking on such a soul in an ekstasis of imagination, similar to that provoked by Ignatian instructions in the *Exercises*, Glaucon sees clearly that the soul he contemplates is full of indignity; slavishly "drawn by a gadfly, it will be full of confusion and regret" (577e). Nor, on consideration, does he feel the full pull of the timocratic soul; he finds himself not keen to endure being "abandoned by his best guardian," a taste for the music of argument. He ends by choosing the kingly man, the man both good and just (544e), as the happiest and best (580c), though he suspects that Socrates "has a still finer city and man to tell of" (544a). Stretched by Socrates' formational tales—he has lived inside each of the possible souls, except the soul of the philosopher, in his imagination—he has been turned a small way around within. He has grown, at least, in his capacity "to distinguish the good and the bad life," and like the most fortunate souls in the Myth of Er, is somewhat better equipped to choose his way (620a).

|| The *Republic* is sometimes seen as a book where Plato exposes himself as an autocrat; it is also infamous as the work where he reveals his "puritanical" disdain for poets: these two misreadings of the dialogue contribute to one popular image of Plato as a cerebral solitary with totalitarian tendencies. But the significance of the fascistic features of the book changes when the *Republic* is understood as an account of an attempt to transform an individual charmed by geometrical thinking and Achillean political idealism.

Socrates' remarks on poets also must be seen as therapeutic to be properly grasped. Glaucon is very much attracted to Homer (607d); his particular reading of the poet has "maimed" his thought (595b), enhancing his love of victory and his pleonexia to the point where the idea of a city where people are selectively bred to produce a successful warrior class appeals to him. The alteration Socrates tries to bring about in Glaucon, the education of his desire, should be understood as an attempt to correct the latter's reading of Homer. Glaucon has an eye for the warrior triumphalism of the *Iliad*; Scorates wishes to expose him to the ecstatic, the philosophical, courage of Odysseus.

Signs of the sublated shamanic pattern within the *Odyssey* appear throughout the *Republic*, especially in the theme of subterranean immurement and return. The book begins with the descent of Socrates and Glaucon to Piraeus in order to view a religious event, a light carried on horseback appearing in darkness; there is the katabasis in the allegory of the cave and Er's descent to the underworld (614b–621b), as well as the counter-example of the crafty, unheroic descent of Gyges' ancestor to steal the magical ring from the immense corpse entombed below the earth. With the exception of that last episode, each echoes the ancient mythic and psychagogic schema of passage to the underworld and renewal found in Orphic mysteries, in the Sumerian myth of Inanna and in the *Odyssey*. Calypso keeps Odysseus "in one place / in a hollow cave" (*Odyssey*, IX 29–30) from which he escapes through the intervention of the gods; Odysseus later descends to Hades where he meets his mother, Antiklea, who urges him to "be eager to go to the light as fast as you can" (XI 223). As well as cave and underworld references pointing to its indebtedness to *Odyssey*, the *Republic* retains the epic motif of a numinous sea journey in the imagery of the triple wave (*Republic* 457b; 472a; 473c) threatening Glaucon's city in speech and in the image of the soul, finally given over to philosophy, drawn "out of the deep ocean in which it now is" (612a) and restored to its "original nature" (611d). Thus Plato reinvigorates the mythic pattern (621c) by reshaping it, removing its violent elements, but retaining its psychic architecture—the epic hero's loss of power represented by Odysseus' loss of his companions; his disorientation and stripping of identity on the trackless sea; his restoration to his homeland—as way of talking about the heroic endeavour of philosophical transformation.

But what of Socratic disdain for Homer in Books III and X of the *Republic* and the banning of all poetry except "hymns to the gods or celebration of good men" (607a)? How to reconcile the view that the *Republic* is the *Odyssey* recast, that Socrates is presented in the dialogue as the new Odysseus and that the structure of philosophy is the structure of the epic hero's quest, an argument made vigorously by Zdravko Planinc in *Plato's Political Philosophy* and elsewhere, with those parts of the *Republic* that appear to be anti-poetic?

There are eight sorts of passages he wishes to "expunge" from Homer Socrates tells Adeimantus early in Book III: those concerning fear of death or loss of any sort (386c–387b); those depicting gods or heroes mourning over "the slightest sufferings" (388d); those showing the gods in derisive laughter (389a–b); those promoting lack of esteem for the truth (389b); those failing to present the gods as "rulers of the pleasures of drink, sex and eating" (389e); those showing them swayed by gifts of money (390e); and those representing heroes as irreverent toward divine things (391c). All poetry which claims "that the gods produce evil and that heroes are not better than human beings" (391d), Socrates claims, have a stunting, contorting effect on a soul and should be suppressed. Glaucon admits he is "very much" charmed by Homer (607d); he has taken a version of the Homeric hero as his paradigm and been harmed by his assimilation of the model (391e). Glaucon fears the bite of loss; what he has he wishes to hold or add on to; his city is rigorous to the point of triumphalism, a garrison against loss, either from the depredations of enemies or a weakening of the warrior excellence of its citizens. Someone with this disposition is incapable of tolerating the erotic ekstasis, the perpetual absence, of the philosophic life. Glaucon is so far from ruling his pleasures that it is difficult for him to even imagine a good beyond pleasure's gratification (509a), and thus he is incapable of a proper demeanour before divine things. He mocks the "excess" of such things and all those who speak of them. Depictions of the gods as preoccupied by sex and quick gain provide him with theological justification for his pleonexia and ingrain this feature deeper in him. Socrates' critique of Homer, then, is not an attack on poetry, not Plato taking a "puritanical," "intellectualist" position in "the old quarrel between philosophy and poetry" (607b), but a chipping away at Glaucon, just as Glacuus has "hammered off" him "shells, seaweed, rocks" which make him resemble "any beast rather than what he was by nature" (611d–612a). Socrates wishes to restore Glaucon to his "original nature" and make him fit to love wisdom and to see his affinity for what is daemonic; this transformation involves a correction of his erotic misalignment formed, in part, by his truncated appropriation of Homeric myth. Glaucon's reading of Homer, devoted though it may be, has been incomplete: he has missed the heroic structure of loss, disorientation and painful return home, Odysseus recovering what he was before he left to seek glory at Troy. Socrates reminds him of the inevitably difficult, wrenching, transformative life of the hero in particular in the story of the cave; a completed reading of Homer, a reappropriation of the whole myth, in particular its elements of katabasis, is one way of doing philosophy.

‖ Some have seen the *Republic* as a cautionary tale against eros itself. The *Republic* is anti-erotic, so this view goes, proposing a philosophy that is "mathematical and ordered" as opposed to the philosophy championed in the *Symposium* and the *Phaedrus*, which is "erotic and rapturous." The spirit of the *Republic*'s version of philosophy is sharply non-Alcibiadean, this argument contends; it is a matter of calculation rather than affect, the intent of which is to uncover the order of the cosmos and do a sort of fractured science. Plato, however, makes no mention of two philosophical paths in the *Republic*, *Symposium* or *Phaedrus*, one with scientific aspirations, the other a matter of the pursuit of longing. He does, though, attempt to draw Glaucon from his attachment to geometrical thinking, seeing it as a pseudo-philosophy, where one might hide if he did not wish to undergo the erotic risk of genuine philosophy.

Socrates speaks of philosophical desire—philosophical "gusto" and "delight"—as "insatiable" in the *Republic,* source of "the truest pleasures" (586d), indeed the *only* true pleasure (587c), but which the lover of honour sees as "smoke and nonsense" (581d) because it brings no honour. Glaucon is the prisoner of both "bastard" pleasures (587c), the love of honour and gain, placing him close to the tyrant, just as he is attracted to what merely seems to be philosophy. Glaucon's complaint is not that he is too erotic, as some have argued, but that he is not sufficiently erotic, that he is not genuinely erotic. Socrates' apparent attacks on eros in the first image of the tripartite soul and the image of the tyrant are, in fact, attacks on what masquerades as eros. Glaucon wants to keep what he has; he prefers his satiety; he wishes to make himself sufficiently esteemed, and he believes he can do this through calculation in politics and war. Glaucon's calculation is an ersatz philosophy; his pleonexia is an ersatz—"bastard"—eros. Absence or kenosis is repugnant to him; the insatiability of philosophical longing is incomprehensible to him—he will never be drawn to the reverence, poverty and unquenchable desire of philosophy, though it alone will give him what he seeks in his feverish city.

Note

1. Ray Monk. *Ludwig Wittgenstein: The Duty of Genius,* The Free Press, 1990, p. 415–22. Monk notes the transformative intent of Wittgenstein's lectures on the philosophy of mathematics in 1939, in which Wittgenstein attempted to dissipate the charm cast by various metaphysical propositions arising from a particular view of mathematics. The episodic form of *Philosophical Investigations* also points to Wittgenstein's therapeutic intent: he is attempting, in the early sections of the book, to undermine attachment to a particular notion of language, the source, he believes, of much philosophical "superstition."

   See also Pierre Hadot, "Wittgenstein, philosophe du langage (II)," *Critique,* vol. 150, November 1959, 973. Quoted in Arnold I. Davidson's introduction to *Philosophy as a Way of Life: Spiritual Exercises from Socrates to Foucault,* Blackwell, 1995, 17–18. Hadot argues for viewing all of Wittgenstein's work from *Tractatus Logico-Philosophicus* to *Philosophical Investigations* and *Remarks on the Foundations of Mathematics* as a therapeutics meant to extricate readers from philosophy as "an illness of language," bringing an end to metaphysical worry.

11
Negative Theological
Meditations
Apophasis and Its Politics

I

Edmund Husserl gave two lectures at the Sorbonne in late
February, 1929, on transcendental phenomenology, his new way of doing
philosophy, the latest of the fresh twentieth-century philosophical sciences.
Husserl told his audience how deeply pleased he was to speak at the home
of French science because he believed the true father of this new philosophy
had been none other than France's greatest thinker, René Descartes. But
phenomenology was neo-Cartesianism, Husserl announced to his no doubt
surprised listeners, without "nearly all the well-known doctrinal content of
Cartesian philosophy" (1).

Husserl's new thinking was Cartesian only in ambition and in its utter
preoccupation with subjectivity. Like Descartes, Husserl wished to provide
all the sciences with an unshakeable grounding, a set of absolute insights
"behind which one cannot go back any further" (2). To do this, he believed,
philosophy needed to be radically rebuilt following a complete destruction

of all previously held philosophical positions; this operation would require, as well, he added, the dismantling of the self of the philosopher.

"First, anyone who seriously intends to become a philosopher must 'once in his life' withdraw into himself, and attempt, within himself, to overthrow and build anew all the sciences that, up to then, he has been accepting," Husserl said.

> Philosophy—wisdom—is the philosophizer's quite personal affair. It must arise as his wisdom, as his self-acquired knowledge tending toward universality, a knowledge for which he can answer from the beginning, and at each step, by virtue of his own absolute insights. If I have decided to live with this as my aim—the decision that alone can start me on the course of philosophical development—I have thereby chosen to begin in absolute poverty, with an absolute lack of knowledge. (2)

Then Husserl adds, echoing Descartes once more, the scientifically grounding insights of philosophy were to be the positions, if any, remaining in the completely effaced psyche of the radical philosopher. The true beginning of all real knowledge was to be the appearance of consciousness in its most harrowed state.

Like Descartes in retirement in Holland, Husserl, in his Sorbonne lectures, later published as *Cartesian Meditations*, selected a single moment to reflect on how he "might find a method for going on" (2). This method, if uncovered with sufficient rigor, would be a prototype for any philosophical initiate following him. It would be, that is, a "transcendental subjectivism" (4), that would leap beyond solipsism and relativism and become a model for all other subjectivities.

|| January 5, 2008, St. Peter's Abbey. I am having difficulty moving on the Husserl essay because I am acutely aware now that I no longer know what my allegiances are, what I love, what I desire. I am unmoored. My present distance from an earlier reading in patristics, I suspect, contributes to this

state. My distance from the sacraments, together with my no longer living in the aspen parkland of north central Saskatchewan, does as well.

|| The Cartesian ego dissolves, with its convictions, under the pressure of doubt; what Descartes wants is the pure diamond of certitude. I want, I think, not an infallible objective knowledge so unassailable it forces belief, but a form of acting and seeing that builds belonging to a place: this mode of living, I have a suspicion, necessarily will be an anti-capitalist therapy since a consequence of late capitalism is a pandemic rootlessness of which I am a victim. What insights are dispositionally and eidetically new will be the rudiments of a new form of residence and a new politics.

|| Aelred of Rievaulx, one of the great twelfth-century Cistercian writers, friend of Bernard of Clairvaux, in his sermon for the feast of St. Benedict, given numerous times during his twenty years as abbot of the reformed monasteries of Revesby and Rievaulx, compared Benedict and his *Rule* to Moses conducting Israel from Egypt. Moses was instructed to establish six cities in the course of this exodus, "three outside the Land of Promise and three within," as "cities of refuge" (Aelred of Rievaulx, *Liturgical Sermons* 151) for those who had committed unintentional homicide, where they might be safe from fatal retribution. Moses' act, for Aelred, prefigures the monastic practices Benedict prescribed that offer shelter to those fleeing "spiritual homicide" (151) at the hands of their passions. Three of these sequestering exercises are physical—work, watching and fasting—and three are contemplative—*lectio*, prayer and meditation. The razed self, I believe, is now itself a "city of refuge" extending protection from the culture-wide, deeply traditioned momentum of destabilizing appetite and cunning; imagination, formed by the hunger of this reduced self, so that it does not observe the usual ontological divisions—animal–human, individual–locale—is yet another city of safety and regeneration.

‖ I always have found Descartes' description of his project, in the first paragraph of his *Meditations on First Philosophy,* alarming. It certainly seems heroic, even if mildly comic in its naïve optimism; but even more it strikes me as deeply chilling.

Several years have passed since I first realized how numerous were the false opinions that in my youth I had taken to be true, and thus how doubtful were all those that I had subsequently built upon them. And thus I realized that once in my life I had to raze everything to the ground and begin again from the original foundations, if I wanted to establish anything firm and lasting in the sciences. But the task seemed enormous, and I was waiting until I reached a point in my life that was so timely that no more suitable time for undertaking these plans of action would come to pass. For this reason I procrastinated for so long that I would henceforth be at fault, were I to waste the time that remains for carrying out the project by brooding over it. Accordingly, I have today suitably freed my mind of all cares, secured for myself a period of leisurely tranquility, and am withdrawing into solitude. At last I will apply myself earnestly and unreservedly to the general demolition of my opinions. (59)

The boldness of the annihilation he proposes makes one wish to turn away. But consider the titanism of his confidence in his methodology to draw down the self. Massive, systematic doubt will accomplish this razing. There is no need of hyperbolic doubt now—everything slides away on its own. Little of depth enduringly compels. We are the sickness of bourgeois vigor, its de-mythologizing, deracinating. I wonder if I should take these energies as ascetical powers and undergo them as shocking means of grace.

I want an affective grounding, an ecological grounding, crave this, I suspect, because I am, I now realize, a foundling of colonial adventure, the settling of Western Canada, my formation the long nineteenth century with its fading imperial convictions, while Husserl, following Descartes, wishes for an absolute certainty on which science may rest. He wants this, as I want a locating, for reasons of identity: a stable science for him will replace a now flaccid religious faith as a shaping teleological end.

"The splintering present-day philosophy, with its perplexed activity, sets us thinking. When we attempt to view western philosophy as a unitary science, its decline since the middle of the nineteenth century is unmistakable" (4), observed Husserl.

> The comparative unity that it had in previous ages, in its aims, its problems and methods, has been lost. When, with the beginning of modern times, religious belief was becoming more and more externalized as a lifeless convention, men of intellect were lifted by a new belief, their great belief in an autonomous philosophy and science. The whole of human culture was to be guided and illuminated by scientific insights and thus reformed, as new and autonomous.
>
> But meanwhile this belief, too, has begun to languish. (4–5)

Descartes' philosophical radicalism was provoked by a philosophical hegemony that was sclerotic with dogmatism. For Husserl, orthodox philosophy was too various and too contentious. The waning belief in the politically foundational powers of scientific insight has this as its clear cause. "Instead of a unitary, living philosophy, we have a philosophical literature growing beyond all bounds and almost without coherence" (5), said Husserl, a "literary" rather than a "seriously scientific" philosophical literature. What will root a culturally formational science anew, Husserl believed, was a fresh, unitary, indubitable philosophy, an apodictic thinking. This new thinking will be found where Descartes found it, in an original, though not idiosyncratic, philosophy of the subject, the self, though, he insists, of a rigorous philosophical introspection, not of psychoanalysis or skeptical dismantling.

"And so we make a new beginning, each for himself and in himself," said Husserl, "with the decision of philosophers who begin radically: that at first we shall put out of action all the convictions we have been accepting up to now, including all our sciences. Let the idea guiding our meditations be at first the Cartesian idea of a science that shall be established as radically genuine, ultimately an all-embracing science" (7). This Descartes-like work Husserl proposes to perform on the self will ground a rejuvenated Enlightenment millenarianism.

But Cartesian introspection, however much he admired its vigor, was compromised, Husserl believed. What Descartes looked for as grounding in the subject rested on what he pre-philosophically believed science and scientific certitude to be. The paradigmatic science for Descartes was geometry, and what he sought in the annihilation of the self were propositions that would be as unshakably fixed as Euclidian axioms from which all else might be deduced. Cartesian doubt, then, was itself compromised since it excluded from interrogation the logic, the shape, of this supposed scientific ideal. This unpurged heuristic then molded Cartesian subjectivity.

Husserl rejected the notion of a normative science, and pursued a subjectivity free of such a formational power, yet still held out hope for an absolute grounding of science, which itself would be re-orienting, re-rooting for European culture in its late imperial phase. What I pursue as foundational is a shared interiority, a transcendental erotics. This will ground, but the form of grounding will be an at-homeness, not a justified belief in scientific veracity. This autochthonicity, the result of a hetero-erotics, is *prima philosophia*, the reliable starting place. How do we know, in this particular philosophical experiment of introspection, what propositions are true and can be safely built upon? We are drowning: whatever floats is, at least provisionally, true.

|| While for Husserl there can be no paradigmatic science, certain constituitive features clearly belong to all sciences. The steps to a putative truth must be repeatable by everyone; this truth is discoverable in experience, and is never absolute, though, added to previous confirmed claims, it helps build a deeper, more expansive account of being with fewer and fewer exceptions. The same features, incidentally, are also found in the interior patterns upon

which mystical theology comments. For Husserl, while no science is a model for his originary philosophy, the generalized method for doing science is.

But he seeks something even more elemental as a starting point than empirical, experimental method and the treating of asymptotic truth as the achievement of a community of knowers. He looks for bodies of evidence that carry, for the philosophical meditator, absolute certainty "if advancing from them and constructing on their basis a science governed by the idea of a definitive system of knowledge—considering the infinity presumed to be part of this idea—is to be capable of having any sense" (14). If such an indubitability exists, he repeats, it can be found only beneath the rubble of the uncritical self, for "the transcendental Ego is antecedent to the being of the world" (18), as the receiver of a mass of competing impressions concerning it, and so the new philosophy must begin with it.

What Husserl discovers as he proceeds is not the monadic certitude of Descartes' *cogito*, the claim marked by the impossibility of non-belief, but the florescent ubiquity of psychic process itself, "the judgings, valuings, and decidings, the processes of setting ends and willing means, and all the rest, in particular the position-takings necessarily involved in them all" (20), which he refuses to receive as truth claims, but experiences as mere phenomena. "The concrete subjective processes...are...the things to which his [the radical meditator's] attentive regard is directed: but the attentive Ego, qua philosophizing Ego, practices abstention with respect to what he intuits." Upon the palpable certitude concerning the existence of such processes, a world of knowledge may be built, even as the philosopher puts "out of play" all claims about the objective world found in psychic phenomena.

|| What is certainty, its nature? In Descartes, indubitability takes two forms: that found in his first, sure assertion, the *cogito, sum* and that found subsequently. With the first, doubt involves a performative contradiction: to doubt that I think, I perform the very mental actions I wish to call into question. The Cartesian certitudes that follow this first truth—concerning the

existence of God, the truth of arithmetical claims and so on—do not have the same form: divinity, for instance, is not asserted in the nature of the act of denying it. Here, with such clarities, certitude is the result of a particular type of psychological experience.

Descartes sets out what he believes to be criteria for truth at the beginning of his Third Meditation, after he has discovered the indubitability of the cogito and while he is in the midst of articulating his several proofs for the existence of God. He restates these criteria, with some refinements, late in the Fourth Meditation. Matters which he intuits "clearly enough" (71), he may doubt, he decides, since God could have made him so that he is deceived by things that strike him with such modest force. He finds he is unable to withhold assent, however, from claims which he perceives "with such great clarity." Before these "clear and distinct" (76), propositions, his affirmation, in fact, is spontaneous, unstoppable.

> I am so completely persuaded by them that I spontaneously blurt out these words: "let anyone who can do so deceive me; so long as I think that I am something, he will never bring it about that I am nothing. Nor will he one day make it true that I never existed, for it is true now that I do exist. Nor will he ever bring it about that perhaps two plus three might equal more or less than five, or similar items in which I recognize an obvious contradiction." (71)

Clear and distinct ideas, he noticed, caused "a great light in my intellect which gave way to a general inclination in my will" (85), so that he "spontaneously and freely" believed them.

Even with the cogito, it is this inexorability of judgment that most persuaded Descartes. It is not so much that doubting the truth of "I think, I am" involves a contradiction in act that convinces him, but this private experience of the unstoppable rush of the will before the sharp clarity of the intuition. Clear and distinct perceptions, he declared at the end of the Fourth Meditation, must, indeed, come from God alone for no other source could give them power to have such an arresting effect on the will. Once such impressions are received, divinity's beneficence assures their truth. To not offer such support would amount to an impossible antinomy in the divine character. These descriptions of truth sound less like exhaustive, systematic conditions than personal accounts of coming to certitude—phenomenologies of the experience of certainty—that Descartes offers as a template to others.

His description of how certitude appears in the psyche is very close to the language of the discernment of spirits. Descartes' implication is that the particular pattern of experience in the reception of clear and distinct ideas is available only to those who have undergone the sort of reduction of self described in the previous three meditations. This suggestion, as well, echoes mystical theology: *phronesis* comes only to those who have submitted to the corrections of ascetical theology, its breaking of old attachments.

|| Absolute certitude is the Cartesian and Husserlian ambition. If, though, the test that confirms certitude is psychological, as it clearly is with Descartes, this achievement of the interior state of delusionlessness is formally close to what is accomplished by a phronetic or formational practice, like that found in Ignatius of Loyola's *Spiritual Exercises*, including, of course, in particular, his "Rules for the Discernment of Spirits," or the method of discernment traced in John Cassian's *Conferences,* though Cartesian ascesis in its extreme subjectivity seems painfully naïve in comparison. Ignatius' and Cassian's method rests on conversation with at least one other possessing extensive phenomenological experience in the matter under consideration. Beside the careful formational methods of Ignatius and Cassian, hyperbolic doubt appears a viciously blunt instrument. The self is hacked down to a stump. Nothing is left to provoke a new rising, except, one comes to suspect, the programmatic ambition that wields the doubt. The method of aggressive doubt also, strangely, leaves untouched a rudimentary Cartesian credulity concerning clarity in its various forms.

|| Another indicator of indubitability in the Christian contemplative tradition, aside from those outlined in Ignatius' "Rules," is the presence of

perduring desire. What is true is what makes for a particular form of endlessness in longing. Here is Meister Eckhart on appetite's infinite range:

> Therefore I say that to the extent a person can deny himself and turn away
> from created things, he will find his unity and blessing in that little spark
> in the soul, which neither space nor time touches. The spark is averse to
> creatures, and favourable only to pure God as he is in himself. It is not satis-
> fied with the Father, nor the Son, nor the Holy Spirit, nor all three persons
> together, as long as their several properties are preserved. To tell the truth,
> this light is not satisfied with the unity of this fruitful conception of the divine
> nature, but I shall go further and say what must sound strange—though I am
> really speaking the truth—that this light is not satisfied by the simple, still,
> motionless essence of the divine being that neither gives nor takes. It is more
> interested in knowing where this essence came from. It wants to penetrate the
> simple core, the still desert, into which no distinction ever crept—neither the
> Father, the Son, nor the Holy Spirit. It wants to get into the secret, to which no
> man is privy, where it is satisfied by a Light whose unity is greater than his
> own. This core is simple stillness, which is unmoved itself but by whose immo-
> bility all things are moved and all receive life, that is to say, all people who
> live by reason and have their center within themselves. (246–47)

Turn away in erotic emptiness and appetite grows, beyond usual imagination. This growing appetite, appearing as twists of dissatisfaction, is certitude. It pulls past propriety, cognitive, intuitional, spiritual, because—it cannot help this and is likely shamefaced before this impulse, shocked by the ferocity of the drive—it helplessly eschews names.

This elemental hunger, the striving of the reduced, untethered self, resembles Husserl's "transcendental ego" (Husserl 65), and Descartes' razed self, only in that it is a point beyond which one cannot go. But here, more appropriately than either the rationalist or phenomenological possibility, is the ground, the first moment of philosophy and of being and thinking, initial home in the exhaustion of the Enlightenment project. And this Eckhartian hunger, fundamental eros—oddly, since it seeks the nameless—is the source of radical, criminal, unitary hope, undecorous, post-hope gestalt anticipation, which expresses itself in a taxonomically transgressive imagination, similar in shape to vital metaphor and to the narrative style of Indigenous North American literatures, such as those found in Robert Bringhurst's Haida translations and in Leonard Bloomfield's transcriptions in *Tales from the Sweetgrass Cree*. Indeed, European culture's chief hope of comprehending, meeting in conversation, this narrative form and being shaped by it—this, I believe, a central part of the autochthonic project—lies in a resuscitation of the noetic and transformative power of imagination and metaphor, in the Western tradition, as it was exercised, for instance, in the Neoplatonism of Iamblichus and Proclus.

Eckhartian hunger and the imagination it fosters: two sequestering practices, two anti-imperial forms of life, cities of refuge. Yet another such city, I make bold to suggest, is friendship, the sort, *amicitia*, Aelred calls "guardian of the spirit" (*Spiritual Friendship* 59), "nothing else but wisdom" (68) and, quoting Sirach (6:16), "the medicine of life," which makes for the engine of conversational conviviality, the friendship he describes at length on his *De spirituli amicitia*.

|| Wednesday, January 9, St. Peter's Abbey. There is another home: it is inside things—empathy, loneliness, a hybristic hunger for the larger place take us there. Poetry, of all the disciplines, is the least surprised by this news; the claim is what it's been waiting to hear. Awareness of our acute deprival and mystical theology are the bearers of this secret. The wolverine whispers in the ear of the river otter. Here is a broader home, a larger room for a more ample self. This self has no need for conscience and compassion: it is what the other is to it.

|| Husserl's foundational self, the transcendental ego, becomes visible only once the philosophical meditator "puts out of play" (Husserl 20), all positions toward the objective world, all efforts to mean, all judgments of probability,

certainty, illusion concerning the nature of being. This, the phenomenolog-ical *epoché*, "parenthesizing," does not leave the radical philosopher with nothing, but with a clear view, at last, of her "pure living," the shimmering expanse of "the universe of 'phenomena' in the (particular and also wider) phenomenological sense" (20–21). Husserl remarks that, having submitted to the reduction of radical philosophy, he now sees himself unerringly "as Ego, and with my own pure conscious life, in and by which the entire Objective world exists for me and precisely as it is for me" (21).

This pure consciousness is the foundation of the world—not in the sense of it being a source since Husserl is not an idealist, but as perspective—and it precedes the objective world as an autonomous existent; for us there is no such purely beheld world. There is no universal world, only a number of idiosyncratic ones, which overlap, creating the impression of universality. Perspective fosters the world. The reduced ego, the ego known in Husserl's transcendental ascesis, "is not a piece of the world" (26), but where the world is gathered. There is not a world, but a world-for-me; there is, then, an infinity of worlds.

Philosophy, as a result, can only be "a pure egology" (30), an only apparent solipsism, which is, in happy fact, a phenomenology of inter-subjectivity and our sole hope for attempting ontology, since consciousness, as Husserl learned from Franz Brentano, is always intentional, always "consciousness of." Mystical theology has a similar shape. It, too, places interiority as a fruitful first philos-ophy: we learn the nature of ultimate reality with less risk of dogmatic distortion by considering the shapes and routes of chastened desire, upon which Being's ground works as a final cause. The object of such consciousness is not safely reachable but its multiple, motile effects on human attention are evident. Mystical subjectivity is a noting and undergoing of these effects.

|| Part of the experience of certitude, residence in the delusionless state, and one source of its characteristic instability, the everlastingness of its reduc-tion, say the mystics, is its imagelessness. Meister Eckhart insists upon this trait of "aghostliness" in erotic understanding, an interior truthfulness, an

effacement experienced initially, surely, as a toppling, but which is, in fact, a mimesis and an availability.

> *How, then, shall I love him? You are to love God aspiritually, that is, your*
> *soul shall be aspiritual, devoid of ghostliness, for as long as the soul is ghost-*
> *like, it is an image and, being imagelike, it will lack both unity and the power*
> *to unite. Thus it could not love God rightly, for true love is union. Your soul*
> *ought to be deghosted, void of ghosts, and be kept so....*
> *How, then, shall I love him? Love him as he is, not-god, a not-ghost,*
> *apersonal, formless. (248)*

A process of negation building on negation is a mark of the passage to truthfulness. This process is not skepticism, or epistemological iconoclasm, or doubt; it is an inching from apparently exhaustive clarities, full renderings of things, both prescribed and proscribed images. But surely the mind needs images to know. Isn't this the point of language, its necessary contribution to understanding? While such a direction for eros, a linguistically fashioned crib for longing, is formationally crucial at the beginning of an interior life, this aid will be jettisoned when it has done a complete job of shaping.

Eckhartian imagelessness is the reduction of the ego. Hybristic transgressive imagination is another form of the reduced ego's hunger, a sign of the complete-ness of its effacement. Hunger is the source of a succouring infinity of worlds.

II

The reduction of self in phenomenology and Cartesian method-ological doubt is impelled by a desire for a state of certainty in the sciences. Apophaticism also drives a dismantling, this, however, the result of an expe-rience of the unknowability of divinity, that degree of beauty. This second reduction is accidental, while the Husserlian neo-Cartesian annihilation is intentional and instrumental. The failure of knowledge, the humbling of knowing, its transformation in apophaticism, brings about a shaping of the self, this shaping a pitched form of noesis since it permits consanguinity.

Apophatic understanding is the achievement of proximity, successive versions of identity, with what one would know: then, only as a consequence of this shaping, knowledge of the objective world is possible through introspection.

You read a world, Husserl claimed, in the subjectivity of another, the sole world at that moment. If attention to numinal beauty shrinks the self to a base on which nothing rests, what does this say of divinity read in the "mirror" of this subverted self? Each instance of apophatic ignorance, of course, is idiosyncratic, but all agree God is no-thing, above images, a not-thereness, upon which, strangely, the heart can fix. All attentive contemplative desire, that is, desire of this sort for anything, brings a person to the epistemological and existential state of apophasis. Apophatic knowing is comprehension in the thrall of undomesticatable, likely unutterable, beauty.

Husserlian "parenthesizing" (20) of the world and the Eckhartian exclusive emphasis on longing force a change in how we imagine the relation between private experience and the polis, indeed even the cosmos. The primacy of the subject in transcendental phenomenology and mystical theology abolishes the old Kantian dilemma of how to know the world as it truly is. The philosophically crucial place of subjectivity means that matters of interiority, cosmology and politics overlap and must, in certain ways, be considered simultaneously.

|| Without the noetic-affective transfixity that preoccupies apophasis, without this working of a final cause, where one is held by an unassimable unlikeness, radical philosophy's annihilation of the self would be dissipation. Apophasis posits both poles: the undermined self and the intact, while unnamable telos, which, while unapproachable by feeling and intelligence, nevertheless acts as beauty acts. Both Husserl's and Descartes' interiority seem too sanguine about the reduction of the self; a razing done without the disarming affective pull of such a telos, or a pull exercised by objects construed as such a telos, is complete extinction, yet in neither Husserl nor Descartes do I read the fear such an obliteration should provoke. What could be the

source of this assurance? The will and a design directed by the will remain in place throughout the rationalist and phenomenological dismantlings. Husserl accused Descartes of allowing a pre-philosophical view of science to slide under his critical gaze, but both are worked on by an unexamined, architectonic ambition, the apotheosis of analytical reason. Both men, then, are merely correcting themselves as if in argument, as they present a simulacrum of meditation, replacing one set of allegiances with another. The meditations are staged; they are a theatre thrown up by eristics; their annihilations are a sham.

|| Saturday, January 12, St. Peter's Abbey. I dream just before I wake that there has been a storm, and some large, beautiful trees, in the front of the house where I am living, fall, at the end of a long lawn. They sag first as I watch them, then cartoonishly revive by what seems an effort of will, then topple completely, blocking the road, two fall. A pair of neighbours comes by and says the trees are diseased; they can smell, they claim, a "chemical" corruption coming from the rotted centers of the trunks. I go back into the house, which is a mansion and hardly seems mine; there is a party going on from which I am excluded. I do not have a saw, I realize, except a laughably inadequate swede saw, no chainsaw to cut up the fallen trees; I imagine traffic backing up on either side of them. I go out after my fruitless search for a saw and find the street-blocking trees have been removed, likely by competent neighbours. I am delighted, relieved by this, but then I see all the other trees, quite beautiful oaks, have been cut down and taken away as well. I am horrified, grieved, enraged by this, and plan to go from neighbour to neighbour—all the houses are shut with grilles—to find the culprit. But I know nothing will come of this. It's not retribution I'm interested in; the only thing is to sit with this horror.

|| *Meditations on First Philosophy* is naïve on the matter of interiority: it renders certitude indistinguishable from conviction. The subsequent Prometheanism of the Cartesian project is a consequence of this naivete:

it wishes to take control of the person and the world for the sake of the person: the intent of its faux egology is not introspective acuity but ego-gain. Perhaps this experience of non-delusional certitude lies outside reason in virtue. Delusion, in the contemplative theological tradition, is met only by a training of the will to connoisseurship. How to teach the will to lean toward what savours of the foundational? Surely the experience of beauty comes at the beginning of this training—Plato repeatedly claims this throughout the dialogues. But an encounter with illness, personal or pandemic, *divina afflictio*, could equally start one toward certitude. Beauty and illness, two doors to identity.

|| I have a sense, desperate, that relief from both private and pan-cultural malaise, a feeling of floating above a place, all places, and colonialism's frenzy for a homogenized more, is to be found under the ground. My last two books of poetry, *Kill-site* and *Orphic Politics*, build from this disquieting intuition. The way out begins in intent Orphic deprival. What will present itself if one waits and listens in the dark? Genuine politics, I am now as certain as I can be, will be small, a contemplative politics.

If This Is Your Land, Where Are Your Stories?, the title of Edward Chamberlin's book, a question a Gitskan elder once asked Canadian officials, is undoing, exposing neatly the colonial, extractive nature of diasporic European residence in North America. At best we are citizens of an equable constitution and substantial natural wealth: the sole "right" these extend us, the single one we've exercised, is an enervatingly limitless self-determination. We have not autochthonic citizenship; we conquered rather than came to this place. Our religion, science and political economy have been rigorously non-syncretistic throughout this long period of conquest: our approach to settlement has been, in Emmanuel Levinas' phrase, "totalizing," an inexhaustible project of making the other the same.

I'd like to hazard a guess at a possible route from colonial totality to the articulation of narratives that may tie us, Europe's children, to the so-called New World. The experience of beauty, let us say, is primary: for us, this has been the moment of the Group of Seven, of Gordon Smith, of Ernest Lindner, Takao Tannabe and many other painters, of the photographers Everett Baker and Courtney Milne, among others, of the southeast Saskatchewan sunsets of Jan Wyers, Emily Carr's trees. But this astonishment, a promising psychagogic start, has deadened into landscape for us, even though it should have led to a quelling and quietening of the self, which could have been the beginning of our philosophical transformation and maturation.

Beauty's dumbfounding might have frightened us—Carr's trees—instead of made us tender, sentimental and dispersed—the many Algonquin autumns—stopped us, removed us from the tremble and distraction of bourgeois tumult. And then we might have found ourselves immured in our own dismantling, available; we might have found ourselves on the other side of residency (who thought there would *be* another side?), in a new way of thinking we could only call imagination, though it would have been closer to visitation, attending to what this land might have said to us.

12

Thinking the *Rule of Benedict* within Modernity

Deans' Lecture Series
University of Victoria, 2005

I

I am a poet and an essayist: I also have a scholarly interest in
Plato, but because the world seems full, or full enough, of Plato scholars,
I've drifted a little and turned, as well, to Christian Platonists of late antiquity, Origen, Evagrius, John Cassian and the like. Perhaps it seems strange
for a poet to have interests like this, but in this country it is not all that
uncommon. I think of Jan Zwicky reading Wittgenstein, the pre-Socratics
and Plato; Erin Mouré, the French theorists and Augustine; Anne Carson, all
the Greeks; Dennis Lee, Martin Heidegger; Don McKay, Emmanual Levinas;
Robert Bringhurst, Dogan, Heraclitus and others. These deep readings of
philosophers contiguous with the writing of poetry may be a Canadian quirk.
I can think of few Americans, aside from Charles Wright, equally engaged in
philosophical thought, and in England only Geoffrey Hill and Don Paterson
of *The Eyes*, both astute readers in the negative theology tradition, come
to mind. It's not that the Canadian poets I mentioned write odes to *The
Critique of Pure Reason*, but that their reading rides as ballast in their work,

and, as a result, this work, at its best, has the exploratory reach of a certain sort of philosophical inquiry. That is, it permits an anagogic reading usually associated with the sort of philosophy I have in mind.

One book that holds my attention now comes from the tradition I mentioned earlier, the Platonic tradition—the *Rule of Benedict*, if not the West's first monastic rule (Pachomius' and Basil's precede it), the first that truly caught on. I have admitted to having a scholarly interest, but, alas, am not a scholar; I read the *Rule* and other books in the Platonic tradition— which I understand as being very much alive, running from Pythagoras to Simone Weil and George Grant, passing through all the Christians who wrote on the contemplative life—as a poet. This does not mean I read these works fancifully. I am too desperate as a writer and otherwise for caprice. I read them with the hunch that they have something to say to me that I must hear—the source of this hunch in a moment—so I read them with as much attention as I can muster, making an effort to understand them both as I suppose their makers wished them to be understood and as heuristics. I read the *Rule* thus as containing a poetics, an ascesis of reading, an epistemology, an etiquette and a politics that are as engaging as they are useful. This last, the politics, should not surprise: a monastery is a polis—kalipolis, the City of God. As a politics, the *Rule* presents no paradigm, is not a blueprint for a state, as some mistakenly believe Socrates' "beautiful" city in the *Republic* to be, but is a psychagogic device aimed at interiority: consider the instructions the work contains and let them alter your fundamental disposition to things. Read the *Republic*, the *Rule*, Pseudo-Dionysius' *Ecclesiastical Hierarchy*— any psychagogic book, any erotic book of the West—with the tentative, expectant, playful mind you would bring to metaphor. I am convinced that the interior practice that poetry calls for, the formation of which is a certain sort of philosophy, is the same as the interiority of an enlightened politics, and in this I am a Platonist.

I have been ruminating for quite a while on the preoccupations of early Western monasticism within the context of modernity, where these preoccupations are discounted, trying to think these concerns as possible epistemological and political therapies helpful to me and perhaps to others. I am not an antiquarian: again, I am too desperate, as well as too lazy. The allegiances of monasticism—to contemplation, to physical work as meditative practice, to idleness (*otium sanctum*)—are discredited allegiances now, and this is partly why I am attracted to them; transgression, heterodoxy, resistance lie this way. I also think there is a way of knowing in contemplation as it's been traditionally understood that resembles the way of knowing in poetry. Poetry, too, is an epistemic practice now discounted: metaphysics, poetry and contemplative idleness—three currently laughable or perhaps culpable enthusiasms. They might not get you arrested, but they could get you fired or at least excluded from the conversation.

The Order of St. Benedict is 1,500 years old; it was founded by Benedict of Nursia in the sixth century, the result of what appears to have been a series of personal disasters, including a revulsion-driven exile from Rome and an attempt on his life; the order rests, as I've said, on one of the oldest rules in the Latin Church. The very earliest clusters of contemplatives, primitive Carmelites in Palestine and the group that assembled around the monk Antony in Egypt, were delightfully ruleless. Such concentrations of devoted, transfixed looking, the ones with rules and those without rules, were not novelties but the latest forms of an ancient tradition—the Therapeutae of Alexandria, Plato's Academy, the friends of Socrates, Pythagoras' community all preceded them. The *Rule of Benedict*, however, takes as its most studied model the earliest forms of Egyptian monasticism as these had been communicated to Europe by John Cassian and his fifth-century book *Conferences*.

The *Rule* is not an act of isolated genius, then, but gathers the wisdom, the contemplative philosophy, of the ancient world. Other books do this; it is the nature of a certain sort of book, a book like this one, to do this. I want to consider seven features of the *Rule* germane to writing, to thinking about our relations with the natural world and to politics. Allow me to repeat at the outset the hunch I have already confessed: the dispositional and noetic allegiances in this work might offer epistemological and political ways out for us. I offer this claim merely as the condition of a thought experiment. Set these elements of the *Rule* beside various intractable problems and see what happens.

1. The *Rule* begins with one of its few commands: "Listen carefully...to the master's instructions, and attend to them with the ear of your heart" (15). *Ausculta, o fili, praecepta magistri et inclina aurem cordis tui.* The sort of listening enjoined here is the substance of the contemplative life, a light, mobile transfixity. John Cassian calls this state *puritas cordis*, purity of heart, and means by it a de-centering, tumbling, affective availability: be like a bit of down, he says, caught in a breeze. This could well seem the description of rootlessness, but is, in fact, an account of being at home, while being homeless or deracinated; it is a description of the homeless, protean cunning of desire itself in its upper ranges. You are caught in a single wind, the wind thrown by beauty—intellectual or moral beauty, physical beauty—and this wind, because of its nature, works benefi- cent alterations. Listen: in order to know, wait: noesis as erotic passivity, poetics the same.

   This opening remark also introduces the matter of the interior senses—an interior sense of taste, sight, smell and so on—a sensorium first sketched by Evagrius Ponticus, who, after Origen, was the chief theo- rist of Egyptian monasticism. Contemplation is a living within such a sensorial world, living by such an interior delectation.

2. Humility. Benedict speaks much of this—the whole of chapter seven of the *Rule*, one of the longest, concerns it. What he has in mind is not self- contempt or an obsequious caving to authority, but letting down the wall of ego and self-direction, and allowing what is there, the *kosmos* itself, say, its nimble order, that lucky, luminous thing, to seep in. Humility, then, is another name for permeability; it is the act of listening seen via another sight line. Noesis as rooted in deference, deference founded on emptiness: here a cognitive methodology, a style of prehension, and a meta-human politics continuous with the project of virtue.

3. Reading lies at the center of Western contemplative practice; this is true of both early Christian mysticism and all of Neoplatonism; both are essentially exegetical. A generous construal of reading, so that it includes understanding a daemonic figure, makes Platonism itself utterly exegetical. What is Plato trying to do throughout the dialogues if not to suss out Socrates? Reading in Cassian's *Conferences*, the *Rule's* foundational book, is heterodox by modern standards. In Cassian, the act of reading takes three forms—hesychastic repitition, *lectio divina* and the discipline of psalmody. I wish to consider two of these, *opus Dei* and *lectio divina*. *Opus Dei,* the work of God, the hours, the discipline of psalmody, the reading and singing of the psalms—poetry—is presented as a reading intended not to gather information or to bring comprehension, but to be a slow engine of transformation, an armature for the mind made by reprisal—reading as theurgy, not fact-amassing; knowledge as trued subjectivity. And look at the dignity, the muscularity, this sense of reading allows poetry: poetry as formational—daemonic, god-making—not ornament, not sentiment, not confessional record.

   Then there is *lectio divina*, divine reading: one reads in this manner not to appropriate system or taxonomy, nor for erudition, but to be arrested—stripped, in other words, disarmed. You become less, though charged, by such a reading, not more. Understanding is change, which itself might be unintelligible to discursive reason. Reason's befuddlement before anagogic alteration is like the puzzlement of love: what is happening to me?

4. At the musical center of the Benedictine charism is a conviction about the complementarity between the body and the mind, physical work and mental work. One is to engage in a daily alteration of *ora et labora*, prayer and work, that should feel pulse-like, not frenetic, lightening (remember Cassian's bit of down), your weight passed from one buoying medium to another. Benedict's attitude to work is not strategic, though

each monastery must support itself, but contemplative—work as a way of gathering attention, work as absorbedness, to use Donald Hall's phrase.

Work is also a form of compunction—work as weeping, as penthic—an aide to the permeability, which is humility's waiting.

5. The imagination of the *Rule* is caught by the quotidian; the short book is filled with paragraphs on sleeping arrangements, menus, dress, times for choir and so on. The book has no plot line but a set of finickity, yielding measurements for tapping into place some large, unnamed, perhaps unspeakable thing—a new-from-the-bottom-up decorum. This attention to the fragments of daily life is much of the ascesis of early Western monasticism: Benedict encourages those in charge of the things of the monastery (shovels, hay rakes, salt shakers, tire crimpers, silage forks, spoons) to treat them as they would the instruments of the altar. If attention is paid here, if respect is here, all will flow well. Being alert to specificity in this way fosters a sort of taking in of the world that steadies and entrances the mind, the eye fed and fed and fed by the spectacle of haecceity, thisness, by the spectacle of the endless, risible show of individuation. Such attention entertains and forms.

6. Mutual obedience: allow yourself to be instructed by everyone, this an undermining and a wealth. Take up the anarchically flavoured epistemological democracy of the cenobium, and see what accrues.

7. Hospitality: here again permeability appears, core contemplative trait, modified by phronesis. Significance lies outside one, or is brought to one, arrives at the door: it is not conferred from within.

I repeat my recommendation to pick all this up with the ludic indeterminacy one brings to grasping metaphor: your love is *not* a red, red, rose. To refuse the playfulness, the tall taleness, the gestural nature, of such a reading, like not getting the joke, not seeing the joke as a joke and thus not receiving the jolt of it, but to take in metaphor or a work like the *Rule* as description or prescription—well, one can see the silliness to which this would lead with metaphor and the authoritarian horrors it might suggest in the case of the *Rule*. The clenched fear of a literal reading, equally fundamentalist in spirit, simply suppresses all perusals of books like the *Rule of St. Benedict*, reproducing the Enlightenment's map of intellectual history where the night of superstition begins on the other side of the fence that defines a narrow field. But metaphor does communicate some truth, a truth that can be uttered only by speaking a lie: in the inebriated error of the claim, the love, the rose, one hears and hears affirmed the whoop of delight in romance. The statement is true, and true in a way that is deeper, more nourishing than the mapping of description, even if its surface is a misdirection.

And this is how I have attempted to read the *Rule*: it isn't true for me as mimesis or prescription, yet it is true psychagogically: yes, I do possess *auris cordis*, a heart-ear: I couldn't be a writer if I did not: how delightful, lightening, it is to acknowledge this. And it is true heuristically or therapeutically: here, in the seven features I have touched on, are rough possibilities for undoing epistemological and political knots by which I find myself bound, the ones keeping me from a full turn to all that poetry is, and the others hindering a return to the larger fire circle of all things.

II

I have been suggesting, among other matters, that poetry and contemplation are communicating rooms, or, to shift the image, that the contemplation succoured by the *Rule* is usable as a kind of preparation for poetry. But *is* poetry, after all, the same as contemplation, or close enough to it, so that a therapy like the *Rule of Benedict* or like the *Republic*, would be equally helpful to a poet as to one keen to live a philosophical life? Poetry and contemplation: maybe I've been too glib in drawing them so closely together. While there have been numerous contemplatives who have been poets—St. John of the Cross, Gerard Manley Hopkins, Wang Wei, Rumi, Rainer Maria Rilke, Hsieh Ling-yün—I have to admit that contemplation, in the end, seems not to be co-terminous with poetry. The contemplative enters a period of unknowing in his or her life of attention, a point in her prayer, where she mistrusts system, discursive reason and the clarities such powers bring; indeed, she is being weaned from such things. During this time, she is blinded, impoverished of cosmology, but her efforts, what she undergoes, still take place within a particular ontology: she is reduced simply to an insistent desire for what some have described as a union with the godhead. And poetry knows no ontological loyalties that I am aware of, nor seeks any such unions.

But there are formal, if not theoretical, similarities between the two ways of speaking and knowing. Poetry, as a linguistic practice, is confident in its failure at the outset of its project; it knows it aspires to say more than can be said: it wants to move beyond the tongue's usual range and this hybristic ambition causes it to break up, drawing into language some of the wildness—the wildness of metaphor, the wildness of incantatory incoherence—we find so attractive. Contemplative language, the language, for instance, of Pseudo-Dionysius' *Mystical Theology*, is equally ambitious, equally fatalistic: it wishes to encircle what lies beyond speech and it fails, it fails, it fails, telling us all along that this failure comes as no surprise: yet each unsuccessful linguistic lunge moves and alters the reader, even as it confesses its inability to illuminate what it seeks to name.

Cognitively as well there are similarities between poetry and contemplation: they both appear incompetent as noesis: they fail to identify, analyze and classify. So spectacularly modest is their achievement, their operation appears to be mere whimsy: they know nothing because there is nothing beyond the range of the sayable: there are water molecules and taxes, but there are no gods and the heart is not capable of a love that can't be broken into parts and understood. Poetry's imprecise speech and apophasis' ambivalence and erasure demonstrate the bracing smallness of the world. If exhaustive clarity is not possible, some say, there is nothing there.

But humour me: let's assume there is something there, but it can't be said, even though it quickens the most feverish speech of which we are

capable; and let us further assume, since we've made it past this first conces-
sion, that poetry and contemplation have picked up the scent of this likely
protean thing and pursue it affectively and linguistically. Let's leave aside
whether what poetry wants to know is precisely what contemplation
wants to know—this takes us too far from epistemology and too early, too
unguardedly, into the dangerous terrain of ontology, and means that all our
answers will miss the mark: we come at the whole matter wrongly so that
any ensuing discussion will be eristic. My hunch, as I've said, is that contemplation and poetry do not share an identical telos, but that what both wants
strikes each the same—as quintessentially compelling and as unutterable.
What I would like to look at instead is the shape of these two knowings, and
here, in their appearance, in their grammar, we find much similarity. Neither
is accumulative, that is, neither gathers a store of facts, categories, certitudes,
but instead both are marked by divestment: the deeper into the practice you
travel, the emptier you become; you lose your bearings; the outlines of the
self become less bold. I am not speaking of sentimental vacuity or an occult
intuitionism or a poetic inspirationalism, those pseudo-wisdoms, pseudo-
poetries, but of real loss: the loss of the sense of language as a tool, the loss
of thinking as an explanatory power, the loss of the image of oneself as a
knower to whom the world is presented. Contemplation and poetry are
forms of knowing where the knower and her powers are first shaved by the
world then are swallowed by the world.

I believe that the emptiness at the heart of poetic knowing and contemplative unknowing must be cultivated through a practice of yielding to loss
(they are thus both mournful or penthic knowings), and that this ascesis is
far more important than putting words on the page or multiplying prayers.
Both knowings issue in plain attention edged with wanting, and the therapy,
the assist, the solicitude of the *Rule* exactly bolsters such attention, such empty
waiting, through its practice of hospitality, obedience, listening to the least,
listening with the ear of the heart and so on. So are poetry and contemplation the same? No, if you think of contemplation as mystical theology, but
yes, if you think of it as ascetical theology, interior alteration. I'm not sure

what poetry truly wants, while it is clear what monasticism is after; but I have some confidence I know what poetry looks like when it reaches for what it wants: it looks empty; it looks erotic; it looks open to all possibility, commodious, surprisable, biddable, abashed—in love—just as contemplation looks. The Romantics exaggerated: we are capable of such states, all of us, but we don't come to them easily, nor are they given to a few privileged, beautiful souls. We cultivate ourselves, are shaped for such forms of knowing, and the nature of this ascesis roughly resembles the rule Benedict wrote.

13

Thomas Merton's Novitiate Talks on Cistercian Usages and Richard Kearney's Theandrism

I

Thomas Merton was novice master at the Trappist Abbey of Gethsemani, located near Bardstown, Kentucky, between 1955 and 1965. There are two things peculiar about this fact: that he held this important position in his community at all and that he held it for such a long time. He was appointed by Abbot James Fox, a conservative churchman and former businessman, with whom the more liberal Merton had many doctrinal and personal battles. A central, later disagreement in the early 1960s arose from Merton's desire to live as a hermit, loosely connected with the Gethsemani community. It was this issue that eventually caused Merton to terminate his tenure as novice master, though his leaving certainly was not a resignation in protest. He took up full-time residence in a cottage near the central monastic buildings with James Fox's reluctant consent and continued to play a significant role in the life of Gethsemani as a concelebrant, spiritual director and writer.

Merton as novice master met frequently with his young monks as they prepared to take their vows within the community following their two-year novitiate. Part of his responsibility was to give lectures on aspects of and influences on the cenobitic ethos such as Cistercian interiority from the early days of the order in the twelfth century and the moods of ancient Egyptian monasticism. One series of lectures, given on a periodic basis between February 1957 and the late winter of 1960, concerned Cistercian usages, the traditional practices associated with monastic life, especially those found within the Benedictinism of the strict observance. *Monastic Observances: Initiation into the Monastic Tradition,* Merton's collected novitiate lectures on monastic usages, is an unusual document to read now, though its original auditors would have found it supremely relevant to the lives they hoped to lead. It contains a formidable series of norms and injunctions concerning how one should conduct himself in all situations in the monastic enclosure from the most minutely quotidian—how to properly enter and leave the common dining area—to the apparently more contemplative—how one should sing the psalms, the center of the community's liturgical life, in choir. This seemingly obsessive concern with the minutiae of individual behaviour could strike a secular modern reader as authoritarian or anti-human, self-preoccupied, or at least aggressively non-spontaneous, but, in fact, the truth is that Merton's lectures offer a glimpse into an important and unfamiliar epistemological posture, a disposition that may be for us part of a rescuing cognitional stance.

|| Running throughout the talks is a particular argument that holds the attention: how one places oneself in relation to objects encountered daily, repeated gestures, collective and solitary activities, one's ascesis in this, determines how one stands, of course, before the world in general, but also the extent of one's knowledge of the truth of the world: indeed the knowledge of singular truth is simultaneous with the enactment of certain dispositions and a burgeoning depth in this relationship to things and acts. This is a rather remarkable claim. Actual apprehension of truth is not the result of objective distance and the supposed impartiality this brings, but of an intensely observed, corrected and shared subjectivity in association with

objects, gestures, even the various nooks and crannies of the physical space one occupies. Just how does such a noetic dynamism work? Merton calls our attention to a set of behaviours that not only shape human essence, but also—or *because* it shapes essence—calls into being in consciousness the actual reality of the world, which is indistinguishable from one's carefully considered relationship with it, a way of holding oneself that determines true ontology. How can we make sense of this?

|| I have been preoccupied over the last thirty years with an attempt to resuscitate and restore to myself what I believe to be a necessary interior substance, which, initially, I had no idea existed. I have pursued this under-taking in a state of unbroken, fluctuating anxiety because it was clear I could not manage the culturally imposed vocation of walking on air, a persistent, unsustainable existential performance required by the late modern European-American fundamentalist allegiance to a narrowly construed employment of reason and to the starvation rations of a brutally literal single-ply empiricism, a form of which had been astoundingly successful when employed within scientific method but which proved disastrously inadequate, menacing even, when re-purposed as a life-structuring mechanism.

It has been a project I have found impossible to pursue within churches or universities, where orthodoxies enforced a narrowing of affective imagina-tion. I sought what I believed to be a deeper, nourishing substance eventually in the place where I came to suspect it may be: in the authentic Platonic tradi-tion of a psychagogic exploration of elemental desire. I needed to approach the "irrational" not as Martin Heidegger had Romantically done, but as Plato's Socrates had done. I continued to read over this long period, a task that likely began in part in a chance encounter with Lars Thunberg's *The Vision of St. Maximus the Confessor: Man and Cosmos* in the old basement library at St. Peter's Abbey during a Saskatchewan Writers' Guild colony in the 1980s. (Later, when I got to know this library better and the community it belonged to, the presence of the Thunberg book in the stacks seemed even more a stroke of luck.) I followed up this discovery with a winter of reading a selection of Maximus' works in translation while I lived on the eastern shore of Lake Superior, a hundred kilometers north of Sault Ste. Marie. I earned my keep by operating a snowblower clearing the long lanes to several houses in the settlement near the village of Batchawana Bay. Maximus was a sixth-century interpreter of Pseudo-Dionysius the Areopagite, whom I also read at this time, as I found myself drawn further into the world of Christian Neoplatonism. Here was the source of a vivifying erotic essence, the origin of the foundational self that, while amplified, ramified in Plato, was also discernable in various pre-Socratic philosophers, Heraclitus, Empedocles, Parmenides and ultimately Pythagoras, and that conceivably, it occured to me later, stretched back into the ceremonial protocols of the Neolithic and Paleolithic and that may be indeed indigenous to the nature of the homo sapiens mind itself. This later supposition received fresh impetus from the paleo-neurological and epistemological work, focusing on Upper Paleolithic cave art, of Steven Mithen, David Lewis-Williams, Jean Clottes and Clayton Eshleman, which I began to sift through from 2006 on, though many of my conclusions diverged from theirs.

It struck me as unlikely that a comparable philosophy of erotic interiority to that which I had found in Plato and his predecessors would not exist outside the European tradition. Later experience confirmed for me this suspicion. Beginning in 1997 and extending for a period of six years, through the great generosity and hospitality of the Cree elder Joe Cardinal, to whom I had been introduced by the poet Louise Halfe and her husband Peter Butt, I fasted each May long weekend at Joe's camp on the Saddle Lake reserve in north eastern Alberta. Lying in that bent willow shelter that first spring, I realized this was the place I'd long been seeking. During my natal being "put out," an extraordinary set of circumstances occurred, and I went over to the side of what they revealed. This is a place where I currently reside. This experience was singular, quintessential, just as the foundational religious experience in my early twenties had been, and was achieved in the face of my craven skepticism.

I saw early on that the practice I had stumbled on in reading Thunberg's book, and tracked elsewhere in numerous places, amounted to a retrieval and vivification of the self. This came about as a result of the recalling of a lost tradition through a deep cultural and existential archeology. I realized as well that this practice must be scholarly *and* ascetical—and that because it was this unmodern amalgam, it would seem anomalous as late twentieth-century reading. The fusion of deep reading and ascesis is the important epistemological insight at the heart of Thomas Merton's exposure of Cistercian noesis through quotidian practice. Understanding here is fundamentally somatic.

|| Ontology, ethics and politics are not the result of analytical philosophical acuity—the rationalist insight severely romanticized in modern European thought—but are inevitable byproducts of both conscious and unconscious epistemological allegiances, wrong worlds as well as true. A true ontology, a sustaining ethics and politics, arises out of a broadly construed, atavistic and superceded cognitive discipline, one that is a shadow of a certain pattern of behaviour or, to put this another way, is aligned by ascesis. The actual world, in its own nature, on its own terms, appears as a result of a particular, decorous way of acting in it.

At the beginning of his lectures on general Trappist usages, Merton drew links between how one performs the infinite acts of living and true comprehension, ultimate affective fulfillment and complete individuation. His audience was a room of young men who had come from high schools, universities or a variety of jobs to spend their lives in Gethsemani monastery. It is winter 1957, Pius XII is still pope; the Second Vatican Council is years away; Eisenhower is president and the Cold War is at its height. These are some of the first words he says to them.

It is important from the beginning to understand what we are doing, in all the observances and practices which we carry out from morning to night. The whole life in large measure [is] made up of these things—they can help or

*hinder our search for perfection. Everything depends on how we carry them
out. Our observances are an integral part in our monastic life. They must live.
[They must be] part of a living organism. They must help us to live, help our
life of charity in the Spirit. [They must assist our] growth as children of God,
[the] formation of Christ in us. [They are the] exact opposite of mere mechan-
ical routine, which diminishes and lessens life [and] obscures the image of
Christ in us, degenerates into formalism, gradually stifles the free breath of
the Spirit [and] kills the spiritual life. [A] wrong understanding and practice
of observances leads to [the] wreck of our vocation. (Merton 5)*

A deep comprehension of the meaning and eschatological aspiration lying in
potency within every act is crucial to the soul's integrity and growth. Identity
is threatened by a failure to see this link or by a misapprehension of it.
Indeed a failure to act in the proper way, a misreading of the nature of acting,
snuffs out genuine eros, the central rudiment of the perduring self.

Then Merton makes a truly astonishing, non-empirical, non-rational,
non-Kantian observation on cognition, a claim that easily could be misread,
caricatured, as piety—

*we have come here to live—to live in Christ, by charity, in the Holy Spirit,
[and] to grow in the works of love—love for God: prayer, liturgical and
private—[to] enter into the prayer of the Church (liturgical gestures and
rites—liturgical action); fraternal union, above all Eucharistic—then, in the
whole monastic day (work, etc.), cooperation, helping one another to grow
in Christ, [through] mercy, forebearance, prayer, instruction and correction
(example). (5)*

What would it be if one's knowing were to be accurately described as "living
in Christ"? It would be the world manifesting itself proteanly, flickeringly,
in the theatre of aligned, isomorphic-with-its-nature and of course (to say
the same thing), generously dilated interiority, vita Christiformus. In the
Holy Spirit? This would be to live in colloquy with Ibn 'Arabi's angel, the

ontologically construed Aristotelian agent intellect, super-potent, gestalt nimble externality of mind, which makes mind.

Thomas Merton continues: "The observances are the visible expression and the outward aid to all this—they are supposed to help us, form us, guide us, show us the way. But we must get below the surface, beyond the letter, and while carrying out the letter properly, penetrate to the full spirit" (5). Noesis, in other words, is enabled, or at least brought into the realm of possibility, by certain ceremonial movements and workplace behaviours, fully probed and savoured, which require, then foster a range of dispositions that facilitate penetrating awareness. Here is Merton's, but more fundamentally Benedict's and Poeman's, theurgy. A structure that is one's own considered way of doing things is school and cognitive performance, in that it forms and speeds the dilated, phronetic activity that is penetrating understanding. And this epistemology is activated in community ("*fraternal union*") that is unintendedly altruistic in an unsurpassibly essential way ("helping one another to grow in Christ"): that is, without conviviality one's behaviour produces no light.

After his introductory remarks, he begins his reading of the earlier parts of the monastic day—a projected Part Two was never completed—by investigating first the occult, dynamizing capacity of places in the monastery, what he calls "the regular places" (7), the daemonia of the polyform site. He again cautions his auditors to not read legalism into his remarks on Cistercian observances, but to see them as attempts at discernment in the uncovering of food caches for the interior person, the seeded human. "We should try to understand the meaning of the monastic plan," he exhorts his listeners, "not necessarily in order to cling slavishly to the letter of the *Usages* on this point, but in order to see why the regular places exist, what they are for, and see whether or not we are failing to achieve any of the purposes for which they were instituted" (7). The point is to comprehend the haecceity, the flavour and the sustaining propulsive power of each particular location, in part, by ingesting the good indigenous to there. *Nemo perturbetur neque contristetur in domo Dei* (Benedict 55): nothing should cause disquiet or en-gloom in the house of God—"everything in the monastery plan is ordered wisely, to prevent useless distraction, worries, cares, agitations, to help a life of prayer and simplicity" (Merton 8), each place a refugia, the location an instruction—the room where the bulk of your interior work takes place is, as Peter the Venerable says, "more eloquent than all teachers," a kind of paradise (William of St. Thierry), allowing *vacare Deo, frui Deo* (to make time—be freed—receive exemption from military service—for God, to enjoy God). In a non-monastic context, one can suppose that places, lightly and contradictorily marked by intentional design, offer a particular succouring of the human submerged in the body—desk, kitchen, reading chair, bedroom window, this certain lamp. But one must be changed to be actually nourished by the sustenance each place offers. This is the opposite of the necessity of some foods having to be altered, by soaking or boiling, say, to be made edible.

‖ The monastic day begins with the hours of the night office, vigils and lauds, each, of course, sung in choir. It involves, as all canonical hours do, the chanting or singing of psalms, the central activity of *opus Dei*, the divine work. The chant creates a power by which it itself is extended beyond its own enactment and it prepares for a deeper interior prayer, which is a savouring and eating. But this is a non-rapturous mastication—it builds essentially on empirical attention to the plain things before one, the psalmic words, the neumes indicating the rise and fall of the communal voice, the individual voices around one, their idiosyncratic timbre, in other words a "material fervor." Here is Merton on chant:

> We do not always have to be explicitly conscious of the material aspect of
> the choir—God forbid. The purpose of the material attention is to give us
> a habitual grasp of the basic material elements of the office so that we can
> handle them spontaneously and without special effort or concern, meanwhile
> devoting our minds to the higher and more important significance of the
> divine praises, and above all, uniting ourselves to God Himself to whom we
> are singing. St. Bernard however insists on material fervor in choir, generosity

in giving our voice, in attention to the words we sing, but above all in order
that we may "taste" the spiritual "honey" of the divine meaning hidden in
the wax of the "letter." (Bernard of Clairvaux, Sermon 7, In Cantica, cited in
Merton 42)

Again, as with places, we have proposed to us latent gracefulness. Thus Merton's remarks on choral prayer make up a peculiar linguistic theory—meaning, autonomous, unlike, outsized, but not anomalous, lies inside meaning—and a strange philosophy of reading. Its platform is plain existential attention, which shifts into "habitual grasp"; it is what we spontaneously do with the sweetness that is a kernel broken out minimally, yet efficaciously, by an enthusiastic, unembellished regard for the *things* of one's practice.

|| How thin is the philosophical foundation, the erotic root, of the diasporic European presence in North America, oddly both enervating and stumblingly violent. It cannot nourish—a foodless zone. What those who live soley in it interiorly dine on is ersatz nourishment trucked in from elsewhere—celebrity, reality T v, managed opinion, and various irritable dissents. Its substance is a severe amalgam: hegemonic, non-contemplative rationalism; a calculative utilitarianism; an evangelism around the Enlightenment which masks colonial endeavour as cultural altruism. Octavio Paz remarks, in "In Search of the Present," his 1990 Nobel Prize lecture, that Mexico's entry into modernity involved a recovery of a vivifying, local past—"Mexico was searching for its present only to find it within, buried deep but alive. The search for modernity led us to discover our antiquity, the hidden force of the nation." Canada, less metissage, more crippled in the mystical part of its natal tradition, is forced to take a more circuitous, laborious route. Dominant white power in this country must recover the esoteric elements in its own wisdom deposit, its sapiential tradition in its Platonic inheritance, and the forks of this tradition in mystical Judaism, Islam and Christianity; then, schooled by these features, it must expose itself, through reading and conversation, to the Indigenous mythopoeisis.

Alain Badiou asks in his *Second Manifesto for Philosophy*, "What is thinking in our times?" (1). I believe it is the recovery of contemplative genius, not as a solitary introspection but as the rudiment of transcultural conviviality. And in other ways, this recovered Pythagorean reason— the available-to-awe exercise of thinking, a contemplative phronesis—is a vigorous activism. To elucidate this claim we must turn to an examination of Richard Kearney's fluid theandric ontology, the sole form of his Whiteheadian theology. Here we will see the depth of the political potency of this restored epistemological ethos.

II

Richard Kearney is an Irish-born philosophical theologian who teaches at Boston College and University College Dublin and whose graduate work in philosophy was undertaken in France in the late 1970s under the supervision of Paul Ricoeur. One of the readers of his PHD dissertation was Emmanuel Levinas. Kearney, in his book *The God Who May Be: A Hermeneutics of Religion*, rejects both the negative theology of Pseudo-Dionysian apophaticism and Scholasticism's Aristotelian metaphysics. Both schools, in his view, regard divinity as a substantial, ahistorical entity, which is nevertheless transcendent of being, even if, between themselves, they would dispute the nature and the extent of this transcendence. In place of Scholasticism's onto-theology, a supreme being, exceptional substance, capable of extraordinary acts, Kearney substitutes a divinity that is essentially possibility, whose "potentiality-to-be is the most divine thing about it" (1–2), a God-who-may-be.

Kearney's deity as emergent possibility is marked by none of the implacable unlikeness of the Pseudo-Dionysian God nor the omnipotence of the Thomistic, but requires human cooperation to existentiate itself as the actualized possibility of the Judeo-Christian kingdom of justice. In this polis, qualifiedly present while remaining anticipated, Kearney's post-metaphysical, eschatological divinity has a double existence: as a final cause, a *posse*, a luring possibility of being; and as embodied in a politics possessing successful orphic and millenarian aspects. This polis-to-be, which is the God-who-may-be, is a theandric achievement, of human nature, drawn by divine possibility. It is "what is promised," the eschatological event. "But precisely because this promise is just that, a *promise*, and not an already accomplished possession, there is a free space gaping at the very core of divinity: the space of the possible. It is this divine gap which renders all things possible which would be otherwise impossible for us—including the kingdom of justice and love" (4). The gap is not the solicitude of the *deus absconditis* but an inevitable feature of an existence in which divinity, that plenitude, is what optimally may be.

Kearney's non-metaphysical, deferredly ontological theology grows out of a long alternative tradition in Western thought. There are elements of Hegel and Whitehead here, as well as features from Nicholas of Cusa, whose influence Kearney generously admits, and aspects from Maximus the Confessor. Divinity as maximal possibility, and beautiful compulsion, appears in human subjectivity as individuating, partly inchoate, partly blind, eros, which nevertheless is discerningly alert to the draw exercised on it, which in fact is its own substance manifest in a different aspect. Between such desire and actualized divinity exists an intimate complicity—with such eros Kearney's God-who-may-be finds voice, as *Geist* in Hegel's *Phenomenology* is the only means for the apotheosis of Absolute Spirit.

Still the desire, which is the shared substance of human individuality and divinity-as-possibility, is not precisely Hegelian spirit in an important sense—it is eschatological, not historical. It is assembled and shaped out of human latency into an unanticipatable ediface, not urged by implicit forces within massive historical process; its judgment falls on individual acts appearing instant by instant, not at the conclusion of history as a whole. It is a desire "for a land foreign to every nature" in the words of Emmanuel Levinas (33–34), not absolute consciousness' becoming acquainted with its own essence, so its achievement is marked by upending, essential surprise. "The desired of eschatological desire exists before memory and beyond anticipation," says Kearney (64).

How does such a desire make a world, indeed an optimal world? Maximus the Confessor is not central to Kearney's theology and emergent ontology, though Maximus' thought throws light on Kearney's project. The human role in the eschatological politics, a mediational role, a creative ontological function, is essential. "For this reason the human person was introduced last among beings," Maximus remarks in *Ambigua* 41, "as a kind of natural bond mediating between the universal poles through their proper parts, and leading into unity in itself those things that are naturally set apart from one another by a great interval" (*Maximus the Confessor*, 157). Maximus' anthropology is a cosmology: the whole of being, as he observes in *The Church's Mystagogy*, is a *makranthropos*, a gigantic human. He means this analogically but also factually. Human beings contain and maintain in coherence a multiplicity that, when ordered, is a protean, complementary, expanding surprising-yet-linked muchness—the cosmos is itself such an infinite array. But he wishes to say more than repeat the ancient commonplace concerning the human as microcosm. It is the human work to fashion such an expanding whole, which is the world in its truth.

There is a causal sympathy between the two instantiations of the human, the erotic individual and *makranthropos*, the putatively gathered cosmos: interior change effects an asymptotic alteration in being. "In order to bring about the union of everything with God as its cause," Maximus continues in *Ambigua* 41, "the human person begins first of all with its own division, and then, ascending through the intermediate steps by order and rank, it reaches the end of its high ascent, which passes through all things in search of unity, to God, in whom there is no division" (157). Here divinity is the polis of the eschatological possibility achieved. This "city" is initially triggered or haltingly approached by a blurring, then erasure, of sexual distinction. The early stages of this new citizenship, this new form of eschatological being, starts in one (and in the world)

> by shaking off every natural property of sexual differentiation into male and female by the most dispassionate relationship to divine virtue....Thus it [i.e.

the human person] is shown to be and becomes simply a human person in accordance with divine purpose, no longer divided by being called male or female. It [the emergent s/he] is no longer separated, as it is now, into parts, and it achieves this through the perfect knowledge, as I said, of its own logos, *in accordance with which it is. (157)*

The confluence of male and female energies in a single interiority, the one made available, opened, to the other is the first healing, Maximus argues, leading to a complete restoration of the cosmos, an utter apokatastasis, in which "the human person unites paradise and the inhabited world to make one earth" (157).

The male-female distinction, occasioned, Maximus argues, like all ruptures, by the fall, is the first separation resolved in the interiority of the apokatastatic individual, making others, like the distance between paradise and the quotidian, capable of healing. Lars Thunberg observes, in his commentary on Maximus' eschatological anthropology-cosmology that with this restoration

it is more the aspect of mortification *that predominates. Paradise is never for Maximus a transcendent reality. It is earth that is divided up in this way. And consequently Christ the man is in the first place the agent of this mediation. Maximus says that Christ sanctified the inhabited world (the* oikoumene*) and entered into paradise after his death....After His resurrection, in returning to the inhabited world, He manifested the restored unity of the whole world. (83)*

In the kenotic consciousness of the Logos, the restored world appears. The second person of the Trinity does this as a theandric force, acting in the combination of human and meta-human energies. Maximus was an orthodox Chalcedonian, his Christology shaped by the Council of Chalcedon's declaration of the two natures of Christ, and this allegiance shapes his eschatological politics.

The Alexandrian Origen allegorically interpreted paradise as the enact-ment of the virtues; the actual, non-allegorical appearance is, then, manifest—created, albeit in an unstable, localized (but how else?) manner—when one takes up a divine, unitary way of being. The world of autonomous, glinting specificity, congruent, bristling with difference, complementary, that bracing gestalt, becomes clear, *obvious*, potent, when one lives, even in the self-conscious way of Merton's novice observing Trappist norms, in a theandric, Christoformic, manner, identity carried in the confluential flow of human and more-than-human (final cause, possibility-at-the-tip-of-imagination) energies. As Thunberg remarks, "This paradise of virtues is not a substitute for the visible paradise, but it is in moral terms a manifestation of the coher-ence of the whole world through the Logos" (84). This makes it a complete ontological sketch, a world. We attend to being in this manner, and the perfections coalesce.

III

14
A Poetics of
Decolonization

A dialogue with Shane Rhodes published in *The Fiddlehead*
Autumn 2012

SHANE RHODES: Your book of poems, *Assiniboia,* published
this spring, is built on an argument that the colonization of the land on
which we live in Canada is not only a process of the past but an ongoing
process that invades and engenders the present of our settler society, our
relationship to land, our relationship to First Nations, our relationships
to each other, and even our poetics. What you seem to be proposing in
Assiniboia (and propose is almost too weak of a word for your insistence)
is a different way of thinking about the past, the present, and colonization. What is some of the thinking that made you want to attempt
Assiniboia? Why now?

TIM LILBURN: The Harper government is advancing a model of this country
that places Western Canada's resource wealth, especially tar sands oil, at its
center. I, along with many others, am uncomfortable with an understanding
of the West that is built entirely on an extractive, and environmentally

irresponsible and dangerous, approach to wealth—the snatch it and leave
strategy, decamping to England or a gated community on Vancouver
Island—the old Hudson's Bay Company, Rupert's Land model, the new
big oil model. I would like an alternative way of imagining where I live.

Any search for an alternative Western Canada, in my opinion,
has to pass through the political and social vision of Louis Riel and
his supporters in the two Provisional Governments at Fort Garry and
Batoche. It's the chief alternative political vision that's been tried (briefly)
under historical conditions. It's no coincidence that Tom Flanagan of
the University of Calgary, an early and crucial Harper advisor, built his
career on an attempt to demolish the credibility of Riel. It's important
to remember that Riel's imaginary society was intended for all people,
included all races. His last secretary, Henry Jackson (Honoré Jaxon after
his conversion to Riel's cause) was a diasporic European from the settler
community around Prince Albert, U of T grad in classics, left-leaning.
Jaxon, along with Sara Riel, the visionary Grey Nun and Louis Riel's sister,
were my way into imagining the polis of *Assiniboia*.

There's something else I was pursuing in the book, and it has to do
with the nature of colonial war. Most, maybe all, imperial wars are really
mythopoeic wars, one cosmology going into battle with and attempting
to vanquish another. There was something deficient in the culture of
Europeans when they first came in contact with the land in North
America and the original inhabitants of that land: European culture had
long ago lost touch with its contemplative root, its own wisdom lineage.
This meant that it had little capacity overall to take in and be ravished
and shaped by the new place, because it was essentially far from the
rapt, persistent attention its own contemplative heritage could have
shaped in it. And, because the contemplative spirit is linked to conviviality, there was (and is) little interest in engaging in open conversation
with Indigenous peoples about the deep structure of being and different
cosmological and ontological accounts. Just read reports of those first
exchanges in the *Jesuit Relations* from the 1630s! *Assiniboia* tries, in

various theatrical ways, to reach toward this restoration—with no great confidence that anything in this line will be successful. I don't want to reduce the book to an extended argument, but these were some of the ideas that were clustered around its origin as line after line gathered. For me, there is a large element of play involved in writing poems, but these ideas or concerns roughly set out the limits of this play for this book.

I am quite intrigued by your suggestion that colonialism is still present, of course, but am even more interested in your claim that it infects our poetics. What do you have in mind here? Also in an earlier email you mentioned that the project you are working on now tracks some of the same themes *Assiniboia* does. What is this new project?

SR: The project I am currently completing is called *X*. Largely using the prescriptive constraints of found poetry (where a poetic text is constructed from previously existing material), much of the poetry in *X* is built using Government of Canada transcripts of the Canadian Post-Confederation Treaties (also called the numbered treaties), their associated documentation, as well as the Indian Act and other First Nations–focused law and policy. Conducted by the Government of Canada over a fifty-year period, the numbered treaties represent one of the largest systematic, colonial land appropriations in the world. Daunting for the history and future they carry and their impenetrable legal diction, these texts are the foundational logic of the current phase of Canadian colonization and of ongoing settler, First Nations, Inuit and Métis relations.

How does colonization affect our poetics? I am increasingly exasperated by poetry (or, why so specific? art in general) that does not in some way interrogate the modes of its production and the environment and geography from which it comes. I'm not asking for postcolonial or Marxist criticism every time I open a book, but I question poetry that doesn't in some way look at where it comes from. I also question the preponderance of our common poetic allusion structures (is there a better word for this?), whether they be to the great European and Western thinkers or

Greek/Roman mythology. Here we are, tens of thousands of miles from the homes of that mythology and philosophy, and most of us know more about it than about the mythologies of the geography and land and people where we live. I speak English, Spanish and French, and nowhere in my education were Cree, Anishinaabe, Secwepemctsín, Inuktitut, or Michif even presented as options.

I am interested in exploring anti-Indigenousness (racism is too general a term for the particular discriminations that have been engineered in Canada) and the ways in which our colonial society builds up and protects the myths at its foundation. How do we hold the idea of living in a just society while also knowing the injustices that exist and continue to exist at our very foundation? How has our thinking—and our thinking even about poetry and what can make poetry—been affected? Beyond just intellectual curiosity, there are reasons why it is easier for us to quote a 500 BC Greek philosopher but say nothing of Deganawidah. And this isn't just an intellectual argument, as I think how colonialism continues to shape our thinking leads directly to our relationship to land and treating land as only a platform for resource extraction.

I am trying to build an uncomfortable poetry that looks uncomfortably at these questions. This is the reason why I'm interested in *Assiniboia* and your thinking behind it. Beyond the mythopoetic structures you mention, how did your thinking about colonization affect the writing of *Assiniboia* and your use of language?

TL: The presence of Indigenous culture and language in settler literature that you hope for has existed previously in less than satisfactory ways. This sort of borrowing or fusion wasn't uncommon a generation back— you can see it in the work of Andrew Suknaski, say, or John Newlove or Robert Kroetsch. And there's another version of it a generation before that in the poetry of Duncan Campbell Scott:

As much as I admire and have been influenced by Suknaski as a writer and even more as a person who inserted himself into the land, I do feel somewhat uneasy about his particular use of Indigenous materials. There is not enough in the poem (or the poet and his culture) to support these presences. With Scott, the move feels like a gathering of artifacts for museums in Europe and major cities in the East, the thought of "a... waning race" (as he put it) stored or displayed. So maybe we need a new way.

Assiniboia is about finding a route into Riel's political and linguistic vision, itself a fusion of the European and the Indigenous North American practices. It isn't about Riel's polis, but is a newcomer's response to and a working toward this broad imaginary state. And I realized along the way that cultural Europeans would have to shed certain things and add others, mostly facets of the West's mystical root—thus speeches from Odysseus, Plato, Suhrawardi (and others which I took out to control the spread of the book)—to complete the journey from one cultural cosmos to another. But I didn't start from some grand, overall idea; I just kept adding phrase to phrase and over time it became clear that there were various distinct voices—Dionysius, Sara Riel, forms on the land like the Cabri effigy—that were talking to one another; figures or forces that mainstream culture had forgotten, interred in silence, were now in conversation. I also was operating no doubt under the influence of Louise Halfe's work, *Blue Marrow* and *The Crooked Good* in particular, and from talking with her over the years, and by the projects of writers like Jan Zwicky and Xi Chuan, who, too, are trying to open up new ways into their social worlds.

Why isn't there more of this, a move toward land awareness in writing and deeper versions of cultural exchange? Well, there is the belief that the problems or complaints that would urge this—the sense that descendants of European settlers aren't rooted here or their literature doesn't echo the Indigenous feel of place (your formulation more or less)—are simply forms of hypochondria. This seems to be the view of Michael Lista in his review of *Assiniboia*, as far as I can make it out—that the feeling of disconnection or unease or unfinished business, which I, and I think others, feel, is just made up or imagined. Then there is the neo-conservative amnesia around colonialism and the free-land source of the country's wealth.

I think your question "How do we hold the idea of justice in our heads knowing the injustices that exist at our very foundation?" is a fine one. Not doing the work of drawing out the foundational injustices from the prescribed forgetting and pulling them into critical and poetic light, surely part of the work of coming to be at home where we are, undermines the entire moral edifice in a surprisingly extensive way. One last thing—are we really that far from the myths and philosophies (Greek, Enlightenment) you would like to see more understated in poetry? They are us.

SR: My concern is much more about why our culture values certain histories and histories of thought above others and this valuation, I think, is intricately tied up with our culture's will to colonize (and the attendant racism and anti-Indigenousness that fuels it) and control. Rather than arguing the intellectual merits of these myths and philosophies, I question why we attach such merit to them and, as a result, what receives little merit at all.

I'm interested in the ideas of time and order with which *Assiniboia* plays. Other than the poem by poem progression in the poems' dramaturgical structure, there is very little here in terms of clear, sequential narrative. Time and sentence structure also become compacted, twisted and shuffled. This is a space where "everything has franchise" and where poetry wanders. Creating this space must have been no small feat of waylaying the need to order and make clear. Why wander?

TL: The poems do move around, slipping back and forth in time and from place to place (the confluence of the South Saskatchewan and Red Deer rivers, Vancouver Island, Batoche), sometimes in myth, sometimes in history, sometimes in the apparent present. This is because the book wants to take in the whole terrain, the temporal and spatial terrain of

Western Canada, old Rupert's Land, over the last hundred or so years. Partly it's an appetite for spectacle, an operatic inflation, that gives the collection this spreading shape, but more than this, it is the desire to think into the roots of settlement and land theft. (*Did* the Hudson's Bay Company actually own Rupert's Land, rather than simply hold a monopoly to trade in various watersheds? Ownership is minimally premised on use and, aside from trading posts and surrounding fields, all the land was used by First Nations people, who were never wards or employees or representatives of the company. The 1869 sale to Canada may have been closer to your local Tim Hortons franchise selling your neighbourhood to China or the State of Washington than we care to think. Imagine the franchise provider as the Queen of Ruritania or a slightly more substantial polity.)

But really the poems' nomadism is only a surface trait, and at a deeper level they are fixed in the present; political history, the aspirations of the dead, age-long philosophical conundra—all these are active and more or less simultaneous in the book, as they are in ordinary consciousness. This is the nature of thought, if you consider, as many daily do, the colonization of the continent. If you move from this multi-ply consciousness, you are mired in ideology or in sentimentality. Where does the complex phenomenon of conquest, and the entrepreneurial shadiness that came with this, with its history and its continuing personal, economic and political effects, live? It certainly doesn't live in a clearly unfolding narrative unless you are content with a cartoon of it. And what interests would be served by such a simplified and minimally true account?

SR: The shifting narrative and time of the poem also has an important connection to doubt. From my research behind the creation of the Post-Confederation Treaties, the Indian Act and related government policy, one thing stands out: the erosion of doubt. It seems that the more sure any government and government official was of what they were doing in terms of "Indian policy," the more disastrous the results. When you take a look at the how the relationships between settlers and First Nations have changed in Canada over three hundred years, one of the key changes on the part of the settlers has been a loss of doubt—moving from a people who didn't know what they were doing in this new world to a people who feel their mastery of it is now absolute. This loss of doubt (and a mounting sense of dominance and superiority) changed what could be seen (at least at the best of times) as relationships of nation to nation to a relationship that is now based more on administration. Read the Indian Act—it is hard to imagine a more discriminatory, anti-Indigenous and hubristic law that tries to control a people all the way down to the minute details of the dances they can dance. Read about the formation of the Indian residential schools. Read some of the statements of Duncan Campbell Scott. Read the Statement of the Government of Canada on Indian Policy (the 1969 White Paper on Indians). Read what is happening right now. This is the thinking of a society and its governments that feel they have the answers and have few doubts about what is right for "other" people—the rest is implementation and administration.

TL: I agree with what you say about "the erosion of doubt," and the building of a terrible certainty that is in conversation with nothing. It yields to nothing because it imagines it is simply common sense. It therefore presents a slippery, seemingly unbudgeable obstacle to even minute attempts to move toward a state of autochthonicity on the side of newcomers. Colonization and its effects over time appear to be just a fact like glaciation. One needn't be in exchange about things like this; the give and take of genuine conversation, that courtesy, is inappropriate when the subject is, say, the temperatures at which certain liquids turn to ice or gas. Against the background of the "certainties" you describe, and their attendant amnesias, what you are doing in *X* and what I attempt in *Assiniboia* is just playing with illusion.

15

Contemplative Experience;

Autochthonous Practice

Presented at the Congress of the Humanities and Social Sciences
University of Victoria, 2013

THE BIFURCATION OF NATURE, the gap separating humans
from the non-human, *res cogitans* from *res extensa*, appears to be unbridge-
able. Little or nothing in conventional religion or politics, or in contemporary
mainstream philosophy, seems able to resolve this split, with its environ-
mental, economic and personal ramifications; indeed in each of these places
of inquiry and practice, human exceptionalism is protected. We appear to
lack the thinking to carry us over. But perhaps an ecocritical interiority, a
psychagoguery of apokatastasis, based on various contemplative phenomenologies, could be a source of promising ways to proceed on this apparently
intractable matter. The return of self to the world, that task in imagination,
carries the same sense of enactable impossibility that marks a number of religious and some philosophical interior dramas. Acting on this hunch of
shared morphology, I will consider two such accounts, Plato's in his famous
description of ascent in the allegory of the cave in the *Republic* and Teresa of
Avila's observations on interior colloquy in the Sixth Mansion of her *Interior*

Castle, in search of clues to a possible autochthonous practice, an ascesis of embeddedness in terrain, the restoration of the human subject to the natural world. Thirdly, I will sift through the poetic practice—the contemplative biography—of the fifth-century Chinese poet Hsieh Ling-yün to provide an example of such a non-Romantic restoration and show, among other things, that a return to poetry can be simultaneous with a return to the wild. I will conclude with a short postscript on contemplative attention in general.

Actual Things

In Book VII of the *Republic*, Socrates announces he will "make an image of our nature in its education and want of education" (514a), that is, he will attempt a depiction of interior or dispositional formation. He begins with the well-known image of a collection of individuals leading a subterranean existence in a cave with an exceedingly long entrance. Within this cave, most of the people live in a manipulated reality: they are instructed, but falsely so, imprisoned in what looks like ideology, the half light of confected thinking.

Previously, in Books II to VII, Socrates, along with his co-conversationalists, has expended considerable effort in imagining a state ideal to, or the inevitable outcome of, the desire life of Glaucon, Socrates' primary interlocutor in the early books of the dialogue. What has resulted is a detailed description of a "feverish" city, with numerous fascistic features, committed to the control of its citizens, its neighbours and environs in order to insure its condition of luxury. Its uniqueness justifies—requires—the internal and social violences it practices. "And hence," Socrates observes, "the regime, once well started, will roll on like a circle in its growth" (424a). Throughout the dialogue, accounts of eros lead to discussions of politics and political descriptions give insight into defining states of desire.

The cave and escape from it are often read as political argument, sometimes as epistemology or as a treatment of ontology. I wish to consider the ascent as a phenomenology, which, of course, has elements arising from Glaucon's particular character but which may be read as well as representative of life within a burgeoning contemplative practice. Like Ibn 'Arabian theophany, it is pinpointedly specific, while being, in a diluted sense, universal. The prisoners in the cave are bound at the neck and ankles and forced to stare at a rock wall on which images are projected. The shadows they stare at are produced by figures carried by guards before a fire burning behind the captives. One prisoner then suddenly is torn from his restraints—the instructional ferocity is remarkable—and is compelled to be free by an aggressive guide who suddenly appears; and this deracination naturally proves painful, unwanted, resisted, and, when successful, causes extreme disorientation, and the surfacing of utterly novel incompetencies in the reluctantly liberated.

"Now consider," Socrates advises,

> what their release and healing from the bonds and folly would be like if something of this sort were by nature to happen to them. Take a man who is released and suddenly compelled to stand up, to turn his neck around, to walk and look up toward the light; and who, moreover, in doing all this is in pain and, because he is dazzled, is unable to make out those things whose shadows he saw before. (515d)

The new illumination, this novel form of seeing, alarmingly eats into identity, undermining the skillful engagement with a milieu that before seemed the basis of a fixed selfhood. The points of certainty of the old world are no longer available. The one thing that seems not in flux is the state of being under the power of an unsought liberator, and this is a disconcerting, incredible form of stability. The loss of the released captive is acutely felt as genuine—the recognitions that previously framed his life strike him, even in the initial moments of his liberated state, as *true*—and the deep insight that will result from his release is not available to him for some time. He is estranged from his new mind; the captive's resourceful consciousness has been taken from him. Skilless, graceless, uncomprehending of the phenomena native to his new condition, mourning the loss of the earlier world picture and his easy and rewarded passage through it, enervated by nostalgia for a lost knowledge map and identity, only half believing, even now, the falsity of both, the captive, in his mind, has dramatically lost intellectual and cultural status, as the subterranean fire remains lit and figures continue to be passed before it. All these distressing features constitute for Plato the initial stages of contemplative attention. This is the feel of interior unfolding for him, his sense of psychagogic education, at least if someone like the noble Glaucon were to undergo it.

The trials of the captive, however, have only begun, and the motif of liberation as assault continues. The freed captive is made to stand and look at the light below the earth, an experience that only stuns and pains him further. The uprooting from the earlier self is ruthless and proceeds through multiple stages during which the former captive is completely unconsoled. In his distressed and outraged condition, nothing reassures him that a disaster is not under way. The substantiality of actual things in the world outside the cave, once he is brought before them, does not impress itself on him; their luminous presence cancels itself ("And when he came to the light, wouldn't he have his eyes full of its beam and be unable to see even one of the things now said to be true?" [516a]). An interior sensorium, furthermore, on these matters has not been activated; there is no way they can appear in the imagination and be savoured there in multiple ways.

Even when he comes to have some ability to approach real things in the world outside the underground chamber—how?—perhaps through will-driven practice, simple non-affect-laden repetition—his distance from them, his consideration of their shadows, seems crucial to his burgeoning formation and understanding; greater, truer intimacy, at this point, is likely to cause further destabilization of the self. Still his return from immurement now has a momentum toward "the things themselves," and this momentum appears to be nascent desire. In the end, he is capable of intuiting not just the quiddities of objects but also the internal patterns linking things and the many complementarities in the assemblage of the real. Thus, after a relentless practice of provisional comprehension and repeated loss, and unwanted correction at the hands of the rescuer, the captive sees, is, one could say, saturated by sight, and is formed by a brimming understanding of the world and, as a result of this cognitive achievement, is specifically suited, oddly enough, Plato tells us, for politics. (How, one might ask, is this series of transformations a training for a political life of balanced interests and persuasive rhetoric? The only response can be that for Plato authentic politics is, above all else, correct ontology. This ontology can't be system but must be the linked autonomies the transformed individual sees.) This new seeing, a unique formation, a politics, is entirely contemplative, with no training in strategy whatsoever in it, but with elements of ravishment and collapse and an experience of a deep, previously unlimned, loneliness, an ontological loneliness, being first felt then met. Things in their autonomy stand out and permit approach. The autonomy in objects may in part be the result of approach, of the subject becoming accustomed to the world outside ideology—in the light of this unencumbered consciousness, things do stand apart with remarkable singularity; yet in their apartness they do not repel human subjectivity, but seem complicit with it.

Vulnus amoris

Teresa of Avila traces another ascent teleology in her *Interior Castle*, written while her earlier *Autobiography* was under investigation by the Inquisition. Like Plato's account of erotic unfolding, the shape of Teresan contemplative practice does not have its source in the subject, her imagination or will. Unlike Plato's interior Odyssean journey, however, there is no sapient, ruthless guide—indeed, with Teresa, guides are often untrustworthy, obstacles to be overcome because their constraining judgments are too literal, conservative or are misogynist—yet, as with the Platonic captive, what the self undergoes in Teresa, while weakly discernable by the self, has a minimal relation to the self's own intention. The Teresan self is as dismayed as the Platonic and as helpless as contemplative regard builds. In the 235 pages of the Peers translation of *Interior Castle*, Teresa gives a daringly generous and detailed phenomenological account of interior change. The description is complex, multi-layered and multi-sided, yet cheerfully accessible, likely since her audience was the community of Discalced Carmelites with whom she lived. Only certain features of her experience can be touched on here.

The Sixth Mansion of the book depicts the midpoint of the elongated event of her philosophical practice, in which the "interior trials" are particularly intense; the self destabilized by *vulnus amoris* (the wound of love) inflicted by the intimate stranger, the Spouse, reels before "[t]hat sight of Him which it has had...so deeply impressed upon it that its whole desire is to enjoy it once more" (Teresa of Avila 126). One is pushed in Plato, pulled in Teresa. The price of this accentuated intimacy, self with Self, for the young Teresa was a series of seemingly insurmountable crises centering around marginalization in the larger affective community; she is disqualified from membership in the group of the right-minded. She accepts the loss of the identifying, buoying community because a more compelling experience of conversational beauty, flickeringly available "at a time when everything really seems to be lost" (127), draws her.

What compensates for the unreliability of guides for Teresa are "locutions," interior experiences that appear to be address. Self-direction, in the sense of attention to an inner colloquy with a second, intimate, yet peculiar mind, seems the only trustworthy way to move at all. But she of course does not counsel caprice or Millian self-determination; discernment is crucial in the matter of contemplative government, a sort of experience-based connoisseurship and an ability to delectate *in ore cordis* (the heart's mouth) all the flavours of each inner movement. How to depict this larger mind, the intimate-yet-strange other in the self? For Teresa, there is no hesitation: she is spoken to by the infinite and infinitely phronetic intelligence of God—or, perhaps more accurately, that this intelligence thinks within her, without displacing her own mind. But there are additional possibilities that have been used in other contemplative contexts, Platonic, Christian, poetic to refer to such direction—address comes from one's *daemonium*; it comes from the inventiveness of one's essential hunger; the ingenuity of Archimedean insight; poetic intuition available in a moment of Keatsian negative capability; the operation of the agent intellect as it appears in Ibn

'Arabī's epistemological angelology. In each of these metaphoric approxima-
tions of the nature of inner address, the interlocutor is the self's alterity, its
best or ideal version. The appearance of this self marks the resuscitation of
the interior sensorium, the recessed senses, the secret body, which for Origen
and later patristic commentators was central to contemplative exegesis. The
"better self" is, in part, a result of this resuscitation, in fact a fundamental
element of its nature.

Such address is a happy injury, the cause for Teresa of a delectable
wounding, a "delectable absorption" (135). The impetus is clear, penetrating,
undoubtable—these are signs of its authenticity. Desire is reconfigured and
increased. Teresan colloquy recalls the multi-positional inner exchange
captured by Marguerite Porete in her *Mirror of Simple Souls*, but it carries
little of the relative quodlibital decorum of Porete's existential theatres.
Teresa describes the moment of communication as perilous, the brush of
the preternaturally sharp mind just out of reach but capable of startling
proximity, indeed able to dislodge the conscious, intentioned self from its
centrality.

This amalgam of distance and shocking closeness is caught in Porete's
name "Farnearness." "Some of them [locutions]," Teresa observes, "seem to
come from without; others from the innermost depths of the soul; others
from its highest part, while others, again, are so completely outside the soul
that they seem to be heard with the ears and seem to be uttered by a human
voice" (139). The proper response, for Teresa, in most cases, is to ignore the
movements—"often, indeed...this may be a fancy, especially in persons who
are melancholy...or have feeble imaginations"—resisting them until they
gradually cease. If, however, they are authentic, they will "not vanish from
the memory for a very long time: some indeed never vanish at all" (142); they
appear to be, in fact, immune to rejection; even if a series of events contra-
dicts them, "a living spark of conviction" remains. This deep grooving of
language into memory does not happen in ordinary communication, Teresa
notes. Nevertheless even such perduring address must be vetted in conversation with a reliable teacher or spiritual director, otherwise one may fall prey

to one's own opinions: being shaped and momentumed by inner colloquy can never be a matter of choice or will, muscular self-determination, Teresa admonishes, but must be the result of obedience to a mutually discerned daemonic pattern, which gives subsequent behaviour, even if substantially out of character, the feel of inevitability, and which comes to term in an unexpected, ego-supplanting form of self-marriage.

Visiting—Mystical Theology Set on Its Side

With both Plato and Teresa, hunger is the first instructor, the real source of dispositional formation. In Plato, one is trained toward a state of authentic appetite; this training, however, does not involve the adoption of an external set of desires, or a non-personal appetitive standard, but is the full articulation of an undeveloped, or malformed, keen appetite already in play—in Glaucon's case, it is his Achillean interest in honour. But once true philosophical eros appears—and with Glaucon, this can occur only once he comes to experience shame for totalitarian outcomes his essential longing urges—it is easily sufficient to push the one enmeshed in ideology past impossible obstacles. Desire for Teresa enables her to place the counsel of various cautious, skeptical advisors under examination, without privileging her own will. A loneliness for land, for sustaining chthonic relationship in this grey, late capitalist time, may be one of our deepest hungers, able to draw a person from the ersatz consolations of global culture, exposing these as ineffectual, inert before deeper need. The power of these consolations, indeed, stops at their ability to mask this unhappy, tireless desire. But hunger, severe examiner, once it, emboldened, clears the rewards of ideology and conservative caution, exposing them as sham states of homeostasis by simply lasting through them, disarmingly deepens and thrusts one into an emotionally trackless terrain. How to enter into relationship with something that actually completes one's human formation, to be caught in a true erotic teleology? And what will mark the way when this teleology must take place within a quest for autochthonicity? What will teach the rudimentary protocols of this relationship, apprenticeship to locale? The culture, in its present form, is committed to denying the existence of such needs.

For descendants of European settlers in North America, with their inherited problematic relationship to land, foundational philosophical appetite, I believe inevitably, involves such an apprenticeship to a particular place. In this work, one will pursue what resembles a mystical theology of non-ascent, one that's been laid, so to speak, on its side. We yearn precisely for what is elementally needful and yet out of range. The ministering land is what a culture of acquisition and mastery—and resulting chthonic anarchy—has driven away. It is possible that the larger self we miss and pursue is a terrain or locale.

At the beginning of the course I mentioned in the Introduction, I argue that there have been three great moments of human artistic engagement with the natural world—the Upper Paleolithic, represented by parietal art preserved in certain Western European caves; the nature poetry of T'ang Dynasty China and that poetry's antecedents; and twentieth-century North America from conservationalist writers like Aldo Leopold and Roderick Haig-Brown to bioregionalists like Gary Snyder, Charles Lillard, Donna Kane and Elizabeth Philips. I had believed previously that the artistic preoccupations of the Upper Paleolithic and mainstream modernity stood in antipodal relation: the Aurignacians and the cultures that followed were interested in the non-human world, the animals they hunted in particular, while we were enthralled largely with the discrete human individual. I see now I've misunderstood the mind in the cave: there are not two foci but one: Chauvet and Lascaux caves offer a more ample, intricate version of the self, the self in transfixed relation to the other-than-human. In eros, the self wants more of the self, not in repetition, but in attachment to the lost, essentially augmenting, fragment. For a self made by the anarchism of capital, what could it want more fundamentally than a rooting spot? Yet in the map of contemporary longing, considered from ideology's point of view, the place where this desire may be met is left blank, but is, in fact, the world of singular things.

It is difficult, yet formationally essential, I believe, to begin a feeding relationship to a place, for in such a relationship is the possibility of the non-atomized, non-central, ecological self, the individual augmented by a crucial, suppressed otherness. As with Platonic and Teresan contemplation, the first gestures in this reach involve quotidian practice, driven by a degree of courage—consider Teresa's resistance to various magisterial voices in order to listen to herself. One approaches this restoration by first simply visiting—looking at the trees on a particular slope, touching them, learning their names, taking them in through the senses, passing them through the various sensorial delectations acute attention makes available. You walk and perhaps lie down; your behaviour grows from a sense of pitched ontic loneliness. In this, eros' experience of poverty, on view in Teresa and Plato as well, human exceptionalism is set aside by the forceful spread of appetite. Autochthonous ascesis is convivial practice, which includes the non-human.

Such pandemic conviviality constitutes unusual behaviour, a heterodoxy of praxis that sets one to the side: to go to the world, you must leave the "world" of apparently sustaining meanings and observances, otherwise you are engaged with the merely scenic. As with Teresa and Plato, you are split off from what you were by out-of-range desire, and this separation is largely and deeply unwanted, even if the vector of eros or the violence of correction is unquestionable. For in chthonic return, erotic lift represents exile from a culture and a prescribed understanding of history that privileges certain humans. Only lonely hunger can carry you on this journey out—this and a conviction you are now without direction.

Under these conditions of poverty and exclusion, you necessarily attend broadly—visually, olfactorily, orally, haptically; your appetite teaches this alertness, the oddness of this permeability: and you pass all you learn through the various pleasures of the interior sensorium. Because my presence is historically, and actually in this moment, colonial, the land may step back before me—or, to say this more accurately, conditions in me will cause it continuously to recede. Nevertheless, my abjectness serves me here, a protean emptiness offering space for approach, and moreover I increasingly

sense in dim outline what would meet my need; further clarity comes as
confidence within heterodoxy grows. I hang around, loitering with loose
intent, wait and see what might come forward. I maintain, as a far as I am
able, a non-Romantic, apophatic anticipation: desire propels me into earth
apprenticeship, and the result of this enterprise is unimaginable.

It is important, I am coming to believe, in this apprenticeship, to learn
the original human language of one's place, at least to see that place through
the lens of ten-thousand-year-old Indigenous proper nouns. More of one's
terrain, it seems then, steps forward, as if in response to this linguistic courtesy. And, if invited, you may give yourself to some of the ceremonial
protocols rooted in your particular territory. Knowing and becoming may
emerge out of action in ritual, which itself is a sort of speaking of a place, and
from the decorum ceremony instigates and shapes.

Shang

The Mountain Poems of Hsieh Ling-yün reveal a phenomenology of a stirring autochthonous self, yet another pattern of contemplative maturation,
which shares some features with Platonic philosophical development, the
self led to the things themselves, and Teresan unitary mysticism. Hsieh
Ling-yün (385–433 CE) came from one of China's high aristocratic families,
and thus played an important role in the imperial court for the greater part
of his youth. But he had the misfortune to back the losing side in one of the
many internecine struggles that fractured the Chin Dynasty and was forced
into a shifting exile far from the capital of Chang'an.

In Yung-chia, the place of his initial banishment, shortly after his arrival,
he fell ill for a period of six months. During this period and subsequently,
he effectively abandoned the minor public post he had been assigned in
the distant province. In recovery, he was struck by the beauty of the place
where he found himself. He began a practice of roaming through the
mountains, recording his impressions as he moved. His passage to an idiosyncratic enlightenment, which he ultimately called *shang*, adoration, began
with deracination and social humiliation, together with physical debility.

Throughout, he lived in enforced solitude, the solitude of estrangement, the uncomfortable immurement of Teresa before the incomprehension of confessors, the solitude one finds oneself in once in the power of philosophical eros, outside the cognitional norm, befriended only by a yours-but-not-yours desire.

Hsieh Ling-yün's prolonged sickness, *divina afflictio*, at the beginning of his exile resembles Teresa's persistent illness in the early years of her contemplative life and is comparable to the extended malaise of Plato's rescued captive. Near the end of this dismantling of a version of the self, Hsieh experienced a moment of *catanyxis* with the horrific realization that up to this point he had wasted his life, and that he was, as a result, useless in his present circumstances.

ON A TOWER BESIDE THE LAKE

Quiet mystery of lone dragons alluring,
calls of migrant geese echoing distances,

I meet sky, unable to soar among clouds,
face a river, all those depths beyond me.

Too simple minded to perfect Integrity
and too feeble to plough fields in seclusion,

I followed a salary here to the sea's edge
and lay watching forests bare and empty.

That sickbed kept me blind to the seasons,
but opening the house up, I'm suddenly

looking out, listening to surf on a beach
and gazing up into high mountain peaks.

A warm sun is unraveling winter winds,
new yang swelling, transforming old yin.

Lakeshores newborn into spring grasses
and garden willows become caroling birds:

in them the ancient songs haunt me with
flocks and flocks and full lush and green.

Isolate dwelling so easily becomes forever.
It's hard settling the mind this far apart,

but not something ancients alone master:
that serenity is everywhere apparent here. (3)

His chief work in the new place became a physical practice of insertion
into the wild through walking (he invented a special sort of cleated shoe to
manage the heights), the visiting of isolated neighbours and locations. He
also completed an extensive mental mapping of his area, drawing on the
ancient names, and recorded it in the remarkable long poem "Dwelling in the
Mountains," this mapping an ascesis of naming as a sort of interior touching
of his terrain. In the course of this discipline of enacted intimacy with place,
he experienced moments of astonishment, which acted as a kind of Teresan
final cause. These slid into a state of adoration, which seemed to him to be
an unstable, yet rich, form of enlightenment or completion. He found himself
home, while remaining homeless: the world appeared as a broader version of
the self, the self as roughly indistinguishable from the mountains and rivers
it savoured.

Attention: A Postscript
Philosophical attention, in Plato's sense, illustrated in the captive's Odyssean
ordeal, erotic, contemplative, sets the quiescent self aside, and nudges one

into a state of appetite for something more—more complex, more interesting, beautiful, multiply engaging. This eros is sorrowful, momentumed,
wounded in the place where noetic rectitude would stand, impoverished
in its plans, yet, as Plato assures us in the *Symposium*, endlessly cunning.
Contemplative attention, eros, fully alert, wants home, the lost, more extensive self, enjoyed before division. The Teresan version of this severing is,
broadly speaking, lapsarian and its resolution is spousal; in Plato, at least
in the *Phaedrus*, it has the feel of an existential loss entailed in birth and
a forgetting of the pre-natal state of vision. Its healing is a return. In Hsieh
Ling-yün the division is the result of a commitment to a narrowly construed
politics, a politics that has no place for the esoteric. All these are ways of
describing the psychic experience of waking to deep deprival, are helpful
analogies for the recognition of loss and the sorrow of the truncated self. The
depictions of separation in Plato and Teresa, it is true, have a metaphysical
tone, but they are most fruitfully read as an inner heuristics. This is because
their origin and sphere are personal experience, and if they gesture toward
ontology, it is as completion of the ecstatic moment, an "it-is-as-if" report,
rather than as parts of a systematic account of being.

Contemplative attention, a state of interior poverty experienced as desire,
turns one toward what would economically feed, the self sensorially dilated
on the outside and inside in this state of realization and non-fulfillment,
fully prepared for delectation, exposed, then, in a state of erotic danger, yet
tumbling forward.

16
Faith and Land

Lecture at Canadian Mennonite University
May 2008

I WANT TO TELL YOU A LITTLE about my family.

What I have to say isn't meant as an extended biographical note, but is an attempt to think through certain cultural predicaments in Western Canada. The story I have to tell is one many others on the Prairies, I suspect, also could tell. It concerns my maternal grandparents, my mother's father, in particular. All thinking is a kind of autobiography, and autobiography always encompasses more than a single life.

This man, whose name was John Blaylock, and whom I remember as quiet, almost unsettlingly gentle (my mother reports he never struck, never shouted) and somehow abashed, came to Canada from one of the poorest districts of Industrial Revolution Birmingham in 1902, and worked for a couple of years for a farmer near Wolsely, Saskatchewan. Railways hadn't been laid yet into the southern part of the province—that's where he was headed—so he bided his time. There were no towns in that part of the world then; the land below the Pipestone River might not even have been surveyed before 1905. When he had saved enough money, he bought a team of oxen and drove them several days southwest through rolling aspen parkland to a homestead fifteen miles out of the newly established town of Creelman. The land, and the house he eventually built, were near a lake, called, in those days, Gooseberry Lake. Today it is nameless, touched by the same forces that have been removing names from the maps of Western Canada over the last forty years; it's now just a rather large slough, where pelicans often nest. There was a hotel at that place then and a dancehall nearby; people took the train out from Regina. The family sold eggs and cream to the hotel.

My grandfather married in 1908, meeting his wife, then a governess, in Boston, where he spent his winters because the possibilities for singing were so great in that city and the cold months on the plains so hard. By all reports, young John Blaylock had a beautiful voice. Things went well for the new couple: crops were good from the first days of homesteading through the 1920s in their area; they bought another farm of a quarter section around an hour away by horse. Times were rather fine for many in those early days: white settlement on the Canadian Prairies was proving to be, in fact, perhaps unsurprisingly, an extension of Europe, a cultural salient of Europe, which solved, completely, with miraculous speed, Europe's two most intractable social ills: landlessness and classism.

Many experienced the homestead years as euphoric as a result. They resemble—and this sounds, I admit, an unlikely comparison—the first days of Egyptian monasticism in the fourth century: a new way of life appeared to have been found. It must have been dizzying. Of course there was an incredible amount of work to be done, but this was set against all night dances in people's houses, local families providing the music, furniture piled in the yard; beef rings; the excitement of threshing crews coming for the rich crops; Christmas concerts at the school; horse-drawn cutters with heated stones set on the floor for warmth—autonomy and a bracing freedom flourished; a local culture was made up as people went along. I've heard tale after shimmering tale.

Then John Blaylock's wife, Florence Densely Blaylock, died, cervical cancer, in 1929. He was left to look after two farms and five children, and then the Depression hit. Soon the family was on the move from farm to rented farm, shedding children along the way, the girls sent out to work on local farms at thirteen and fourteen. "Necessity" (38), as Simone Weil called the steel edge of the world, came down hard. John Blaylock's escape from urban European poverty was brief and came only and very quickly to an entirely new sort of poverty on the blown-out plains.

My grandfather ended up an itinerant hand roaming from farm to ranch to farm through Western Canada. He had a little over twenty good years on the land, and, after this, his family was scattered everywhere and he was more or less homeless. He was never on the streets that I know, but he didn't own any of the places he occupied after 1931, a rented farm at Beemerside, the hired man's room on Gus Link's farm near Kipling—during the last years of the war, in his fifties, he was working on a ranch somewhere west of the Okanagan. I remember visiting him in a rooming house on a busy street in Regina when I was in my early teens. There was space for a bed and a chair and, I think, a small stand-up radio. He took his meals at a boarding house several blocks away.

Everything I write, I sense, is about this life or is somehow founded by this life. I am not completely sure I know what I am confessing when I say this, but the conviction is there. It comes from the feeling that when we give an account of a parent's or a grandparent's life we are offering a predictive rendering of our own. I don't mean that the earlier life is a template or a kind of fate, but I do want to register the sense that one's own days can seem an aspirational result or echo of others' days. Perhaps I am simply saying that essential tasks, those that are particularly difficult or seem foundational, can get spread over generations. The tricky, major work of autochthonicity doubt-less is one of these.

One of my grandfather's children, a daughter, my aunt Marjorie, married a farmer who managed to survive in farming in the area, and most of her descendants still live not far from the old homestead: four generations, a hundred years in my family's first place on this continent, a ragged beginning.

I now live in Victoria, where a remarkable discovery made it into the news last winter—a bison skeleton, found locally, carbon dated to 14,000 years ago. This find means that southern Vancouver Island likely was not under ice at that point, as before had been believed, but was prairie. Another interesting feature about this skeleton is that its spine is broken, strongly indicating human involvement in its death. There are other signs of what look like methodical butchery on the bones.

This would be surprising if it's true because, according to usual theories, there shouldn't be humans in this area then. The date is at least 5,000 years too early. Human beings should appear around the mouth of the Fraser, snaring salmon, digging clams and living in pit houses no more than 9,000 years ago, after the melting of the ice in the last glaciation. This is the account that accords with the conventional theory of the populating of the Americas—people crossed from Siberia on the Bering land bridge and scooted down the east side of the Rockies between two huge sheets of glacial ice, the Laurentide and the Cordilleran. The quick-footed immigrants eventually turned up in what is now eastern New Mexico, near the present town of Clovis, where they left their famous spear points at megafauna kill sites. Some of them then, after a few thousand years, curved back up north to invent and perfect the crafts of the fish trap, of whale harpooning and the buffalo pound.

It's likely now that the earliest date for human settlement eventually will be pushed back from the 12,000 years ago date the traditional Clovis First theory calls for. The first humans on the North American continent, more than a few scientists now believe, possibly came by boat along the coast, though, no doubt, they moved on foot in and through various ice-free refugia. They weren't explorers; it's probable that the first people did not think they were in a new place at all, but in a reach of the old place, north east Asia, Beringia—thus the absence in Indigenous legends of mention of migration. Archeological dates for human settlements in that area, eastern Siberia down to the Amur River, are very old, 30–40,000 years old, even older if you move farther south into northern China or a little farther west in Siberia, into the Altai Mountains region, where Neanderthal sites have been unearthed in the last few years.

Evolving controversies in the world of North American archeology aside, non-Europeans have been here—this place thought of as including old Beringia, the North Pacific, as well as the coast and possibly the prairies of Western Canada—a very long time, between 40,000 and 14,000 years versus 100 years or so for European settlers. There is a form of belonging to land that is deeper than having a local address. It could be called chthonic citizenship, earth-belonging. Residence may give you a bit of familiarity, but it alone doesn't offer you this sort of attachment, the feeling or sense you flow from the ground where you stand, that this ground has taken you in and names you and comforts you, that a particular place is a sort of larger version of your own body.

I once made a fifty-dollar bet with a class of first-year philosophy students at St. Peter's College, where I taught during the 1990s. The students were third- and fourth-generation denizens of rural north central Saskatchewan. The bet was that they couldn't name five indigenous species growing in Wolverine Creek valley, which we could see easily from the windows of our third-floor classroom. Philosophy professors say the strangest things, perversely saving the oddest for the fifteen minutes before lunch. Wolverine Creek, by the way, flowing behind the Benedictine Abbey south of Muenster is the northwest tip of the Assiniboine River's drainage. The Wolverine, never more than a small stream, passes into Last Mountain Lake, which feeds into the Qu'appelle. I was pretty sure I'd keep my crisp, red bill safely in my wallet because I guessed there were only a couple of people in the whole province then who could win this bet, the naturalist Trevor Herriot and the novelist Sharon Butala.

But chthonic citizenship is an even deeper enfolding into the land than terrain literacy, and while it is assisted by long-term residency and includes this literacy, it requires something more, a particular form of interior or epistemological practice, a certain sort of looking. This is the lifelong, daily attention of the hunter and gatherer, fixed, alert, pliant, empty, permeable,

drinking in day by day the lay of the land. Empty, alert, welcoming everything, the mind of those people who ran down that bison many years ago
at the foot of the Sooke Hills—this is the fixity in which any land, in all its
characteristics, unfailingly impresses itself deeply and transformatively on
human consciousness.

Few know this sort of attention as an economic necessity now—we
no longer need this sort of openness to survive—but this doesn't mean it's
entirely foreign to us. What does this description of a kind of caughtness, a
being alert, an absorption, look like? Something flickers in the noetic operation as we imagine it; clearly it resembles something we do know. I believe
it resembles prayer. I don't mean liturgical prayer or petitionary prayer or
confessional or praise prayer or vocal prayer of any sort, but contemplative prayer. This is the prayer Teresa of Avila describes in her *Interior Castle*,
say, or Meister Eckhart talks of in his sermons, or Aelred of Rievaulx in his
Speculum Caritatis (*The Mirror of Charity*). The hunter-gatherer mind
shares a form with the transfixed mind. Chthonic citizenship requires we
bring this sort of contemplative keenness, the optic power of the heart, to
the place where we happen to live. If we don't bring this sort of seeing to our
engagement with where we find ourselves, length of residence won't bring
us home to it. We still won't know the names of those plants even after a
hundred generations: we'll be filled only with the shimmer and distraction of
whatever global commercial culture remains.

So being deeply in a place requires some psychic labour, a work in the soul;
in fact it demands, I believe, what amounts to an impossible labour, which
has at least three elements. The first of these is turning away from what
clamours, reaches for attention and splits this attention into a thousand pieces,
turning away and stowing this dispersive force in a cloud of forgetting, as
another early contemplative would have said. This particular work is called
anachoresis by the old monastics of Egypt like Evagrius or John the Solitary,
the gift of withdrawl, retraction of the ego with its stickiness, its credulity
and omnivorous appetite; and there are many spiritual exercises that make
this sequestering of focus possible; one of these, ascetical manuals call "modesty

of the eyes." The necessary labour also involves stability, a staying putness, a prime, elemental contemplative state, an ascetical, politically charged state in the anarchism of capitalism. And lastly the needed work involves a resuscitation of the spirit and gnosis of contemplation in a Christianity that's been preoccupied by doctrinal clarifications and the construction of coherent, complete theological systems since the Arian controversy in the fourth century. This last requirement is perhaps the most tricky, the one most difficult to imagine happening. And these unlikely achievements must occur roughly simultaneously, not serially. I don't mean to suggest obligation here, but to express a hunch about an inevitable pattern.

No wonder so many diasporic Europeans in North America have bolted into Eastern religions, known through accommodating English translations, or into an equally flattering creative animism or Christian literalism or into some other placating, endearing devotion. This behaviour fits with the prevailing imperial spirit of perpetual movement and protean self-service. A hard, almost unimaginable labour of retrieval, withdrawal and unmodern attention awaits anyone who wishes to stay within the Western tradition and settle truly where she is. Why would anyone want to pick up this deep work? Why not just head for the world of continental and global trading and consuming systems, where everything is carefully straightforward and encouragingly, universally the same, and nothing requires a penetrating gaze? Everything there, in fact, shuffles off such a look, gives it back, with a kind of unintended honesty; there is nothing within the objects in that context or their arrangement that can hold the full weight of our affections, and so the things, with a sort of eerie truthfulness, shake off our complete love, leaving us interiorly unhoused, exactly nowhere.

I don't mean to suggest, by the way, that chthonic citizenship is possible only if it is built on Christian contemplative practice. This is simply my particular, almost-fogotten home. The beginning of this citizenship can be built on any spiritual or esoteric tradition deeply, authentically heard. But Christianity has a particular work to do now in the New World, a work of re-invention and retrieval.

Some of us will choose this labour of tackling the tasks, three or more, contributing to embeddedness, because we are thirsty, lonely for where we are, and feel helpless in this. We want that strange, vivifying friendship with a terrain, grove of trees, want something to talk to us this way; we want to lose the unnerving sense some of us have of floating. We want some other, more exact, yet commodious, identity uttered into us. And also some will pick this work up because they are in terror of what we will do as we act in our usual state of disengagement and hovering, using the land as if it weren't our greater bodies—pesticide use, mono-cropping, oil sands and so on.

These are, I admit, peculiar ideas in our particular cultural context. This is a good sign for the ideas. The strangeness indicates the philosophical standing of the ideas. As Plato reminds us (in the *Phaedrus*), there are madnesses that are not to be feared, but that are beneficent, in fact gifts. Lyrical imagination is one of the kind, seizing insanities; poetry, as a result, is one of the places that welcomes strange talk, poetry acting as a repository, a room for augmenting peculiarity. This makes poems devices of unusual political power: through them, the unlike appears.

Poetry, as a transformative, political instrument, cuts two ways, into the author as much or more than the reader. I worked on a collection of poems called *Moosewood Sandhills* in the early 1990s. The book comes from that time in my life when I first realized, with a shock, that I had no skill to be where I was. One of the poems in that collection is called "How to Be Here?" This is a question that has preoccupied me now for almost twenty years. It seems to be our central political and cultural question, though it is rarely, if ever, asked.

I published *Orphic Politics*, another book of poems, in 2008. It tracks a period of illness I went through, 2004 to 2007. Much could be said about sickness in the project of meditative absorption. All contemplative traditions speak of the importance of kenosis, *mortificatio*, the necessary breaking down of the self, because, as Pseudo-Dionysius the Areopagite says, all human thinking about divinity is "a kind of error." Or, as Nicholas of Cusa says, there is not even the possibility of analogy with God—which makes, perhaps, even the doctrine of the Trinity chiefly a way of making sense of interior experience. Illness—*divina afflictio*—can be a kind of effacing preparation for shapeless, spreading attention. Illness, or losing much, can be part of the pattern of contemplative fixity, a feature of this phenomenology. Illness can have this meaning; and if it is read in this way, it, too, has political power.

LATE SUMMER ENERGY

Sunflowers, wet sparrows,
grind in their throats into a vinegar fog over the ground,
where Pythagoras lies, stroking the bear,
putting fruit and bread into its mouth, whispering to it;
they're on the second terrace, under the dried Chinese lantern plants,
disguised as dog-range invisibilities, fox not quite turned
                    into people, the last Final Causes;
in the bear's skull, the ordered light returns
and rims correctly. Pythagoras has planted
three two by fours into the bear, who has been eating people recently,
                    to fingernail the cosmos' veering, fluid weight,
until Being's own speed treasurechest will cradle it.
Fruit and bread, touching the hair around the mouth.
The bear scents the swooping slosh of crowned, deeply thighed light
that corners and corners in him; he will soon follow a braid of it
                    up the gathering mountain,
and we, in the houses, will taste our sickness rising
                    on ladders from skin lakes. (Orphic Politics 62)

Poetry receives aberrance, heterodoxy, "madnesses" (Plato, *Phaedrus* 244A), not as a place of containment or a hospital, but as a reliquary holds bone shards; poetry houses the unusual in such a way that the transformative power of the anomalous is exposed. Indeed poetry releases this power—which is inert or even destructive outside poetry, outside inspired diagnosis, outside prediction and outside erotic love, Plato's four benefi-cent, self-building, culture-building derangements. Poetry releases the power of the heterodox, of the appetite-haunted insight, and in fact serves as its maieutically enhancing instrument, whereby this slightly unsettling power may disassemble de-eroticizing certitudes, make a person strange, new, fixed. Poetry may disarm and thrust you into an intimate unusualness. Then trans-gression names, bringing breathtaking identity, and, as this, it heals—that is it brings together parts separated. It breeds a permeability that will allow one to hear whatever might speak, including a piece of land. Poetry, intently yielded to, can lift the furniture in a room.

17
Nothingness

Summer 2010

The high priest Hilkiah said to Shaphan the secretary, "I have found the book of the law in the house of the Lord." When Hilkiah gave the book to Shaphan, he read it.

Then Shaphan the secretary came to the king, and reported to the king, "Your servants have emptied out the money that was found in the house, and have delivered it into the hand of the workers who oversee the house of the Lord." Shaphan the secretary informed the king, "The priest Hilkiah has given me a book." Shaphan then read it aloud to the king.

—2 KINGS, 22.8–10

GIGANTIC INSECT AND BUFFALO herd shapes of clouds move through eastern Alberta into Saskatchewan, as canola stands in bloom and roads are washed away farther east; it is the wettest June on the prairies in years. It's just beginning to dawn on people that we are entering an era of extreme weather, the likely result of climate change. I am driving south on Highway 38 near the Sheercross coal-powered generating station, a heavy, six cable line dipping between X-shaped towers on the east side of the road, then crossing over to the west, land on either side mostly empty pasture, grass and wild flowers thick and plush. I am heading for Gleichen, where I will gas up, check the oil, then turn south again, keeping clear of Calgary, now in Stampede week.

|| Christendom seems on the point of being used up. Ten Anglican churches were closed in Victoria last year; others will follow. Sexual crimes and their cover-ups have undermined the Catholic Church. Christianity in late capitalism seems to be withering away as the state was said to do in mature communism. This strikes many as both inevitable, in a cultural evolutionary sense, and welcome, an old hegemonic limit to individual freedom at last meeting its end. The just and only real arbiter of behaviour, the unassisted, unsubsidized rationality and will of individual persons, has emerged, the apotheosis of historical change, as the unchallenged source of human action. Here is the victory of intelligence and human maturity; the church, insofar as it has any role to play in the contemporary world, now exists as an anachronistic assisted living arrangement for the credulous and timid.

Yet the individual alone, at least in these days, seems incapable of generating ethical grace; instead, what is brought forward for admiration from that place is an apparently unfoolable cunning, often clothed as irony. Yet the fear of Thomas Hardy, agnostic, though "churchy," still seems prescient, that without a Christianity shaped largely by a tradition of contemplative practice the West would lack a moral substratum or aquifer, and this absence over time would brutalize culture. In this country what we most admire for their powers of amelioration—free access to medical care, for instance, a tolerant multi-culturalism, an ambition for social equality—comes from a mild socialism in the middle years of the twentieth century that had its roots in a particular savouring of the New Testament in places like a certain

Baptist church in Weyburn, Saskatchewan that, during the Great Depression, was under the charge of Tommy Douglas. Yet the psalms sung at vespers every late afternoon, last sun coming through blue bands in the stained glass window at St. Peter's Abbey, still sound sweet.

I turned sixty this June and, without putting much planning into it, spent the weeks around my birthday wandering through places in Saskatchewan that meant something to me, Thunder Creek valley, where Helen's parents have a farm; my hometown of Regina, where I went to university and where I experienced the conversion that made me a Catholic; and St. Peter's College, where I taught philosophy for fourteen years. I have been trying, I suppose, to tie things together in these peregrinations, to make it all somehow cohere. Some elements, however, resist any tug toward explanatory shape. I am unrelievedly puzzled by the evanescence of the apparently permanent bearing walls of my early life, rural Saskatchewan, the church, my family. All that is solid melts into air. And I am puzzled, as well (what conceivable architecture makes this possible?), and disconcerted by the strange spectacle of the mammoth civilization in which I live resting on a surprisingly thin, unenergized noological base. I spent part of one afternoon in the old Regina Cemetery trying to find the graves of my paternal grandparents—which turned out to be nowhere near where I thought they would be. A helpful cemetery worker tracked down the small white stone for me of Hugh and Mary Lilburn, at the northwest edge of the large graveyard, he dying in 1947 and she in 1953, immigrants from a small holding near Dromore, Northern Ireland, citizens of Regina, janitor and homemaker, for the last third of their lives. I stared at the stone, which surely no one has visited in decades, for some time, looking for a kind of clue. Something is here and it is true, but it does not manifest itself as clarity. The lightness I experienced before the stone—perpetual, it seems, irresolvable—is part of what it means to be a member of settler society in North America.

|| I am reading Marguerite Porete's *The Mirror of Simple Souls* this summer. I have been wanting to stray into it for years. Once in, I encountered a

texture or flavour of thought that resembled what I had found in Meister Eckhardt and John Ruusbroec, the spectacle of the confident, luminous, limitless individual self, the full stretch of that one's desire reaching out beyond the reductions of authority.

Marguerite Porete was burned to death in Paris at the Place de Grève on June 1, 1310. In her condemnation, she, a beguine, was referred to as a "pseudo-mulier" (false or fake woman), charged with being a relapsed heretic and the author of a book "filled with errors and heresies" (Porete 5). This book, the longer title of which is *The Mirror of Simple, Annihilated Souls and Those Who Remain Only in Will and Desire of Love*, begins with an address to the author's particular reader by Love on behalf of the Soul which has been "lifted to the seventh stage of grace," the very interiority this work has the power to help shape. "As for you actives and contemplatives, and perhaps those annihilated by true love, you will hear some powers of pure love, of noble love, of the high love of the Unencumbered Soul; how the Holy Spirit has placed his sail in her as if she were his ship" (80).

Marguerite Porete's book was condemned twice. At some point between 1296 and 1306, it was denounced by Guy of Colmieu, Bishop of Cambrai, who ordered that the volume be burnt in the presence of its author. She then was warned to cease distributing any other copies of the work that may exist on pain of death. But Porete continued to send transcriptions of *The Mirror* to other bishops, religious and lay people. The problems with the book, from the Church's perspective, were both doctrinal and political. Some of its claims appeared to resemble those made by followers of the condemned Free Spirit movement; but action against the book and its author likely was part of a larger effort to suppress or control semi-autonomous, non-cloistered religious groups, in the early years of the fourteenth century, including certain types of beguines. The chief target of this campaign, however, from the point of view of civil authorities and their ecclesiastical supporters, was the Knights Templar, who had grown increasingly powerful and who controlled significant tracts of land.

The beguines grew out of the new spirit of humanism spreading through northern Europe in the late years of the twelfth century and, further, out of a revolutionary understanding of religious practice that favoured an apostolic, preaching form of life over a cloistered, purely contemplative one. It was chiefly a movement of women, though some men, called beghards, were also members. The women tended to live together in semi-regulated, formal communities, some of which were quite large. The Great Beguinage of Paris, established in 1264 with the support of the French crown, housed over four hundred women, some living a community life in dormitories, others in houses they had built, all surrounded by a wall. There was an infirmary, school and well within the enclosure; women came and went from the area with relative ease. A mistress and her council governed the whole community. The Dominican prior of Paris provided spiritual support when required.

Women who chose to live outside of such communities, as Marguerite Porete did, had none of the civil and ecclesiastical support the enclosed beguines of Paris enjoyed. Mendicant orders like the Franciscans, exemplars of the new apostolic religious way, were instructed to shun these often solitary wanderers. Marguerite Porete gives no clues in her book about how she maintained herself and where she lived, but she was clearly unconnected to any fixed group. She was an itinerant conversationalist in northern France and Belgium, moving within a loose group of interlocutors, a collection of friends and auditors that appears to have been broad. When she was re-arrested in 1310, she was detained with the beghard Guiard de Cressonessart, who presented himself as her defender. He, however, "confessed" to heresy once both were threatened with death while in custody. Marguerite Porete maintained a complete silence through the three months of her imprisonment and trial.

|| *The Mirror of Simple Souls* is both a phenomenology, that is, an account of interior conversations making up a single life, and a helpful guide. It is a treatment of the humbling of rationality and a healing of the strain and distortion that "Reason" suffers as the controlling existential power, by

placing it under the governance of its "mistresses," love and faith. It is the
story of the affairs of the human within this new economy and a description
of the "unencumbering" of the soul, slipping free from Reason's deter-
mined decorum, the moral norm arising from a certain logic associated with
Christian Aristoteleanism.

> Love: This Soul by such love, says Love herself, can say to the Virtues that for
> a long time and for many days she has been in their service.
> Soul: I confess it to you, Lady Love, says this Soul, that there was a time when
> I belonged to them, but now it is another time. Your courtliness has placed me
> outside their service. And thus to them I can now say and sing:

> > Virtues, I take my leave of you forever,
> > I will posses a heart most free and gay;
> > Your service is too constant, you know well.
> > Once I placed my heart in you, retaining nothing;
> > You know that I was to you totally abandoned,
> > I once was a slave to you, but now am delivered from it. (84)

Marguerite Porete's "annihilated soul," her "unencumbered soul," possesses
Evagrian impassivity, taking "account of neither shame nor honour, of neither
poverty nor wealth, of neither anxiety nor ease." (84) This soul is willess,
living "by understanding, by Love and by praise," beyond, as she makes clear
in the passage quoted above, the dominion of the virtues. Such a soul has
twelve names; among them are the very marvelous one, the not understood,
the foundation of the church, the destroyed by humility. Her final names
are oblivion, forgotten (87–88). Her choosing, her erotic motion, is that of
"Farnearness," the divinity in inchoate apophatic focus, and her state is unconsoled, insufficient, full: she possesses all, she possesses nothing; she knows
all, she knows nothing; her thought is in a rest place, which she identifies as
the Trinity, but this thought is an opacity since it does not report the ipseity

or location of this power that contains and supplants the core of the self. The annihilated soul is not comprehensible to the Church, nor is she identified wholly by herself, even as she intuitively moves, the virtues serving her in her drunkenness. Hers is a loaned inebriation, an osmosis effect driven by the delirium of divinity ("But the clearest wine, the newest, the most profitable, the most delicious and the most intoxicating is the wine from the tap at the top. This is the supreme beverage which none drinks but the Trinity" [106]). The unconsoledness of this soul does not budge, though she swims in a sea of joy. She is not-Church, not-individualism, a third possibility.

Soul: ...what He possesses is more mine than what I possess or ever will. (113)

Love: ...if you understand perfectly your nothingness, you will do nothing, and this nothingness will give you everything.... (115)

Soul: ...since He will never love...eternally anything without me, I say therefore that it follows that He never loved anything without me. In addition, since He will be in me through love forever, therefore I have been loved by Him without beginning.
Reason: Watch what you say, Lady Soul! (116)

|| Who after Kant is not an epistemologist? Who after, say, Gershom Scholem is not at least a little curious about the gnostic powers of the affections? It might be tempting to suppose that Marguerite Porete's reconstruction of human interiority corrects Plato's tripartite soul outlined in the *Republic*. But such a supposition would misconstrue Plato, for all three of the soul's powers in that anthropology—reason, spiritedness and appetitive force—are unmistakably erotic, with a certain sort of rationality, the formed soul's chief faculty, a sensuous organ, ravishable by the beauty beyond being, seeking that beauty with an asymptotic hunger. But by Marguerite Porete's time, reason had lost access to this range of longing.

|| The deepest knowing is savouring—a savouring that is double. The two forms of understanding, or enjoyment, delectations of the ear that is inner, leagued in delight with the one outer, are amplifications, adumbrations of one another, as memory stands to experience though not with the unvarying sequentiality of this relation. Contemplative savouring is intensified, brightened, made nimble by the sensorial.

This means only the individual is authentically knowable and real since nothing courts the interior mouth, for example, the heart's sense of taste, as specificity does. And if haecceity is presence, as Emmanuel Levinas suggests, all knowing, whatever it may call itself, is theology. Another way to make this claim: if noesis is non-erotic, it is bogus (and perhaps dangerous), and all eros is theological.

> Reason: Ah, Lady Love, says Reason, what do you call wise?
> Love: The one in the abyss of humility, says Love.
> Reason: Ah Love, ...who is the one in the abyss of humility?
> Love: The one...who has no injustice in anything and knows
> he has no righteousness in anything. One who is in this understanding of his
> injustice sees so clearly that he sees himself beneath all creatures in a sea of
> sin....
> Love: ...And so she has thus lost all her senses in this practice to the point
> that she knows not how to seek nor how to find God, nor even how to conduct
> herself....She must be excused from everything.
> Fear: Ah Love...where is such a Soul since she is no longer with herself?
> Love: She is where she loves, says Love, without her feeling it. (120–21)

This image of the unconscious, unlocated, probing, erotic soul resembles the portrait of the lamentable, confused, stubborn, wayward adept in the *Tao te Ching*. A sort of sprawl and a stupidity, from a distance, marks this life even for the one who leads it.

|| What will characterize contemporary interior practice, the mystical theology, that particular account of yearning, of the late twentieth century, the early twenty-first century? How may it seem from the distance of a hundred years? Surely one of its features will appear to be a preoccupation with the human estrangement from the natural world, that loneliness; another will be a raw, barely articulable inclination to hasten the ascesis of decolonization, this driven, on the settler side, in part, by the sense that suppressed memory of theft fogs all understanding. It thus will seem a mystical milieu saturated with unappeasable ontological mourning. And it likely will stand out for its mistrust of instrumental, hegemonic rationality and a search for a reconstructed, realigned cognition, which, as it becomes less Romantic, may appear more Pythagorean. It will be distinguished by anachoresis, daemonic withdrawal, as all contemplative eras are, differing only in the intensity of the custody claimed over the interior sensorium. The custody exercised in this time, I suspect, will be recognized as light, protean, informal, unsuspicious of conviviality.

|| Marguerite Porete's example and her examination of the operation of "fine love" on the annihilated soul rescues us from the trap of a naïve vitalism, a mythological affective epistemology driven by the "heart" and intuition, which confuses certain preferences for insight, though Porete's way itself lies in the emotions and is intuitive. It is, that is, savouringly attentive, discerning, absorbed by what catches and anagogically moves, rather than systematic and deonotological. The root of this discernment is the confusion, the not-knowingness of her annihilated soul. This ascesis, an inevitably dispositional practice arising from being love, yields an ontology, for the unencumbered soul knows the world only as sufficient and so exquisite as to be "hers." This alignment or address to being urges a decorum that is richer than ethics.

|| When one, without personal will, takes on the affective life of the Trinity, she fully comprehends the world, even while she remains in a state of shifting ignorance. The Holy Spirit, in *The Mirror of Simple Souls*, addresses

Love on the affairs of the soul in this way—"all that I possess is of the Father and the Son. And since she possesses all that I have, and the Father and the Son have nothing which I do not have in myself, says Love, thus this Soul possesses in her, says the Holy Spirit, the treasure of the Trinity, hidden and enclosed within her" (122). Note the overlapping of the speech of Love and the Trinitarian third person. The noetic deposit born in this overlaying makes the soul the true church, for Marguerite Porete, and Holy Church becomes "Holy-Church-Below-This-Church."

|| Marguerite Porete distinguishes between those who are "lost," obedient to reason and the virtues, while still and surely saved, and those who are "sad," who remain in will and desire, attentive to the practice of the virtues, yet plucked by an intimation that a region lies beyond. Indeed this comprises the wisdom of the soul in the second state, a persistent sense that an additional band of experience exists. This belief, however, "gives them so little understanding and sufficiency in their being that they maintain instead that they are miserable and sad" (134), in a state of unbroken longing.

The annihilated soul enters a disposition beyond this penthic absorbedness as she wills nothingness and "this nothingness...gives all things" (154) to her. From it the soul receives her real name, which is the absence of a name, since this soul is the fluid state, unstable, unnominable, in which love transforms her. The work of this soul, therefore, in part, is astonishment, "pondering nothing about the nearness of Farnearness" (159). She is wealthy and impoverished, inert, attentive, everywhere, obedient to the slightest touch, unmovable, indifferent to enemies, owned by all that is, owning all. This is the self upon which the wealth of what the church knows falls, one source, in its unknowing, of moral beauty. Let the church, indeed, be overcome, but not by the powers of the liberal, assertive, Enlightenment, autonomous self alone. There is too much that would be lost in such a victory; all that is included in interiority and its politics, our current central need, is endangered by it.

Epilogue

At the Foot of ẈMÍEŦEN

BEHIND THE SHED where I read and think, a ferned cliff, its
Garry oak and Native plum, hold language as pitchers hold water. Some of
this speech, I am told, is older than the time of trees and ferns; some nouns
come from before the last glaciation. Humans didn't make these words, but
the land itself, seeking linguistic form, did. If you know them, you can sense
the words move in the trees, flowers and stones; and in this state of perceived
animation, they become porous to human attention, somewhat more available in a convivial way to you—ĆEN̲IŁĆ (Garry oak), ȾEXEN IŁĆ (Native
plum).

   To come to this place, to see it as an aide, indeed one's extended body, to
arrive at its essential language, *prisca sapientia*, I've discovered, you must
set out from a point of courtesy that can be reached, among other routes,
through revivified contemplative practices that once stood at the center of
European thought but that are now suppressed or forgotten. The renovation of Western philosophy required to imagine a post-imperial world is a

work that is substantial and, while dislocating, delightful. This re-making
cannot be achieved by invention but only by a retrieval, exact as possible,
of lost cultural parts. It will entail the resuscitation of a larger version of the
self, deepened interiority that is sustained by conversation with a range of
interlocutors, not all of them human. I have tried to track such a return in
this book by reading and enacting the phenomenologies of some of the
West's masters on the inner life from Plato to Ibn 'Arabi, Teresa of Avila and
Marguerite Porete.

The writing of these contemplatives holds a residue of the wisdom of
the Upper Paleolithic, its caves, juniper wick lamps, vulture wingbone flutes,
ochre handprints and long narratives, our oldest extant thought, receiving it
through orphism and Pythagoreanism, then through Diotima, Plotinus, Jesus,
Mohammed and Benedict of Nursia. Savouring these inner routes can be a
discipline of pre-conversation for diasporic Europeans in North America, and
may bring them to a place where they may be ready for plunging interior
exchange with First Nations interlocutors drawing on the restored ceremonies, should these people be willing to be partners in conversation. Here
is where the undergoing of events like Porete's nothingness may take us.
This place of possible daemonic exchange would be close to the old interior sensibility of the first symbolizing homo sapiens, Aurignacians and
their cousins farther east, from whom both groups ultimately come. The
orphic retrieval I hope for and seek will help, at least, to place both parties
on similar psychagogic pages, lifting the block on the European side that has
existed from before contact. A self that is "non-discursive, uncalculative, intuitive, mystical" (53), in the words of the Cree thinker Joseph Couture, a self
embodying a non-Cartesian style of rationality, becomes possible. Such a self
issues, says Couture, from the "emptying of self through attentiveness."

Autochthonicity is a long, likely uncompletable walk; meanwhile climate
change, the new reality, presses us. Will there be sufficient time, as seas rise
and species meet extinction, to achieve the dispositional changes that will
return us to the land? This seems to me the wrong question. A better one
is, what does justice now ask of us? For me it is an ascesis of contemplative

acts within the natural world, which offers no strategic efficiency, yet nevertheless contains within itself the germ of the sole durable politics. It also
could foster a conversational permeability, a Levinasian spirit of infinity. The
re-said parts of the orphic tradition in this book, re-staged, passed through
the body, can produce a modest ability to listen.

‖ I spend the morning pulling invasive species on the west slope of the
mountain, Scotch broom, ivy, Spurge Laurel, Himalayan blackberry, all
plants newcomers brought to this island to remind them of home. The
vegetative expression of untreated nostalgia, an emotion allowed to speak
over other feelings, digs into the land. The alien plants now spread over
the cliffs without check. Winter, during the rains, is the best time to attack
them, when the ground is saturated. But even then some of the stalks are
so large, you can only clip them at the base with the big secateurs and hope
for the best. If left unattended, the broom and ivy would cover the mountain, the ivy adept at smothering and killing trees. It's especially thick at
the northwest boundary of the park where it abuts a block of houses, some
homeowners encouraging it to climb their front yard oaks. You must exercise caution when extracting ivy and laurel here since a few of the residents
find this activity suspicious, encroaching, a sneaking up on their property.
Yanking broom and pulling English ivy is like removing colonial names
from land forms. On municipal maps W̲MIEŦEN is called Mt. Tolmie after a
Hudson's Bay Company employee; it is one of many sites is southern British
Columbia and Washington State that bear the fur trader's name.

‖ I first met Kevin Paul in the mid-1990s when he was a young poet
studying in the University of Victoria's Department of Writing with Lorna
Crozier, Patrick Lane and Derk Wynand. I was visiting Victoria to give a
reading and asked him to send me some of his work, since I was then poetry
editor at *Grain*. I was bowled over by the early poems I had seen, many of
which made it into his first book *Taking the Names Down from the Hill*,
which went on to win the Dorothy Livesay Prize. This book was followed

by *Little Hunger*, which received a Governor General's Award nomination. Both books are attempts to express the nature of w̲SÁNEĆ culture and sensibility in the peculiar medium of the English lyric poem. I believe Kevin is one of the most talented writers of his generation. I re-met him in 2004 when I came to the University of Victoria to teach, and we've been good friends since. He became my language teacher a few years back, and I meet with him every few weeks to learn SENĆOŦEN, the original tongue of the Saanich Peninsula.

The language for me has proved to be a singular gift. The illness I fell into when I came to the coast was partly the result of an estrangement from the land. I didn't know how to be in my new place, to be fed by it, to be connected to it so that, through it, I could fully breathe. My enacted self felt as though it bounced back to me off the surface of things here. I've had some difficulty learning the primal language of this peninsula, especially its "under the tongue" sounds, which imitate, Kevin tells me, the sound of rocks loosened and played by the tidal ebb and flow; these sounds, he assures me, always give w̲NIETEM (newcomers, people who came from nowhere) difficulty. Initially the language drew me as a way to extend my friendship with Kevin, but as I mastered more nouns a surprising bounty appeared.

With the appropriate names for things, the trees, birds, plants "opened their eyes," or so it seemed. This animation was a reduction of the distance between objects in the land and me, as well as an apparent shuffling aside on the part of oaks, stones, salal, which permitted space for me in the forest. While I struggle to speak phrases in conversation with my teacher, SENĆOŦEN remains for me largely a chthonic language; I use it to address the place in which I live. It is a potent and calming pneumatic tool; the language seems to me to be a living being, instructor, trail-sharer, friend, source of companionable beauty, a larger, autonomous, communicating mind. And Kevin's instruction has given me the true names for landforms I look at and walk in—P,KOLS (white tip mountain), TENE̲N (stirred, moved, slope), TIQENE̲N (place of blessing). By these names, I believe I have been introduced to some of the presences within this land, so that a relationship can enter its earliest stages. As well as being a poet, Kevin stands at the center of a project of language restoration on the Saanich Peninsula and the Gulf Islands. With linguist Timothy Motler and other native speakers within his community, he is working to complete the first SENĆOŦEN dictionary, as well as a collection of traditional stories. This is courageous political, world-building work. From the names, the land beneath the used land rises up.

The land, from which language emerges to end up in human mouths, and its creatures, in the world Kevin occupies, are also themselves performers of ceremonies, custodians of insight.

CEREMONY

A crow walks
its muddy
kneeless walk
across
a freshly ploughed field.

In this light,
I see the crow
as crows are –

so much seems possible. (11)

When creatures and humans mix, identity and placedness are born, as happens in this fragment from "When the Mask Opens."

Inside the raven's mouth
an ancient man's face is carved,
capturing the moment he wept
large tears, potent enough
to put us here forever.

Whatever we call ourselves now.
Whatever we will call ourselves.
It was that ancient man inside the
raven's mouth, driven by loneliness
to despair, who put us here forever. (14)

‖ It's the May long weekend, northern Alberta, and I am at Joseph P. Cardinal's camp on the Saddle Lake reserve, about to be put out on my first fast. Peter Butt, Francis Whiskeyjack and I have spent the morning cutting young willows to construct our lodges. The willow poles have to be sturdy enough to bear the weight of a tarp and any rain or snow that may collect on it, yet sufficiently supple to be bent and tied by their own branches to another pole two yards away. I have just erected the skeleton of my lodge, and I lie inside it to see if I have the right measurements—the space must contain my sleeping bag and me. As I lie, looking up at trees and sky through the grid of tied willows, I think with an electric shock of surprise: this is where I have wanted to be for decades.

Louise Halfe, over coffee at a place on Broadway Avenue in Saskatoon months earlier, had extended me the great honour of inviting me to come with her and her husband, Peter, to the camp of her elder Joe, and join in the May ceremonies. She and I had been friends for years and met frequently to talk about poetry and interior matters feeding poetry. This was the first time we had spoken of the fast, a three- to four-day period you pass in silence, in the bush, with no food or water, under the guidance and protection of an elder. Fasting, she said, was preparing for death, the practice of dying. OK, I thought, I've heard that phrase before; it came from the mouth of Socrates. This was philosophy's work.

Joe Cardinal had begun a sweat lodge on his reserve in 1971, after he had met and been instructed by the great Arapaho elder Raymond Harris. This was twenty years after the ban against spiritual ceremonies had been lifted in revisions of the Indian Act. Sixty years of suppression of ceremonies and two generations of the residential school system meant that very few in the community observed the old protocols. In 1983, Joe added Cree practices to the Arapaho sweat he'd learned in Wyoming. I draw these details of Joe's history from an essay on healing by Ross Hoffman, who joined us that long weekend in the bush.

I have not met or been taught by many like Joe Cardinal. Only a pair of Benedictines, the Cistercian Ambrose Davidson and the hermit James Gray, approach him, but really, Joe was in a class of his own as a teacher, a master capable of triggering liberating insight, though he would always claim any healing did not come from him. He was part of a remarkable generation on Saddle Lake reserve that included Joe Couture, Harold Cardinal, Eugene and Mike Steinhauer, along with Joe's wife, Jenny, involved in the restoration of the old spiritual ways. I am still meditating on what he said to me after twenty years.

Philosophy has another work: it is remembering. Louise Halfe begins *Blue Marrow*, one of Canada's great long poems, with an invocation of many women, most of whom died unknown in the nineteenth century, calling on their spiritual power, thus feminizing and indigenizing the familiar Catholic litany.

On my left breast was a hoofprint. It disappeared when I began the
walk for them:
  okâwîmâwaskiy
  full of grace;
  The Creator is filled with thee
  Blessed art thou among iskwêwak
  and blessed is the fruit of thy womb,
  Holy Mother of all
  Pray for us kitânisak,
  now and at the hour
  of our death. Amen.

Adeline Cardinal. Emma Woods. Sara Cardinal. Bella Shirt. Nancy
Gladue. Fanny Sunchild. Round Faced Woman. Charlotte. Ah-gat.
Bernard Woman. Pray to them.

> *Glory be to* okâwîmâwaskiy
>
> *And to* nôhkom âtayôhkan

wâpsôs—Up at Dawn Woman. Frying Pan Woman. Vera. Pauline
Johnson. Shawndit. Waskedich Woman. Wet Pants Woman.
Carter Woman. Rubber Mouthed Woman. Louiza. Ehnah-Sarcee
Woman. Pray to them. (3)

"The prairie is full of bones" (2), says Halfe. She bids them to stand and
be heard. This is remembering. This is thinking. Remembering is one of the
chief springs of ethics—*okâwîmâwaskiy* (Mother Earth); *âtayôhkan* (Spirit
Beings). Remembering is courtesy, is regard; it brings forth the full self of the
one who recalls.

|| Could it be that the appropriately named land, the land existentiated by an
ontological courtesy, is the Ibn 'Arabian agent intellect, that more expansive
sensibility, intimacy that is strangeness, there when one has lost enough,
been broken sufficiently in intention, to be available for visitation? When
I walk on P,KOLS, the contesting gestalts align themselves, and I see what I
must do—the place is a source of acute understanding in justice. How much
of an ethical self would I have if this experience weren't possible, if these
trees did not exist? True noesis isn't premised on self-monitored rational
distance but on a being claimed that has little to do directly with choice.

|| Europe came maimed to North America. The culture of the West had
divested itself too completely of the more than 40,000 year old homo
sapiens attachment to a form of gaze that was the experiential core of
the Upper Paleolithic Revolution, its cosmologies, its artistic mimesis, its
careful attention to animals, their emergence from the walls of caves. When
Louise Halfe formally responded to the lecture I gave at St. Thomas More

College, which stands as the first chapter in this book, she passed around a large picture album of cave art and encouraged the audience to recall and reoccupy the mindset of their deep ancestors. Europeans' most intimate, immediate stripping of the esoteric, a renunciation making modernity possible, was of Platonic orphism and Christianity's most feral mysticisms, two platforms that would have sustained an absorbed, contemplative look.

With these losses, Europe misplaced the capacity to begin conversations—as opposed to evangelizations—with other cultures with the esoteric, the transfixedly interior. It has disciplined itself not to begin reflection with the state of contemplative absorption, taking this refusal as a sign of the achievement of the human apogee, producing a sort of reasoning that Val Plumwood called hyper-rationality, the cognitive lymph of turbo capitalism. Thus it is unable to recognize non-intentional contemplative alertness, permeability, as a venerable and crucial form of thought. Little surprise then that its cultural occupation of the New World came to be totalizing.

|| Neal McLeod, in his remarkable book *Cree Narrative Memory*, recounts stories of the disappearance of animals and spiritual presences with the coming of settlers to Western Canada. His great-grandfather Peter Vandall, *kôkôcîs*, reported that during the 1870s and 1880s, in the first years of reservations, thousands of buffalo would gather at Redberry Lake, a former fasting location, south of the Sandy Lake reserve, just as ice got thin in March. They would stand on the surface until they broke through and drowned. There are also stories of spiritual beings and animals retreating into the earth at that time. This withdrawal was a prelude to the "spiritual exile," "the internalization of being taken off the land," which was deepened by the multi-generational experience of residential schools (McLeod, *Cree Narrative Memory* 57–58). These vanishings are dramatic instances of the interring of the esoteric, the chthonically spiritual, in the contemporary world.

The convivial community, in the traditional Cree imagination, the living polis, extended beyond human culture. McLeod records the memories of Charlie Burns, of the James Smith band, of long journeys in his youth to *manitow sâkahikan,* Manitou Lake, near Watrous, Saskatchewan, where people would collect a healing salt to take back home. Such locations, says McLeod, were places where Cree people "communicated with the landscape," where "the *nêhiyawak* were able to communicate with other beings and the powers of the land around them, the *âtayôhkanak,* the spiritual grandfathers and grandmothers" (26).

Cree Narrative Memory is committed to the recovery of *nêhiyâwiwin* (Cree-ness), founded on collective remembrance "anchored in places and landscapes" (19), to "a coming home through stories" (61). Each of these three writers, Paul, Halfe and McLeod, is engaged in the act of retrieval of a culture and an epistemological performance and a multi-ply ontology that is currently beyond the margins of sanctioned, contemporary thought. This retrieval will establish the possibility of living vitally now. As Taiaiake Alfred says in *Wasáse: Indigenous Pathways of Action and Freedom,* "It is time for our people to live again....The journey is a living commitment to meaningful change in our lives and to transforming society by recreating our existences, regenerating our cultures and surging against forces that keep us bound to our colonial past" (19). For Waaseyaa'sin Christine Sy, in her "Through Iskigamizigan (The Sugarbush)," in Neal McLeod's *Indigenous Poetics in Canada,* this coming home has meant a long process of decolonization that, she says, allows her to exist. Its parts are the reclamation of her language, Anishinaabemowin, and a re-identification with the land, in particular with the Ontario maple sugarbush, "a place through which to decolonize" (187).

|| *The Larger Conversation* has been itself a project of resuscitation, in its case of the psychagogic heart of Western thought, the deep philosophical roots of politics. An Evagrian, Boehmean, Poretean, Teresan mystical life had been a rickety, imperfect, marginal carrier of the orphic deposit, the Upper Paleolithic's reach into the near present, in the European line of thought, but it, like the animals in Peter Vandall's stories, has retreated into the earth. This disappearance has left a wound, a wound like Glaucon's that causes further misery, a spreading malaise. Europeans in North America, no matter

the ancestral length of their stay, can lay claim to no sustaining self, I believe, unless they find and take on the land's friendship; and one can't come to the land without the esoteric, the interior, without contemplative availability to it. The self-severing, heart from land, as I've argued, has ecological, as well as psychological, significance. The land also will step back from newcomers if we do not bring a sense of colonial history with us, if we do not bear in mind Indigenous people, their epistemologies and dreams, their languages, which the land has fostered.

|| ȾIW̱EṈ—have pity—S̱OS SEN—I am poor—I say to the oaks, arbutus, camas and stones as I walk on the mountain behind the house. Take me in. Deer wander into the yard from the top of the cliff. IYES IṈGES—you are beautiful young deer; I note their careful steps. As they fold themselves into their habitual beds under one of the fir trees, I thank them, HÍSW̱ḴE SÍAM, for their wary, lounging regard.

Disaster is often the precursor of great contemplative ages—strain in the Roman Empire and doctrinal stresses setting the stage for Antonian eremeticism and Pachomean cenobiticism in the Egyptian desert, World War II and its aftermath quickening the growth of American Cistercianism, where Merton found a home. We have nothing and we pause and look around. As awareness of the extent of climate change sinks in, its multiplying effects, one chain of response will be a contemplative muting, building alertness and compunction. This needn't be a global phenomenon, but may be regional and flickering like the growth of monastic communities in eastern Nigeria and the western Cameroon following the collapse of the State of Biafra. Grief around the vanishing of starfish in the Pacific northwest, around endless fires in the boreal forest, must find some lodging place in our interior lives.

If response to this grief in places turns out to be contemplative, I suspect it will not take traditional forms, which seem exhausted, perhaps not in their essences, but almost certainly in their external cultural expressions. But, as this book claims, *The Rule of St. Benedict* still has much to say to us, as do Ignatian and Cassianic rules for the discernment of spirits, along with

Platonic and Neoplatonic spiritual exercises, Porete's interior theatre and Ibn 'Arabi's angelology and his observations on phenomenological stages in the contemplative life. It will serve us well to listen in on this old talk. I can't see how the new form of singleheartedness will not lean toward the secular; indeed it will be immersed in the quotidian world, will be ad hoc, marked by a Taoist-like lightness and mobility. I sometimes imagine I see such an absorbedness forming now within the building panic. We come to nothing and we look around, our attention chastened, sharpened, hastened by our emptiness.

Dramatis

Personae

HENRY CORBIN (1903–1978)

Corbin was a French Islamologist, who taught in both Teheran and Paris. He had a particular interest in Shi'ite Sufism and in the philosophy of Ibn 'Arabi and Suhrawardi.

IAMBLICHUS

Born in the ancient Syrian city of Chalcis around 240. As a philosopher, he attempted to link Platonism with more ancient forms of thought, chiefly Egyptian and Chaldean. He studied with Porphyry, Plotinus' disciple, but later vigorously disagreed with him on the subject of theurgy. Porphyry, like his teacher, did not claim numinous significance descended deeply into the physical world; Iamblichus did. He taught in Apamea for many years until his death in 320.

IBN 'ARABI

Born in Murcia, south east Spain, in 1195. Pilgrimages in North Africa and to Mecca eventually led him to Damascus, where he lived for the last seventeen years of his life, dying in 1240. A voluminous writer, his chief works are the *Futuūhāt Makkiyya* (*The Meccan Openings*) and *Fuṣūṣ al-ḥikam* (*The Ringstones of Wisdom*).

ISAAC OF NINEVEH

He was a seventh-century hermit living in the mountains of Khuzistan. He was born in Qatar. Much of his work has been lost. His collected instructions for monks on the spiritual life, however, are central texts in the Syrian Church.

JULIAN OF NORWICH

A fourteenth-century English mystic, possibly a Benedictine nun, who lived as an anchoress in the churchyard of St. Julian in Norwich. In May 1373, she received a series of visions, which she described in her *Revelations of Divine Love*.

OSIP MANDELSTAM

One of the major Russian poets of the twentieth century. He was born in Warsaw in 1891 and died on route to a prison camp in the Russian far east in 1938. Part of the generation of Akhmatova, Pasternak, and Marina Tsvetaeva, his prose work *Conversation on Dante* contains most of the elements of his mature poetics.

THOMAS MERTON (1915–1968)

Trappist monk of the Abbey of Gethsemani, Kentucky. Poet, autobiographer, activist, practitioner of *lectio divina.*

ORIGEN

He was a resident of Alexandria in the late second century and worked in that city for most of his life as an unordained catechist. As a writer, he was chiefly an exegete, but his *On First Principles* provided the first extensive treatment of Christian spirituality and metaphysics.

MARGUERITE PORETE

The date of her birth is unknown but that of her death is well documented: she was burned at the stake in Paris as a "relapsed heretic" June 1, 1310. She was a beguine who wrote a single book, *The Mirror of Simple, Annihilated Souls and Those Who Remain Only in Will and Desire of Love*. During her trial and condemnation, she maintained complete silence.

JOHN RUUSBROEC (1293–1381)

A priest in Brussels, then later a solitary attached to the small religious community at Groenendael, where he worked as an author and spiritual director.

GERSHOM SCHOLEM

The originator of Kabbalistic studies in the twentieth century, he emigrated from Germany to Palestine in 1923. A close friend of Walter Benjamin, his *Major Trends in Jewish Mysticism*, based on a series of lectures given in New York in 1938, was dedicated to the philosopher.

SUHRAWARDI

He was the founder of the Ishraq or Illuminationist school, which blends Islam with aspects of Zoroastrainism and Neoplatonism. His major work is *Ḥikmat al-Ishrāq* (*The Philosophy of Illumination*). Born in northwest Iran, he was murdered in Aleppo in 1191.

TERESA OF AVILA

A sixteenth-century Spanish Carmelite, she was the author of numerous books, including her *Autobiography* and *Interior Castle*.

Glossary

annihilation

In Marguerite Porete, the word refers to the formation of "the unencumbered soul,"
which takes "account of neither shame nor honour, neither poverty nor wealth, of
neither anxiety nor ease," (84–85), its dynamism the desire life of "Farnearness," the
divine eros, so that "all that I possess is of the Father and the Son," a wealth based on
emptiness (see *fana*).

apokatastasis

When Origen writes in *On First Principles* "the end is always like the beginning"
(Bk. I, VI.2), he is not thinking of an efficient causality operating in history, but he is
expressing himself aspirationally, in confidence of providence. Apokatastasis is "the
perfect restoration of the entire creation" (Bk. III V.7), which begins with the truing
of elemental desire in individuals, and proceeds "by word, by reason" and "courses
of discipline and periods of time." This notion of return has psychological, but also
cosmological implications, since what is returned to are the accords of paradise. In the

medicine of the ancient world, the word also referred to the return of the ill body to a previous equilibrium.

apophasis

Speech about divinity in negative theology, reduced, checked, undermined, yet not stopped by recognition of the uncircumscribability of its object. Longing, in this circumstance, continues, and it wears a succession of plausible suits of linguistic clothing. *Apo* (prefix): "from, away from, asunder, separate"; *phasis*: "speech" (*Klein's Comprehensive Etymological Dictionary*).

fana'

"Creation is a concatenation of theophanies" (Corbin, *Creative Imagination* 202). Each of these is a manifestation of a divine name and the occultation or nudging aside of a limited, not fully imagined individuality at the moment of the disclosure of divine being, a setting aside of the self to make a route for the numinous. To "become absent from yourself" in the words if Ibn 'Arabi (*Futūhāt* II 554.3 in Chittick 176), facilitating the appearance of a larger self, more lit.

haecceity

From the Latin *haecceitas* (this, thisness). In the philosophy of John Duns Scotus, it is the property of a thing that creates individuating difference, by which it is *this* thing and no other. "It is always necessary that the primary formal reason for just this singularity stems from something intrinsic per se to the singular in question" (Duns Scotus 2.24). The property of haecceity makes an object or person striking, unparalleled, except in broad strokes.

katabasis

A philosophic or orphic descent. A medical term in the ancient world for the decline of a fever, "a going down," "to go down" (*Klein's Comprehensive Etymological Dictionary*).

lectio divina

Divine reading. It is a form of reading that places a systematic understanding of a text below the experience of being pierced by an aspect of it.

penthos

A "word" associated with the desert monk Poemen shows the supreme value the earliest Christian monks in Egypt placed on tears—"Truly you are blessed, Abba Arsenius, for you wept for yourself in this world" (Ward 18). Eros arrives at a certain non-resolving sorrow and persists as this. It is an emotion core to contemplation: "I will moan like a dove" (Isaiah 38.14). For Gregory of Nyssa, it "is a sorrowful disposition of the soul caused by the privation of something desirable" (Hausherr 18). A breach in the contemporary world that could trigger it is alienation from the world, one's particular place.

theurgy

From the Latin *theurgia*—divine work. In the thought of Iamblichus, this is a form of philosophical rite more efficacious than intellectual discourse. The practice is drawn from the *Chaldean Oracles* and the *Corpus Hermeticum*, and, he believed, was known to both Plato and Pythagoras. By it, one was able "to purify and dissolve our human passions, or ward off some of the dangers that menace us" (Iamblichus I, 11). The specifics of the rites in the ancient world are unknown, because its practitioners followed the discipline of secrecy, but they seem to have involved the ceremonial use of physical objects (cereals, stones, wood, statues) or words considered as physical objects, in order to achieve interior insight, "the tending of the soul within us." Such ceremonies, ceremonial performances, says Iamblichus, Heraclitus called "remedies." The ontological conviction in Iamblichus and Plato that the numinal reaches deeply into the physical world makes theurgic practice not only possible but central to thought.

Acknowledgements

"Thinking the *Rule of Benedict* within Modernity" was first published in *Fiddlehead* (Summer, 2006); an early version was given as a seminar presentation at the symposium "In the Field," at St. Peter's College, 2004. "Faith and Land" appeared in *Prairie Fire* (Spring, 2009), "A Poetics of Decolonization" in *Fiddlehead* (Autumn, 2012) and "A Mandelstamian Generation in China" in *Brick* (Winter, 2014). Thanks to all editors involved.

I wish to acknowledge the support provided by the University of Victoria Book and Creative Work Subvention Fund.

I also wish to express my gratitude for the helpful people at the University of Alberta Press, to Peter Midgley in particular, who has been a committed supporter of *The Larger Conversation*. I finally wish to thank Dr. Michael Lahey and Duncan Turner for their assistance in seeing the book through its last stages.

Reading

Aelred of Rievaulx. *The Liturgical Sermons: The First Clairvaux Collection, Advent–All Saints.* Translated by Theodore Berkeley, Cistercian Publications, 2001.

——. *Spiritual Friendship.* Translated by Lawrence C. Braceland, edited by Martha L. Dutton, Cistercian Publications, 2010.

Alfred, Taiaiake. "Opening Words." *Lighting the Eighth Fire: The Liberation, Resurgence, and Protection of Indigenous Nations,* edited by Leanne Simpson, Arbeiter Ring Publishing, 2008, 9–11.

——. *Wasáse: Indigenous Pathways of Action and Freedom.* Broadview Press, 2005.

Alter, Robert. "Foreword." *Major Trends in Jewish Mysticism.* By Gershom Scholem, Schocken Books, 1995, xi–xxvii.

Badiou, Alain. *Second Manifesto for Philosophy.* Translated by Louise Burchill, Polity Press, 2011.

Benedict of Nursia. *The Rule of St. Benedict in English.* Edited by Timothy Fry, Liturgical Press, 1981.

Brock, Sebastian. "General Introduction." *The Syriac Fathers on Prayer and the Spiritual Life.* Cistersian Publications, 1987, x–xliii.

Chittick, William C. *The Sufi Path of Knowledge: Ibn al-'Arabi's Metaphysics of Imagination.* State University of New York Press, 1989.

Clottes, Jean. *Cave Art.* Phaidon Press, 2010.

———. *What Is Paleolithic Art? Cave Paintings and the Dawn of Human Creativity.* Translated by Oliver Y. Martin and Robert D. Martin, University of Chicago Press, 2016.

Corbin, Henry. *Avicenna and the Visionary Recital.* Translated by Willard R. Trask, Routledge and Kegan Paul, 1960.

———. *Creative Imagination in the Sufism of Ibn 'Arabi.* Translated by Ralph Manheim, Princeton University Press, 1997.

———. *Spiritual Body and Celestial Earth: From Mazdean Iran to Shi'ite Iran.* Translated by Nancy Pearson, Princeton University Press, 1977.

Couture, Joseph. *A Metaphoric Mind: Selected Writings of Joseph Couture.* Edited by Ruth Couture and Virginia McGowan, Athabasca University Press, 2013.

Descartes, René. *Discourse on Method and Meditations on First Philosophy.* Translated by Donald A. Cress, Hackett Publishing, 1993.

Duns Scotus, John. *God and Creatures: The Quodlibetal Questions.* Translated by Felix Alluntis and Allan Wolters, The Catholic University of America Press, 1975.

Eckhart, Meister. *Meister Eckhart: A Modern Translation.* Translated by Raymond B. Blakney, Harper and Row, 1941.

Freidin, Gregory. *A Coat of Many Colors: Osip Mandelstam and His Mythologies of Self-Presentation.* University of California Press, 1987.

Grudzinska Gross, Irena. *Czesław Miłosz and Joseph Brodsky: Fellowship of Poets.* Yale University Press, 2009.

Hadot, Pierre. *The Present Alone Is Our Happiness: Conversations with Jeannie Carlier and Arnold I. Davidson.* 2nd ed. Translated by Marc Djaballah and Michael Chase, Stanford University Press, 2011.

Halfe, Louise Bernice. *Blue Marrow.* Coteau Books, 2004.

Hausherr, Irénée. *Penthos: The Doctrine of Compunction in the Christian East.* Translated by Anselm Hufstader, Cistercian Publications, 1982.

Heidegger, Martin. *Martin Heidegger: Basic Writings.* Edited by David Farrell Krell, HarperCollins, 1993.

Hoffman, Ross. "Perspectives on Health within the Teachings of a Gifted Cree Elder."
  Pimatisiwin: A Journal of Aboriginal and Indigenous Community Health vol. 8,
  no. 1, 2010, 19–31.

Hsieh Ling-yün. *The Mountain Poems of Hsieh Ling-yün*. Translated by David
  Hinton. New Directions Press, 2001.

Husserl, Edmund. *Cartesian Meditations: An Introduction to Phenomenology*.
  Translated by Dorion Cairns, Kluwer Academic Publishers, 1993.

Iamblichus. *On the Mysteries (De mysteriis)*. Translated by Emma C. Clarke, John M.
  Dillon and Jackson P. Hershbell, Society of Biblical Literature, 2003.

Ibn 'Arabi. *The Ringstones of Wisdom (Fuṣūṣ al-ḥikam)*. Translated by Caner K.
  Dagli, Kazi Publications, 2004.

Ignatius of Loyola. *The Spiritual Exercises*. Translated by Louis J. Puhl, Loyola
  University Press, 1952.

Isaac of Nineveh. "Discourses." *The Syriac Fathers on Prayer and The Spiritual Life*.
  Translated with an Introduction by Sebastian Brock, Cistercian Publications,
  1987, 246–63.

———. "Headings on Knowledge." *The Syriac Fathers*, 264–71.

Julian of Norwich. *Revelations of Divine Love*. Translated by Clifton Wolters, Penguin
  Books, 1966.

Kadloubovsky, E., and G.E.H. Palmer. *Early Fathers from the Philokalia: Together
  with Some Writings of St. Abba Dorotheus, St. Isaac of Syria and St. Gregory
  Palamas,* Faber and Faber, 1981.

Kearney, Richard. *The God Who May Be: A Hermeneutics of Religion*. Indiana
  University Press, 2001.

Klein, Ernest. *Klein's Comprehensive Etymological Dictionary of the English
  Language*. Elsevier, 2003.

Levinas, Emmanuel. *Totality and Infinity*. Translated by Alphonso Lingis, Duquesne
  University Press, 1992.

Lingenfelter, Andrea. "Translator's Introduction." *The Changing Room: Selected
  Poetry of Zhai Yongming*. By Zhai Yongming, Zephyr Press and the Chinese
  University Press, 2011, xi–xviii.

Mandelstam, Nadezhda. *Hope Abandoned: A Memoir*. Translated by Max Hayward,
  Collins Harvill, 1989.

Mandelstam, Osip. *The Poems of Osip Mandelstam*. Translated by Ilya Bernstein, EPC Digital Editions, 2014.

———. *Selected Essays*. Translated by Sidney Monas, University of Texas Press, 1977.

———. *Selected Poems*. Translated by Clarence Brown and W.S. Merwin, Atheneum, 1974.

Maritain, Jacques, and Raïssa Maritain. *The Situation of Poetry: Four Essays on the Relations Between Poetry, Mysticism, Magic and Knowledge*. Translated by Marshall Suther, Philosophical Library, 1955.

Maximus the Confessor. *Maximus the Confessor*. Translated by Andrew Louth, Routledge, 1996.

———. *Maximus Confessor: Selected Writings*. Translated by George C. Berthold, Paulist Press, 1985.

McLeod, Neal. *Cree Narrative Memory: From Treaties to Contemporary Times*. Purich Publishing, 2007.

———, editor. *Indigenous Poetics in Canada*. Wilfrid Laurier University Press, 2014.

Merton, Thomas. *Monastic Observances: Initiation into the Monastic Life*. Edited by Patrick F. O'Connell, Cistercian Publications, 2010.

Mithen, Steven. *The Singing Neanderthals: The Origins of Music, Language, Mind, and Body*. Harvard University Press, 2007.

Neruda, Pablo. *Canto General*. Translated by Jack Schmitt, University of California Press, 1991.

———, and César Vallejo. *Neruda and Vallejo: Selected Poems*. Edited by Robert Bly, translated by Robert Bly, John Knoepfle, and James Wright, Beacon Press, 1971.

Origen. *On First Principles*. Translated by G.W. Butterworth, Peter Smith, 1973.

Paul, Philip Kevin. *Taking the Names Down from the Hill*. Nightwood Editions, 2003.

Paz, Octavio. "In Search of the Present," Nobel Prize Lecture, 1990, www.nobelprize. org/nobel_prizes/literature/laureates/1990/paz-lecture.html.

Plato. *Phaedrus*. Translated by Alexander Nehamas and Paul Woodruff, Hackett Publishing, 1995.

———. *The Republic of Plato*. Translated by Allan Bloom, Basic Books, 1991.

———. *Timaeus and Critias*. Translated by Desmond Lee, Penguin Books, 1977.

Ponticus, Evagrius. *The Praktikos and Chapters on Prayer*. Translated by John Eudes Bamberger, Cistercian Publications, 1981.

Porete, Marguerite. *The Mirror of Simple Souls*. Translated by Ellen L. Babinsky, Paulist Press, 1993.

Pseudo-Dionysius. *The Complete Works*. Translated by Colm Luibheid, Paulist Press, 1987.

Riel, Louis. "Memoradum." Special Collections, University of Victoria, FC3217.1 R53A2 1970z. Victoria, BC.

Rothenberg, Jerome. *Poetics and Polemics: 1980–2005*. University of Alabama Press, 2008.

Rumi. *Mystical Poems of Rumi*. Translated by A.J. Arberry, University of Chicago Press, 1979.

Ruusbroec, John. *John Ruusbroec: The Spiritual Espousals and Other Works*. Translated by James A. Wiseman, Paulist Press, 1985.

Scholem, Gershom. *Major Trends in Jewish Mysticism*. Schocken Books, 1995.

———. *Walter Benjamin: The Story of a Friendship*. The Jewish Publication Society of America, 1981.

Suhrawardi. *The Philosophy of Illumination*. Translated with an Introduction by John Wallbridge and Hossein Ziai, Brigham Young University Press, 1999.

Sy, Waaseyaa'sin Christine. "Through Iskigamizigan (The Sugarbush): A Poetics of Decolonization." *Indigenous Poetics in Canada*, edited by Neal McLeod, Wilfrid Laurier University Press, 2014, 183–202.

Teresa of Avila. *Interior Castle*. Translated by E. Allison Peers, Image Books, 1961.

Thunberg, Lars. *Man and the Cosmos: The Vision of Maximus the Confessor*. St. Vladimir's Seminary Press, 1985.

Vallejo, César. *The Black Heralds*. Translated by Rebecca Seiferle, Copper Canyon Press, 2003.

Wallbridge, John and Hossein Ziai. "Introduction." *The Philosophy of Illumination*. By Suhrawardi, Brigham Young University Press, 1999, xv–xxxvii.

Ward, Benedicta, translator. *The Sayings of the Desert Fathers: The Alphabetical Collection*. Cistercian Publications, 1975.

Ward, Jean Elizabeth. *Li Qingzhao: An Homage*. Translated by Lucy Chow Ho, Starward Studio, 2008.

Weil, Simone. *Gravity and Grace*. Translated by Emma Craufurd, Routledge, 1995.

Wolin, Richard. *Walter Benjamin: An Aesthetics of Redemption*. University of California Press, 1994.

Xi Chuan. *Notes on the Mosquito: Selected Poems*. Translated by Lucas Klein, New Directions Press, 2012.

————. "Style Comes as a Reward." *Almost Island*, Winter, 2012, www.almostisland. com/winter_2012/special_issue_style/style_comes_as_a_reward.html.

Zhai Yongming. *The Changing Room: Selected Poetry of Zhai Yongming.* Translated by Andrea Lingenfelter, Zephyr Press and the Chinese University Press, 2011.

Permissions

Excerpts from *Mystical Poems of Rumi* by Rumi, translated by A.J. Arberry, University of Chicago Press, 1979. Copyright 1979 by Ehsan Yarshater. Used with permission.

"On a Tower Beside the Lake" by David Hinton, from the original Chinese by Hsieh Ling-yün, from *The Mountain Poems of Hsieh Ling-Yün*, copyright ©2001 by David Hinton. Reprinted by permission of New Directions Publishing Corp.

Excerpts from *The Syriac Fathers on Prayer and The Spiritual Life* by Isaac of Nineveh, translated by Sebastian Brock © 1987 by Cistercian Publicatons, Inc. © 2008 by Order of Saint Benedict, Collegeville, Minnesota. Used with permission.

Index

"On a Tower beside the Lake,"
206–07
Huaizhao, 94
Hudson's Bay Company, xiii, 107–08,
193, 231
human exceptionalism, 195
humanism, twelfth century, 223
human settlements in North America,
212–13
humility (Rule of Benedict), 164
hunger. See appetite; eros
Husserl, Edmund
annihilation of self, 156–57
Cartesian Meditations, 143–44,
147–51
nothingness, 62
radical philosophy, 58, 144, 147–49,
154
transcendental ego, 152, 153–54

Iamblichus, 83, 110, 126, 153, 241, 247
On the Mysteries (De mysteriis), 15
Ibn 'Arabi, 241–42
agent intellect, 9
the angel, 26, 45, 122–23, 200–01,
239–40
himma, 51–52, 54
identity and annihilation, 120–21
imagination in, 36
individuation (Name), 116–17,
118–19, 120
kenotic individual, 40
in Mecca, 48–50
passion, 42

reading transformation, 28–29, 33
Sura Yasin as a figure, 44–45
identity. See self
Ignatius of Loyola
The Spiritual Exercises, 135–36, 138,
151
illness, 45–46, 59, 158, 206, 216–17, 232
Illuminationist school, 74, 75, 80
See also Suhrawardi
imagelessness, 64, 154–55
imagination
creative, 26
imagelessness, 35
Socratic exercises, 134, 137–38
transformative power of, 153, 159
"world of the Idea-Images," 35–36
Imagination (active), 44, 51
iconoclasm of capitalism, 60
Indian Act, 193–94, 234–35
Indian residential schools, 11, 194,
234–35, 237
Indigenous communities
Christian churches and, 10–11
conditions for conversation with, 11,
15, 230, 237
Indigenous nations, treaties with
Canada, 108
Indigenous North American literatures,
153
Indigenous scholarship, 12
individuality
community achievement, 5
self-recognition, 72–73

individuation
attention to specificity of things, 166, 172–73
contemplative practice, 118–19
intimacy and, 120, 122
liberal individualism and, 43
passion as, 42
song and, 121–22
intelligence (active), 26, 51
See also imagination
Intelligence (of Avicennism), 37
interiority and interior life. See also psychagogic meaning; self-knowledge
aesthetic of interiority, 47–48
the angel and, 39, 44, 47
contemplative phenomenology, 31
contemporary practice of, 227
exercises for (Socrates), 137–38
"feeding the Angel," 50–51
in Interior Castle (Teresa), 199–202
interior senses, 164
male–female distinction, 182–83
Recital of Hayy ibn Yaqzan (Avicenna), 75–80
roots of, 4
as world, 116–18
interior senses, 9–10
intuitive philosophy, 81
irony, 116
Isaac of Nineveh, 42, 61–62, 63–68, 242
Discourse, 65–66
Islam. See also Ibn 'Arabi
individuation and, 117
Suhrawardi and, 70

Jackson, Henry (Honoré Jaxon), 188
Jesuit Relations, 1630s, 10–11, 188
Jesus Prayer, 19
Jewish mysticism, 24–25, 27–28
Jintian (Today) journal, 101
John, Gospel of, 117
John Chrysostom, 134
John of the Cross, 19
John the Solitary: anachoresis, 214
Joseph the Visionary, 65
Julian of Norwich, 19, 45–47, 61, 242
justice
as a category of good (Socrates), 129, 131, 136
climate change and, 230–31
colonialism and, 190–92

Kabbalistic writings, 24–25, 27–28
Kane, Donna, 203
Kant, Immanuel, 5, 10, 30, 57, 156
katabasis, 246
Kearney, Richard: The God Who May Be, 180–84
kenosis, 9
Khlebnikov, Velimir, 84
Kings, 219
Klein, Lucas, 94, 99
Kroetsch, Robert, 190

land. See also place, experience of
experience of loss of, 8–9
language and languages. See also Acemeist movement; names, nomenclature; poetry
in Assiniboia, 192–93

transformation, 13, 25
mystical Orthodoxy, 67

names, nomenclature. *See also*
    language
  of annihilated soul, 224
  Indigenous language, 232, 236
  individualizing word, 88, 118–19,
    120
  intimacy with place, 207
  Mandelstam, 82
  seeking the nameless, 152–53
  Suhrawardi, 73–74, 78, 83
  Whitman's American, 84–85
nationalism and language, 84–85
nature. *See also* locale; place,
    experience of
  bifurcation of, 195
  contemplation of *(theoria physike)*,
    7, 121, 214–16
  human homology with, 8
negation (apophaticism), 155–57
Neoplatonism, 15, 26, 83, 110, 117, 126,
    153, 165, 239–40
  See also Avicenna; Maximus the
    Confessor
Neruda, Pablo, 96, 110–11
  Canto General, 110–11
  "Let the Woodcutter Awaken,"
    111–14
  "The Heights of Macchu Picchu,"
    111
  theurgical powers in poetry, 113–14
Newlove, John, 190

Nicholas of Cusa, 181, 216
Noah (and other prophets), 120–21
North America, human populating of,
    212–13
nothingness, 62–63, 224–25, 227–28,
    230
  See also annihilation of self
numbered treaties (Canada), 189,
    193–94

obedience, mutual *(Rule of Benedict)*,
    166, 169
oddness, 122–23, 216
  See also musicality in poetry
oriental wisdom (Suhrawardi), 43–44
Origen, 9, 14, 161, 164, 184, 201, 242
orthodoxy and ontological clarity, 127
  See also certainty, certitude
Our Lady of the Prairies Abbey, 20–21
Ouspensky, P.D.: *In Search of the*
    Miraculous, 19
Ouyang Jianghe, 97
  Double Shadows, 105

Pamirs Poetry Journey, 95
panic, 29, 58
  See also despair
paradise: enactment of the virtues, 184
passion as individuation and thought,
    42
Paterson, Don, 161
Paul, Kevin, 232–33, 238
  "Ceremony," 233
  Little Hunger, 231–32

shape of poetic thought, 115–16

techne's identity as *poeisis,* 40

theophanic, 55–56

transformation politics, 13, 97–100, 103–05, 110–11

transformative force, 15, 217–18

way of knowing, 163

politics and political transformation

Allegory of the Cave and, 198–99

contemplative politics, 158, 199

difficult language, 52, 54–55, 98

"How to Be Here?," 216

illness, 217

imaginary city in *The Republic,* 131–32, 134, 162

imagination, 36

kataphaticism, 51–52

lifelong practice of, 12–15

Neruda's poetry, 110–11

new epistemologies, 68

poetry as floatation device, 109–10

poets of China, 97–100, 101–02, 103

theurgical powers in poetry, 113–14

through reading, 32–33

Porete, Marguerite, 9, 223, 239–40, *242*

Mirror of Simple Souls, 10, 201, 221–25, 227–28, 230

Post-Confederation Treaties (Canada), 189, 193–94

poverty

cultural poverty, 26–27

genuine political practice, 32

power, displays of state, 99–100

prayer. *See also* contemplative interiority

activism of, 29

choral (chanting), 178–79

coherence of song and, 116–17

contemplation of nature *(theoria physike),* 7, 121, 214–16

contemplative focus, 9

as corrective stirrings, 62

effects of highest, 67

emptiness, 66

eros and, 42, 66

hesychasm, 67–68

hunger for or appetite for, 63

Isaac of Nineveh's thinking, 64–66

"prayer of fire" (Cassian), 36

preoccupation with, 60

reciprocity of, 55

sitting with, 61

of thanksgiving, 65

Proclan theurgy, 62

Proclus, 15

provinciality and reading practice, 26

Psalms, 57, 67

psalms *(Rule of Benedict),* 165

psalms, chanting of, 178–79

Pseudo-Dionysius the Areopagite, 61, 126, 191, 216

Ecclesiastical Hierarchy, 162

Mystical Theology, 168

psychagogic meaning

contemporary poetry and, 37

meditation on the Names, 49

reading of the *Rule,* 162, 167

sitting with prayer, 61–62

Socratic devices, 130, 135–37

transformation and, 114

psychology, political weakness of, 68

publican's prayer, 67

Pythagoras, 8, 174, 180

radical philosophy, 58, 144, 147–49,
    154–56

Ray Monk, 142n1

razed self, 145, 152, 153

reading

    features of practice of, 26–29

    Rule of Benedict, 164

Redberry Lake, 237

Red Deer River, 192

Red Toryism, 14

Regina Cemetery, 221

Republic (Plato's Socrates), 125–42

    Allegory of the Cave, 68, 76, 126–30,
        195–99, 202, 204, 206

    the divided line figure, 136–37

    eros in, 141–42

    Glaucon, xi, 78, 127–42, 196, 202

    imagined cities, 75, 78, 134, 137–38,
        196

    journey narrative, 80

    Odyssey, 138–41

    shame in, 133–35, 202

    Thrasymachus, 37, 128, 129, 134

    tripartite soul, 225

Rhodes, Shane, 187–94

    erosion of doubt, 193–94

    valuing histories, 192

    X, 189

Ricoeur, Paul, 180

Riel, Louis

    Assiniboia, xiii

    Provisional Governments, 188

Riel, Sara, 188, 191

Rilke, Rainer Maria: *Sonnets to
    Orpheus,* 8

ritual

    observances, 176–77

    political theurgical powers in
        poetry, 113–14

    transformation exercise, 13–14, 15,
        48–49

    use of objects from nature, 8

Rivera, Diego, 113

Robinson, Marilynne, 14

Romantic poetry, 36–37

Rose, Gillian, 14

Rule of Benedict, 162–70, 239–40

    germane to writing, 164–67

Rumi, Mawlana Jalaluddin, 47–48

Rupert's Land, xiii, 107–08, 192–93

Russia: October Revolution, 84

Ruusbroec, John, 19, 31–32, 222, *243*

    A Mirror of Eternal Blessedness, 29

Saanich Peninsula, 7, 9, 232–33

Saddle Lake reserve, 174, 234–35

sadness of philosophical eros, 25

St. Augustine

    Confessions, 75

    De Trinitate, 10

Steinhauer, Eugene and Mike, 235

St. Gregory of Palamas, 67–68

St. John of the Cross, 61

St. Maximus the Confessor. *See*
Maximus the Confessor
St. Petersburg: Stray Dog cabaret, 94
St. Teresa of Avila, 26, 61
Salamun, Tomaz, 95
Sandy Lake reserve, 237
Saruddin Qunyawi, 47
Saskatchewan, 221
Schlink, Bernhard: *Guilt about the
Past*, 11
scholarly and ascetical practice, 175
scholarship, 13–15, 24, 25, 38, 41
Scholem, Gershom, 27–28, *243*
Major Trends in Jewish Mysticism,
23–25
utopian program of interpretation,
32
*Walter Benjamin: The Story of a
Friendship,* 27–28, 29–30, 32
Schumann, Robert, 115
science and scientific insight, 39–41,
147–49, 173
Scott, Duncan Campbell, 190–91, 194
Second Vatican Council, 14
Seiferle, Rebecca, 52, 55
self, well-formed
appearance of, 5
becoming your self, 120–21
within every act, 175–76, 184
self as ampler ecology, 6, 9
See also locale
self-knowledge. *See also* interiority and
interior life
intuitive philosophy, 81

self-recognition, 71–75
SENĆOŦEN, 232–33
sexual differentiation, 182–83
shame, 133–35, 202
catanyxis, 134
Shams al-Din Shahrazuri, 80
shang (adoration), 205–07
Simpson, Leanne: *Lighting the Eighth
Fire,* x
singing, activism of, 29
See also musicality in poetry
Siqueiros, David, 113
skepticism, 33
Slavoj Zizek: *The Fragile Absolute,* 62
Smith, Gordon, 159
Snyder, Gary, 203
Socrates. *See* Plato; *Republic*
solitude of estrangement, 206
song and individuation, 121–22
See also musicality in poetry
Song Lin, 105
Sooke Hills, 214
soul or human innerness, 7–8
South Saskatchewan River, 192
spiritual exercises, 135–36, 138
Sufism and angelology, 38
Suhrawardi, 69–81, *243*
doctrine of presence, 80–81
*Ḥikmat al-Ishrāq (The Philosophy
of Illumination),* 70
"lights," 87–88
names, 83
oriental wisdom, 43–44
therapeutic nature of philosophy,
126